CAUGHT IN COURT

By the same author

Legibus. A History of Clifford-Turner 1900–1980
Published privately by King, Thorne & Stace, 1980

JOHN SCOTT

CAUGHT
—*IN*—
COURT

A SELECTION OF CASES WITH
CRICKETING CONNECTIONS

Foreword by
COLIN COWDREY C.B.E.

ANDRE DEUTSCH

To Janet

First published in Great Britain 1989
by André Deutsch Limited
105-106 Great Russell Street London WC1

ISBN 0 233 98479 8

Phototypeset by Falcon Graphic Art Ltd
Wallington, Surrey
Printed in Great Britain by
Billings and Son Ltd, Worcester

CONTENTS

FOREWORD
BY
COLIN COWDREY

When John Scott asked me to write a Foreword to a book that he was writing on cricket and the law, the Packer case immediately sprung to mind and I expected to be presented with a slim volume to which a couple of introductory paragraphs would be appropriate. I was surprised and intrigued, therefore, to receive over three hundred pages of typescript, covering more than 150 cases.

On reading *Caught in Court* I found that I had, in fact, heard of several of the cases but that I knew only in outline what most of them were about. I found it fascinating, therefore, to read the full stories of those cases and also to read about the many of which I previously knew nothing. As John mentions, apart from giving the facts he has also explained the legal issues involved and I feel that he has done this in a way that makes them interesting and intelligible to mere laymen like me, as well as to his fellow lawyers.

The cases cover a wide variety and much research was involved in writing the book. John has also set them in their cricketing contexts and identified connections which most people would have missed as, for example, those of the judge in the Odiham Cricket Club case. His knowledge is, perhaps, not surprising as he has been a lifelong cricket lover and a member of Sussex since he was a schoolboy. Like many who have got pleasure from the game, John has put a lot back into it and he is a trustee and former committee member of Sussex and the treasurer of the City of London region of The Lord's Taverners, – and so a friend and a colleague of mine.

When reading the book I was reminded of the close affinity between cricket and the law. In my early years of first-class cricket the then Sir Walter Monckton was President of MCC and invited as guest speaker Sir Norman, later the Lord,

Birkett, pre-eminent in his field and at the height of his powers. The combination of Monckton and Birkett on their feet after dinner – and they truly loved their cricket – was a feast to savour.

Different cases will appeal to different people, but there were some which I found particularly interesting. Among these are poor old Bill Bestwick's manslaughter case, the tragically unlucky accident that killed Ted McDonald, the 1892 case concerning The Original English Lady Cricketers and the case arising from the Kent player, James Seymour's, benefit match. I was fascinated to read about the different kinds of cases involving West Indian Test cricketers; the Hylton murder, the Constantine hotel case, the assault by Gilchrist (who was terrifying enough with a cricket ball let alone an iron!) and the libel on Clive Lloyd and his team. Of the cases involving Australian Test cricketers, I was intrigued by the Coningham divorce case and the action brought by Sidney Barnes, the Turnstile Hurdler – although I came to know him as a remarkable extrovert I never actually played against him.

Although cricket and cricketers seem to have featured in the courts recently and attracted much publicity, the book shows that cricket cases go back nearly four hundred years and that well over a hundred years ago disputes with umpires led to riots and assaults. Cricketers of the past were, it seems, more rugged than their modern counterparts. Perhaps this is not surprising, but somehow I had imagined that the giants of the golden age did not, like the rest of us, have feet of clay. Nevertheless, some of those who 'finished second', like Vallance Jupp, were probably unlucky and I feel that the cases have been written up fairly, as John has not taken sides and has mentioned extenuating circumstances where they existed.

There are so many new cricket books it is surprising that there is a niche still to be filled, but John has done just that with *Caught in Court*. I congratulate him on having written an original, interesting and entertaining book, ideal as a straightforward read or to dip into as a bedside book, provided you do not want to go to sleep too quickly!

Colin Cowdrey

PREFACE

Two cases which feature in this book first gave me the idea of writing it in the early 1950s, when I was still a law student. The cases were *Bolton* v. *Stone*, which to lawyers is probably the best-known case concerning cricket, and *Rex* v. *Hylton*, which is one of the most sensational cases involving a well-known cricketer. For over thirty years the idea lay dormant, but when I retired from full-time practice as a solicitor I thought it worth finding out if the idea was worth pursuing. I therefore approached Tom Rosenthal, whom I knew as a distinguished publisher and cricket enthusiast, to find out whether, if I decided to write such a book, he thought that any publisher might be interested in it. Considerably to my surprise, he not only said 'Yes', but also that Andre Deutsch would like to publish it.

The thread that runs through all the cases in the book is cricket. Every case involves either a well-known cricketer or the game of cricket, cricket equipment or a cricket field and in many cases more than one of these. It can justly be said that in some instances, such as the 'Peeping Tom' case, the link with cricket is tenuous. This I accept, but it was I who marked out the boundaries of this particular field and, thus, the decision as to what to include was mine alone. The cases, which include none heard after 1988, can only be a selection, as there must be many which I do not know about. Some cases which qualify for inclusion and of which I do know have been omitted and these include ones where I have been unable to trace enough information to warrant including them, run-of-the-mill traffic offences and, with two exceptions, divorce cases. One or two cases have also been omitted where an offence was committed many years ago and the offender is still alive, but has since rehabilitated himself.

As will be apparent, the cases are written up according to subject matter and within each category I have generally dealt with the cases chronologically. In most instances where I know them, I have given a person's forename the first time he is mentioned, although I could not bring myself to refer to W.G. as William Grace! For subsequent references I have usually used the surname only, rather than using the prefix 'Mr' or adopting the increasingly prevalent modern practice of referring to people just by their first names. Where I know that people have subsequently been knighted or ennobled I have so indicated, usually by means of a footnote.

In several of the cases, especially those in the 'Financial Allsorts' and 'Taxes and Wills' chapters, I thought it would be interesting to indicate the approximate current value of sums of money referred to and I have therefore done this. The expression 'current value' throughout the book means 1987 value and I have calculated this from a table of the purchasing power of the pound going back to 1825, which appeared in *The Sunday Telegraph* in 1982, updated by the official Retail Prices Index. One has got so used to continuous inflation that it is interesting to note that in previous generations the value of money rose as well as fell. Thus the pound in 1914, although worth less than it was in 1889 - 25 years earlier – was worth more than it had been in 1864 - 50 years earlier.

I have given the sources at the end of the book and, as I hope the book will be of interest to lawyers as well as cricketers, I have also listed those cases in the book which are in the law reports and given the references of the reports I have used. This only applies to about 20 per cent of all the cases, but with such cases I have attempted to explain the legal issues involved, as well as giving the facts of the case and the decision of the court. I hope that this will add more for those interested in the legal technicalities than it will detract for those for whom such matters have no appeal.

Clearly it is very important in a book such as this not to make mistakes and I, and some of those who have helped me, have striven to eliminate these. Inevitably, a few will have slipped through the net and if any reader spots one I shall be glad to hear about it (via André Deutsch). Likewise, I shall always be interested to hear of cases, both old and new, which would qualify for inclusion in the book.

I would like to express my warm appreciation to all those listed in the Acknowledgments. The bare statement of thanks in that section does not adequately convey my gratitude to them for all their help and encouragement. Finally, I would like to thank Colin Cowdrey for writing the Foreword. He and I were contemporaries at Oxford but I did not get to know him until later, as our cricket was played at very different levels. I do, however, remember his first hundred in first-class cricket, which was scored in the Parks for the Free Foresters against the University in 1951, the year before he went up. Hugh Bartlett, whom I knew and who was also playing in the match, commented to me enthusiastically on Cowdrey's performance and predicted a bright future for him. The former Sussex captain's confidence was fully justified as that hundred was followed by another 106 centuries, the captaincy of Kent and 114 caps for England.

ACKNOWLEDGMENTS

I would like to thank the following for their help:

John Bright-Holmes, Gerald Brodribb, Gill Clarke-Jervoise, F. Collins *(Cheetham CC)*, Ian Crawford, Geoffrey Cuthbertson, Timothy d'Arch Smith, Bernadette Dunne, John Ford, Edward Grayson, Stephen Green the curator at Lord's, Malcolm Hooker, Philip Hustwitt, A. S. ('Jeff') Jeffares, Martin Kane, Carol Lander and Angela Heale *(Clifford Chance library)*, George Lee *(Uxbridge CC)*, Stanley Lowy *(Gunn & Moore)*, Perran Newman, H. A, ('Ossie') Osborne *(Sussex CCC library)*, Frank Peach *(Derbyshire CCC)*, W. F. Pearce *(Bromley Environmental Services)*, Clive Porter *(The Cricket Society)*, Andrew Railton *(Waltham St Lawrence CC)*, Jackie Ranston, Bob Rham, W. J. ('Sam') Russell, Teresa Sapsted, Perry Simson, Graham Smith, Roger Tolman *(Locksbottom CC)*, Tony Vann *(Yorkshire CCC)*, Anne Vickers and John Woodcock.

The staff at various libraries and record offices, especially those at the Newspaper Library at Colindale, the Law Society Library and the East Grinstead Library, the staff at the offices of several newspapers, especially some of the local papers used as sources.

In addition, I would like specifically to thank those who have provided me with photographs and/or permitted me to reproduce illustrations which are subject to copyright:

Nottingham Evening Post, Doncaster Library Services and Sheffield Newspapers, The Cricketer International, Bolton Evening News, Marylebone Cricket Club, Miss N. Rheinberg MBE, David Frith, The Times, The Press Association, Adrian Murrell and Allsport UK, Yorkshire Post, Thorsons Publishing Group, Daily Mail, Sport & General, Birmingham Post & Mail, Allan Glenwright, Jack Pollard and Angus & Robertson, Graham Gough and the Wolverhampton Express & Star.

I

SUDDEN DEATH

The origins of cricket are obscure because the game was not invented but developed over the centuries from an elementary game with bat and ball into the one which is played today. Stephen Green, the curator at Lord's, has listed[1] over fifty references to cricket before 1700 of which all but about a dozen were in the seventeenth century. Of those before 1600, most relate to some form of game played with 'bat' and ball, not necessarily known as 'cricket' or any variation of that word, while several of the references in the seventeenth century are to legal cases involving cricket. One of the earliest of these cases concerns a death resulting from an injury sustained during a game of cricket.

Although sudden death is not something usually associated with cricket or cricketers, even before the days of helmets and protective clothing the game could prove a dangerous pursuit and it has always produced a steady stream of injuries and fatalities. Cricketers, too, although seldom involved in cases of murder or manslaughter, seem to have had an unhappy proneness to suicide, which until the Suicide Act of 1961 was itself a crime. Among the notable cricketers who took their own lives are Andrew Stoddart, Albert Trott, Harold Gimblett and Raymond Robertson-Glasgow, who was also one of the most entertaining writers on the game. A suicide inevitably results in an inquest but the proceedings of coroners' courts, not being of an adversarial nature, are outside the scope of this book and, in any event, a catalogue of well-known cricketers who committed suicide would make depressing reading.

Some old cases
Litigation has sometimes arisen from personal injury or damage to property caused by some aspect of the game but, as far as I

---

[1] The *Journal of The Cricket Society*, Autumn 1981.

know, none of the instances where someone died as the result
of an injury sustained while playing or watching cricket has been
followed by the dead person's personal representatives suing the
club or individual concerned. This may partly be due to the fact
that such an action could not have been brought before 1934,
when an Act[2] was passed which enabled the estate of a person
killed as a result of another's negligence to recover damages. It
would be impossible to compile anything like a comprehensive
list of the occasions upon which someone's death has arisen
from an injury sustained while playing or watching cricket, as
many were not recorded at all and others lie buried in short
paragraphs in old national and provincial newspapers. In any
event, as with the cases of suicide, even those deaths which
resulted in an inquest are strictly outside the scope of this book
but the earliest of these is worth describing as it occurred over
350 years ago and, like the Boxgrove case which is described
later, seems to support the view that in the early days of cricket
it was permissible for a batsman to hit the ball twice.

On 28 August 1624 Jasper Vinall and Edward Tye, husband-
men of West Hoathly, a village near East Grinstead in Sussex, were
playing a customary game called 'crickett' with various others on
Horsted Green at Horsted Keynes, the neighbouring village,
when Tye hit a ball into the air and tried to hit it again as it
was dropping to the ground. Meanwhile Vinall ran up behind
Tye to try and catch the ball but Tye, who did not see him,
unwittingly hit Vinall with a small staff called 'a crickett batt',
which he was holding in his right hand. Vinall received a wound
on the front of his head from which he died on 10 September.
Two days later an inquest was held at West Hoathly where the
jurors, one of whom bore the famous Sussex cricketing name
of Langridge, held that Vinall had not been killed feloniously
but by misadventure and through his own carelessness.

This case shows that by 1624 cricket was 'a customary game'
and established in Sussex and also gives some clues as to the
nature of the bat in that it is described as a 'bacillum', meaning
a little staff. This is, to an extent, corroborated by the fact that
Tye held it in his right hand, but then Ian Botham holds even his
heavy modern bat in one hand when running between wickets.

[2] The Law Reform (Miscellaneous Provisions) Act 1934.

The inquest has also been considered as providing evidence that in the 1620s a batsman was permitted to hit the ball twice other than 'for the sole purpose of guarding his wicket', the only circumstance in which this is permitted under the present laws. Moreover, although it is impossible to be certain, the account of the inquest lends credence to the theory that the ball could be hit twice by a batsman, not only to prevent himself being caught but also to score runs, and that obstructing the field, at least unintentionally, was also allowed. Certainly by 1744, when the first code of the laws of cricket was produced, Tye would not have been allowed to leave his 'running ground' to prevent a catch or to hit the ball twice, except to protect his wicket.

From 1939 to 1957 I lived in the village of West Hoathly without ever having heard of Jasper Vinall or Edward Tye. However, looking back, I remember that then, as now, there was a crossroads on the edge of the village called Vinols Cross[3] where there was a public house of the same name, and that about a mile outside the village there was another road junction called Tyes Cross. Were they perhaps named after the unfortunate cricketers involved in the fatal accident in 1624?

In 1647 another person died in Sussex from an injury received from a cricket bat, but this instance does nothing to clarify further the position regarding hitting the ball twice as it is not even clear whether the injury was sustained in a game of cricket. At the West Sussex Quarter Sessions held at Arundel in January 1647 Margaret Brand stated on oath that her brother, Henry Brand of Selsey, told her that he had recently received a wound in the head given to him by Thomas Hatter, also of Selsey, with a cricket bat. Brand died a month later and Hatter's wife and mother offered Brand's widow £1 6s. compensation, which she accepted. There is no indication of the circumstances in which the injury was sustained but, if it was correctly described as 'recently' received in the month of January, it seems unlikely that the incident occurred during a game of cricket.

One death which did, however, occur during a game of cricket was that of George Twigg, who was killed 'in a cricket

---

[3] The local telephone directory shows several Vinalls and Tyes, but no Vinols.

match' in May 1775. The incident is reported in the following paragraph from *The Leeds Mercury* of 15 August 1775:

> Tuesday ended the assizes at Derby, when Mr Justice Blackstone passed sentence of death on William Wright and Thomas Sheffield, convicted of sheep stealing, who were afterwards reprieved. Thomas Reynolds, found guilty of Grand Larceny, was ordered to be transported for seven years. William Slack, convicted of Bigamy, in marrying Ann Bloore, at Calke chapel in July last, his former wife being in full life, was burnt in the hand, and to be imprisoned one year. William Waterfall, charged on the coroner's inquest, with unlawfully killing George Twigg, in a cricket match at Bakewell common in May last, was found guilty of manslaughter, burnt in the hand, and to be imprisoned nine months.

Drewry's Derby Mercury of 4–11 August 1775 also mentions the case but, apart from giving Twigge an ultimate 'e', discloses no further information except that it was Waterfall's left hand which was burnt. It does, however, give more details of Thomas Reynolds' grand larceny: he stole a black sow belonging to William Bryant and then drove it to his house five miles away. Apart from these two reports, I have been unable to trace any other account of the Waterfall case, although the coroners' records reveal that John Mander, coroner for the honour of Tutbury, was paid a fee of £1 for holding the inquest on Twigg's body.

Sir William Blackstone, the judge who sentenced Waterfall, was one of the great jurists of English law. He was Oxford's first Vinerian professor of law and between 1765 and 1769 he published his *Commentaries on the Laws of England*, which for some hundred years was an indispensable textbook for lawyers and remains the best general history of English law. In 1770 he was made a judge of the Court of Common Pleas but he made no mark as a judge and his fame rests on the *Commentaries*, which have passed through many editions and have been translated into several languages. *The Leeds Mercury* and *Drewry's Derby Mercury* also show the severity of punishments imposed two hundred years ago for a range of offences. Of the five sentences mentioned in the extract quoted above, Waterfall, having committed, at least in modern eyes, the most serious offence, received the lightest punishment.

Two other incidents, the facts of which may or may not in some way be similar to those which caused Twigg's death, are reported in the August 1987 and February 1988 issues of *The Cricketer International*. The first, which occurred in Sri Lanka, relates that:

> M. Nilam, an 18 year old cricketer, died as a result of a blow dealt by the umpire with a stump during a 25 over game played at Mahagastota, in the Nuwara Eliya district. The deceased had apparently been dissatisfied with a decision made by the umpire, resulting in hot words. The umpire is alleged, at this stage, to have plucked one of the stumps and dealt him a blow – which sadly proved fatal.

In the second incident it was the umpire who was killed:

> An Indian umpire, Uday Vasant Pimple, aged 20, was killed by an irate wicket-keeper after rejecting his appeal in a match at Nagpur, Central India, at the end of December. The wicket-keeper, who has subsequently disappeared, disputed the decision given by the umpire and then smashed him over the head with a stump. Pimple was rushed to hospital but died shortly afterwards.

Two vital differences from the 1775 case are that in the two recent cases the assailant would seem to have been guilty of murder, rather than manslaughter, but I have not been able to trace whether or not there was a prosecution in either case. Perhaps, however, Pimple's death helps to explain the pressures to which umpires are subject in some parts of the world and the, albeit unintentional, reflection of those pressures in some of their decisions.

The generation after the Waterfall case saw two other games of cricket which apparently gave rise to violent deaths, although neither occurred during the game. The first of these is reported in the *Whitehall Evening-Post* of 10–12 August 1786. The report reads:

Wednesday se'nnight an unfortunate affray happened at Haverhill: Several farmers servants having been playing at cricket, a quarrel arose between one Stephen Boreham and another person, when they agreed to fight; Abraham Goodlad to be sidesman to Boreham, and Robert Webb to be sidesman to the other, who was his fellow servant. In the course of the battle, the sidesmen quarrelled, and went to fighting; after a few blows had passed between them, Webb drew a knife, and threatened his antagonist that he would stab him if he struck another blow; which Goodlad not regarding, advanced to renew the battle, when Webb stabbed him with such violence into the bottom of his belly that the knife penetrated to the back bone: and a brother of Goodlad's running to his assistance, the blood-thirsty wretch attempted to stab him also, and would have effected his purpose had not a by-stander providentially caught hold of his arm. – The poor wounded young fellow languished till four o'clock on Thursday morning, when he expired. The Coroner's Jury sat on the body, and brought in their verdict Wilful Murder by Robert Webb, who was thereupon committed to Chelmsford gaol.

On the wording of the report it is not clear whether the quarrel was, in fact, in any way related to the game of cricket which the farmer's servants had been playing. Nor can I be certain, whatever the verdict of the coroner's jury, that Webb was subsequently tried for murder, as I have not traced any record of the case.

The circumstances of the second death are described in three contemporary newspapers but *The Bury & Norwich Post* is the only one which refers to cricket. The issue of 21 June 1809 contains the following item:

Fatal Duel. At about 2 o'clock on Thursday afternoon, Ensign P. Mahon and Assistant Surgeon Lewis O'Hara, of the 11th regiment of foot (now lying at Maldon in Essex) met upon Woodham Mortimer Common and exchanged a shot each without effect; but, upon a second fire, Mr O'Hara fell mortally wounded, having received a ball from his antagonist's pistol in the body; and about six o'clock the following morning expired. The quarrel arose at a game of cricket. Immediately after the fatal occurrence, Mr Mahon was taken into custody, but found means to elude the vigilance of the constables, and effected his escape. The seconds absconded immediately.

A short account in the *Chelmsford Chronicle* gives no additional information but the *Essex Union* of 20 June gives the following account of the inquest:

On Saturday last, an inquest was held at Maldon, before Wm. Codd, Esq. on the body of Lewis O'Hara, Esq. 2d assistant surgeon, of the 2d battalion, of the 11th regiment of foot, who was killed in a duel upon Woodham Mortimer Common on Thursday last, as mentioned in the greater part of the impression of our last paper. The investigation continued from seven o'clock in the morning, till three o'clock in the afternoon, owing to the great number of witnesses who were examined, but as none of them could identify the person of the survivor, the jury, after deliberating about five minutes; returned a verdict, Wilful murder against person or persons unknown.

On Sunday at one o'clock the remains of this unfortunate young man were interred at Maldon with military honours. The procession consisted of the 11th regiment, part of the 5th dragoons, and a division of the East Norfolk Militia (which had halted on their way to Chatham; from Stilton Barracks). The band of the Norfolk attended, playing the dead march in Saul; and the whole moved in slow order down the line, formed from the barracks to the church. The other surgeons of the regiment, Col. Stothard, of the volunteers, &c. attended as chief mourners. The deceased was 23 years of age, of very handsome appearance; 6 feet 2 inches high, and very generally beloved.

Mr. Mahon, the survivor, was taken into custody previous to the inquest, but escaped from the constable.

It seems rather strange that if eight hours of investigation failed to 'identify the person of the survivor' the *Essex Union* was able to conclude its account by naming him.

Surviving army records contain no direct references to the duel, but do give some information about the contestants. For the months of April to June 1809 Mahon is shown as being on the strength of the 1st Battalion of the 11th Foot,[4] but as 'doing duty' with the 2nd Battalion, which was stationed at Maldon. O'Hara is on the pay lists of the 2nd Battalion and is shown as having signed for his pay due up to 24 June and then as 'Died': he seems, therefore, to have been paid a week or so in advance, as he died on 16 June. Not only were there apparently no disciplinary proceedings against Mahon, but the muster rolls show that on 6 August, less than two months after O'Hara died, Ensign Peter Mahon was promoted to lieutenant. He continued to serve in this rank until the 1815 *Army List* recorded him as a 'casualty since the last publication'.

One can only speculate as to the cause of the quarrel which gave rise to the duel but, possibly, especially if the game was a single-wicket match, the dispute may have related to a bet or to some incident in the game which had a bearing on the outcome of a bet. As with the Waterfall case, the Indian sub-continent provides the only, possibly related, case which I have traced. *The Sunday Express* of 1 November 1987 contained the following paragraph:

> In Bombay a quarrel over a 100 rupees (less than five pounds) bet on which teams would make it to the World Cup semi-finals ended in one of the punters being stabbed. Two others have been charged with murder.

Among the instances in the mid-nineteenth century where people were killed during a game of cricket, or at least died of injuries sustained during a game, were some very strange ones. A book published in 1897[5] lists twenty-six instances of accidents which resulted in the death of a player, seven in the death of a spectator and two in the death of an umpire. I will digress to describe four of the most bizarre. On 25 August 1835 John Walker, who was aged 67, tripped on a tuft of grass while bowling, ruptured himself and died nine days later. In 1855, while playing at Templecombe in Somerset, a man called Tucker was killed by being crushed between some railway trucks, which were being

[4] The 11th Regiment of Foot was The North Devonshire Regiment, subsequently The Devonshire Regiment and now part of The Devonshire and Dorset Regiment.

[5] *Curiosities of Cricket* by An Old Cricketer (A. L. Ford).

shunted, while he was looking for the ball which had been hit on to the railway line. Nine years later, in February 1866 at Nowgang in India, Fusilier Goddard fielded a ball, ran to the wicket, ball in hand and knocked a stump out of the ground at the same time falling on it. The brass tip of the stump pierced Goddard's neck and he 'never spoke again and was dead in less than ten minutes'. All except one of the nine instances of the death of spectators or umpires listed were the result of the individual being hit by the ball. The one exception occurred on 1 October 1870 at Callington Grammar School in Launceston, Cornwall, where a young man called Bishop 'incautiously got close to the wicket, at which a batsman was striking with all his might at a tempting ball, but which he missed, and the bat came with such fearful force on his head that he died almost immediately'.

The Bestwick case
The first case in the twentieth century which qualifies for inclusion does so not because the death happened during or arose out of a game of cricket, but because one of the men involved was a well-known bowler who took 1,457 first-class wickets. The player was William Bestwick, a fast-medium bowler who played all but two of his 323 first-class matches for Derbyshire. His career extended from 1898 until he retired after the 1925 season in which, at the age of 50, he took 35 wickets at 15 runs each. Had he not departed for the South Wales league in 1909, only returning to Derbyshire after the Great War, his record, which in 1921 included 10 Glamorgan wickets in an innings for 40 runs, would have been even more impressive. Bestwick's career is also notable in that on 5 June 1922, in one of the five matches in which his son Robert played for Derbyshire, father and son were the two bowlers operating against Warwickshire, whose two batsmen at the time were William Quaife and his son Bernard. This is probably still, as *Wisden* said at the time, 'unique in county cricket'. On 27 January 1907, however, after he had been with Derbyshire for nine years, Bestwick was charged with manslaughter in that he did 'unlawfully and feloniously kill and slay one William Brown at Heanor on the 26th of January'. To examine this case, apart from the details of his cricket career, one needs to know something of

Bestwick's background and circumstances and also those of William Brown.

Bestwick[6] was one of the fourteen children of George Bestwick, a miner, and he was born at Heanor, which is about nine miles north of Derby, and had lived there all his life. During the winter months he, like his father, worked in the pit and in January 1907 Bestwick and Robert, his only child, lived with his father and mother as his wife had died in the summer of 1906. Brown was also a miner and almost six years older than Bestwick and, like him, was born and bred in Heanor and had started work at the age of eleven. When he was sixteen Brown emigrated to Canada where he remained for fifteen years doing various jobs in the Toronto area. While in Canada, Brown met an Irish girl called Penelope and she and Brown were married in about 1889. Some ten years later Brown and his family returned to Heanor, where he resumed his occupation as a miner. In all Brown's wife bore him ten children, of whom seven were still living in 1907.

Bestwick and Brown knew each other and their life in the pit and in the close mining community of Heanor, where they lived less than a hundred yards apart, threw them together. Both were 'strong and muscular' and Bestwick is described as having 'a harmless temperament' while, until he suffered an accident about two years before his death, Brown was regarded as a 'bright cheerful man' and the Browns as a very happy couple. The accident, which comprised a series of nasty cuts to the head, had a dramatic effect on Brown for after it 'he became morose and suspicious, with one idea praying on his mind that his wife had not been faithful to him'. In fact Brown's suspicions were groundless but subsequent to the accident, whenever Brown tasted drink he became 'a terror to the household'.

On Saturday 26 January Bestwick spent part of the evening with his brother, George, and a friend called Alfred Kemp at the New Inn. The three of them left the inn at about eleven o'clock and in Burnt House Road on their way home they met

6 Most, but not all, of the account of the Bestwick case is taken from the 1 February 1907 edition of *The Ilkeston Pioneer* newspaper, which is now defunct. Quotations, unless otherwise indicated, are from that source.

Brown, who had left his home at about a quarter to eight having had his tea. In the three hours after he left his home Brown 'appears to have got some drink, and was soon in a half-maudlin state. Neither was Bestwick sober.' When he saw Bestwick, Brown went up to him and shouted, 'That's the . . .[7] who's been with my wife.' Bestwick, presumably hoping to defuse the situation, held out his hand, saying, 'Good night, Mr Brown; good night.' They appeared to shake hands but, as Kemp put it at the inquest, Brown 'seemed to use a bit of talk' and the two men started fighting.

They fought for a minute or two, both men falling to the ground where they continued struggling. Kemp and George Bestwick made no attempt to separate them until William Bestwick cried out that Brown was biting him. Bestwick's brother, Kemp, and also Mrs Kemp who had now appeared on the scene, parted the combatants and took Bestwick, who was bleeding from his face and hand, to his brother George's house at 40 Burnt House Road. Similarly Brown, whose nose had been fractured by a blow from Bestwick, also went to the house of a brother where, in addition to his sister-in-law, was a neighbour called Albert Gillott. Brown, 'who was wild in appearance, and carrying half a brick in his hand', then rushed into his own house where 'he took a running kick at the table . . . threw the pots up to the ceiling, and shouted that five or six men had been on to him and broken his nose.' Brown then picked up two large knives, sharpened them and, dropping one, ran out of the house.

Meanwhile, Bestwick had been in his brother's house where George's wife, Sarah Alice, bathed Bestwick's hand which was bleeding. After she had done this Bestwick said, 'I think I'll go home and get to bed' and left. In well under a minute, however, Bestwick staggered back into the house with blood pouring down his face and cried, 'Oh, Sarah Alice! I'm done.' She asked Bestwick what was the matter and he replied that Brown had stabbed him and he fell with his face on his sister-in-law's apron, soaking one side of it with his blood. Bestwick then called for a pen, ink and paper so that he could make a will 'and do

---

[7] The blank is *The Pioneer*'s not the author's. The same observation, with appropriate changes of source, applies to other similar blanks.

what I have to do for my lad'. Fortunately, although Bestwick's
wounds were serious, they did not prove fatal, but he needed
nine stitches in the left side of his face and five in the right side.

In the few seconds that Bestwick had been out of his
brother's house, Brown had lost his life and his body was
discovered at about five minutes to midnight by two youths,
George Benniston and George Parkin, lying in the road opposite
Benniston's home. Brown had several knife wounds to the head,
including one behind the left ear, which was the main cause of
the haemorrhage causing his death and which, the subsequent
inquest was told, could not have been self-inflicted. The
police were called and, in the early hours of Sunday morning,
Superintendent Daybell charged Bestwick with manslaughter.
Bestwick was then 'conveyed to Langley Mill lock-up' and the
next day, Monday 28th, was remanded by the magistrate until
after the inquest, which was to be held on the 29th. *The Pioneer* reports that Bestwick's friends, especially cricketers, stood
by him and promised him support. In a splendid example of
Edwardian journalese *The Pioneer* relates that the anxious time
which Bestwick spent in the coroner's court 'must have been
enlivened by the cheery telegrams he received from various
quarters. One of his correspondents was Mr A. E. Lawton,
the old Derbyshire captain, who had spent many a happy
hour on the green sward with him in seasons past . . .' The
inquest was held by the coroner, W Harvey Whiston, and a jury
of fourteen at the Jolly Colliers Inn at Heanor. Bestwick was
present, with his head swathed in bandages, as also was his
solicitor, Horace Clifford of the Derby firm of Clifford and
Clifford. The proceedings started at half past eleven and, with
only a quarter of an hour's break for lunch, did not finish
until after half past seven in the evening. Except of course
for the unfortunate Brown, most of the dramatis personae in
the events of the fatal Saturday night gave evidence, including
Brown's widow and Doctors William Turton and Ernest Eames,
who had conducted the post mortem on Brown.

Evidence given at the inquest revealed the events, which are
narrated above, leading up to Brown's death and the finding of
his body. Exactly how Brown met his death, however, remains
something of a mystery as there were no witnesses to the final
meeting of the two men and, although it took place very close

to several houses in Burnt House Road, it seems that 'perfect silence must have reigned while the two men struggled in that fatal encounter'. What does seem clear is that when Brown ran out of his brother's house with a newly sharpened knife, he walked past the house of Bestwick's father and towards George Bestwick's house shouting as he went, 'Now for Mr Bestwick.' Coincidentally Bestwick emerged from number 40 on his way home just as Brown was approaching from the direction of Bestwick's father's house. Thinking the approaching figure was his father, Bestwick called, 'Hallo, father,' but did not receive a reply. Bestwick then turned to go home and was immediately struck with a knife on his right cheek. He then turned round to return to his brother's house and was struck on the left cheek before staggering back into number 40. At the inquest Bestwick's solicitor had asked him:

Did you touch him? – No.
Where was the last you saw of Brown? – When I got the blows.
Did you see what they were given with? – I saw it was a knife of some sort.
You went into the house, and have no idea how Brown came by his death? – No.
You did not try to take the knife away? – No.
You are quite certain you didn't do that, and that you did not try to stab him. You tell the jury on your oath that as soon as you got the blow you turned back? – Yes.

Bestwick himself had in fact been lucky to escape with his own life. Doctor Turton said in his evidence that one of Bestwick's wounds was near the temporal artery and that, in any event, Bestwick 'would probably have succumbed to his wound . . . if he had not had prompt attention'.

After Bestwick had given evidence the coroner summed up and told the jury that if they thought 'Bestwick did inflict this wound, it would be for them to say whether he did it wilfully and feloniously, or whether – if he did it at all – it was simply done to save his own life'. After three-quarters of an hour the jury returned with the following written verdict:

The opinion of the jury is that William Brown met his death in a struggle with William Bestwick, the latter acting in self defence.

The next day Bestwick was again taken before the magistrate who was told by Superintendent Daybell that, as after a very careful inquiry, the coroner's jury had returned a verdict which amounted to justifiable homicide, the police intended to offer no further evidence against Bestwick and asked that he be discharged. The account in *The Pioneer* concludes, 'The proceedings terminated and Bestwick shortly afterwards was conveyed in a cab to his home in Burnt House Road, Heanor.'

As had been indicated, this unhappy event did not interrupt Bestwick's cricket career, although he was conspicuously less successful in the 1907 season when he took only 61 wickets for Derbyshire compared with 111 at a significantly lower cost in 1906. *Wisden* makes no mention of the injuries which Bestwick had sustained or of the anguish which he must have suffered, merely commenting that his performance 'showed a sad falling-off'. Nevertheless, with Arnold Warren, Bestwick continued during 1908 and 1909 to bear the brunt of the Derbyshire attack, but after the 1909 season, in spite of having taken 75 wickets for his county, he was dismissed from the county staff owing to his intemperance. *Wisden* merely states that: 'Bestwick's connection with Derbyshire has ceased, the committee having determined not to play him any more.' Happily, after a period of exile in the South Wales league, he resumed playing for Derbyshire after the Great War and in fact played for another seven seasons, although owing to league commitments, he only appeared once in 1920.

After his playing career was over Bestwick was appointed to the list of first-class umpires and stood as an umpire until the 1937 season when illness forced him to retire. He died in May 1938. The best-known incident of Bestwick's umpiring career also has a connection with drink, although not necessarily of an alcoholic nature. In his first match for Middlesex, Denis Compton, batting at number eleven, had scored 14 when Bestwick gave him out l.b.w. As E. W. Swanton relates in his biography of Gubby Allen[8] who was Compton's partner, Allen went up to Bestwick and more in sorrow than in anger said

'Bill, that wasn't a very good l.b.w. decision, was it?', to which Bestwick replied, 'Very sorry, Mr Allen, I had to pump ship.'

The Peeping Tom case

The next case, which took place at Leeds Assizes in 1925, also involved two miners and a charge of manslaughter – as well as one of murder – against one of them for causing the death of the other. The connection with cricket in this case, however, is not in the identity of either party but in the location of the death. This was on Doncaster Town Cricket Club's ground, about 10 yards from the new pavilion, which had been opened on 19 April 1924. The case, known as 'The Peeping Tom case', proved of more than local interest, so that even *The Times* carried quite a long account. This may partly have been due to the accused being defended by Sir Edward Marshall Hall KC, one of the most eminent and colourful advocates of the period.

About half past three on the afternoon of Saturday 6 December 1924, Albert Needham, who lived in the village of South Kirby, left his home on his bicycle to go to Doncaster, which is about 10 miles from South Kirby. On this occasion Needham did not tell his wife, Margaret, why he was going to Doncaster, a journey he had been in the habit of making nearly every Saturday for the previous two years; Needham used to say that it was an outing and he enjoyed the ride. His wife knew that he visited a friend who lived in Doncaster, called Thrustle, whom she had never met and whose Christian name she did not know. The friend was in fact Wilfred Thrustle, a 33-year-old labourer, who was employed at the Doncaster Cemetery.

It is, perhaps, understandable that Needham did not tell his wife the precise purpose of his weekly visit to Thrustle, which was to accompany him to the cricket field and other promising locations to spy on courting couples. Nor was this spectator sport confined to Needham and Thrustle, but was apparently quite a popular recreation in Doncaster. Thrustle later maintained that there were 'hundreds who are spying on couples as a regular thing', including well-known businessmen, although not presumably all at the same place and time. One of these 'hundreds' was Samuel Bishop, who with Needham and

[8] Later Sir George Allen.

Thrustle, set out on that Saturday for an evening's 'viewing'. They each had torches and, while Thrustle wore an ordinary cap, Needham wore a woollen one which would make him less easily recognisable if spotted. In addition Needham was equipped with a pair of rubber knee caps made out of straps and an old motor tyre, which kept his knees dry and made silent movement easier in the proximity of his prey.

James Doyle was a 23-year-old miner, who worked at Bentley Colliery and lived with his parents in Doncaster. During the Great War Doyle, who was the eldest of six brothers, joined the navy but had been discharged as being under age. At the end of the war he had enlisted in the King's Own Yorkshire Light Infantry and served in India, but had contracted malaria and been invalided out after two years' service. Doyle was engaged to Doris Wilford, a 17-year-old domestic servant who lived and worked in Thorne Road, Doncaster, and whom Marshall Hall described as 'a fresh-complexioned pretty girl'.

On the evening of 6 December Doyle took his fiancée to the local theatre, the Arcadia, which they left at about twenty past ten. They walked down to the cricket field where they stood talking about what they would do at Christmas. By this time Needham and Thrustle had been in position for some time, although Bishop had left at just about the time Doyle and Miss Wilford arrived. Perhaps a chilly December evening had not been conducive to any of the couples under observation engaging in activities which appealed to Bishop.

At the trial three months later, there was a conflict of evidence as to exactly what happened next, but what is not in dispute is that Doyle spotted Needham and Thrustle and went up to them and that in the ensuing altercation Needham was stabbed and fatally wounded by a knife which Doyle was carrying. Doyle, apparently not realising that he had killed or even seriously injured Needham, left the cricket field with Miss Wilford and they walked towards an area with street lights. They had just crossed the road when, according to Doyle's statement, Thrustle came up to him 'from behind, smiling, and said "You've done it now; you've killed him." I then said to Doris "Hold my coat (meaning my overcoat). I'll knock that smile off his face." He ran back again and joined another fellow who seemed similar to the one who had attacked me.' Doyle, in his statement, described how he thought that Needham was the other man with Thrustle when the latter approached him and that he was smiling, so Doyle discounted the allegation that he had killed Needham and went to Miss Wilford's sister's house, where they arrived at about eleven o'clock.

Two days later, on Monday 8 December, Doyle saw from the newspaper that someone had in fact been 'murdered' at the cricket field and the following day, after consulting with his parents and his fiancée, Doyle went with his father to the offices of Corbin, Greener & Co, solicitors and then accompanied one of the partners, William Crawford, to the police station, where Doyle made a statement. Later the same day Doyle was formally charged with the murder of Albert Needham.

Thrustle's version of events, which came out at the adjourned inquest held on Monday 22 December and at the subsequent trial of Doyle, was significantly different from that given by Doyle. According to Thrustle, after the struggle he went over to where Needham lay, lifted up his head and spoke to him and saw that Needham was dead. Thrustle then went after Doyle and Miss Wilford and when he caught them up said to Doyle, 'Young fellow, do you know you have killed that man?' to which Doyle replied, 'Yes, and I'll . . . well kill you.' Thrustle's version then alleged that, on continuing to follow the couple, Doyle had threatened him with a weapon, which he could not identify, but that Miss Wilford had said to Doyle, 'Come along with you,' that the couple had then turned and gone away and that he had continued to follow them, but had lost them when they turned a corner. Thrustle said he then went to Bishop's house and told him what had happened but Bishop, no doubt relieved to have left the cricket field just before Doyle spotted Needham and Thrustle, said he could not do anything as he had not been with them when Needham had been killed. Thrustle then went back to his own home, told his wife that 'something terrible' had happened and the two of them went to the police and reported the matter.

Both Doyle's statement and Thrustle's evidence, which the jury also heard at the adjourned inquest, gave details of their differing versions of the quarrel and of the struggle which led to Needham's death. After a hearing lasting over four hours the jury returned a verdict against Doyle of 'manslaughter,

under great provocation'. The coroner accordingly committed
Doyle for trial at Leeds Assizes. A voluntary subscription list
was opened to pay for Doyle's defence and the money raised
enabled his solicitor to brief Sir Edward Marshall Hall, then
nearing the end of his career, to defend Doyle. The case was
tried at Leeds on Wednesday 25 March 1925 before Mr Justice Branson. Sir Herbert Neild KC led for the prosecution,
assisted by R. F. Burnand,[9] while Marshall Hall was assisted by
J. A. Greene.[10] In spite of the verdict of the coroner's jury, the
prosecution decided to persist with the charge of murder, as
well as that of manslaughter. Doyle's hope of acquittal, at least
on the capital charge, clearly depended mainly on whether the
jury of nine men and three women believed Thrustle's version
of events or preferred that of Doyle and his fiancée.

Apart from admitting plans and photographs of the cricket
field to evidence, Thrustle was the first witness called. He
told how he and Needham were standing near the gate when
a man came up to them and said, 'What's the game then?' to
which Needham replied, 'Nothing, man; what's the matter with
you?' The man then said, 'I'll show you what's the matter,' and,
drawing something which glittered from his body, struck a blow
against Needham. According to Thrustle, Needham seemed to
ward off the first blow but the man struck at Needham again
and caught him in the body. Needham then staggered away
saying, 'My God, Wilf, he's done it!' Thrustle said that the man
then attacked him but Thrustle shot his foot out and caught the
man in the chest, that there was then a struggle between them,
during which the man struck several blows at Thrustle with the
weapon, but that Thrustle eventually prevailed and threw the
man off. After he had run through his evidence with his own
counsel, Thrustle was subjected, as *The Doncaster Gazette* put
it, to 'the incisive and deadly questions' of Marshall Hall, to
which Thrustle 'returned determined answers, never flinching'.

In response to Marshall Hall's questions Thrustle denied
that he and Needham were on the ground when Doyle first
saw them, denied that he and Needham 'provoked Doyle by
a blow from the knee in the lower part of the body' and

[9] Later Sir Frank Burnand.
[10] Later Sir John Greene.

denied also that he 'bashed' Doyle's hat over his eyes and knocked him on to the ground. Marshall Hall then went on to suggest that the mark of Thrustle's foot on Doyle's coat could only be consistent with it having got there when Doyle was on the ground, as Thrustle would have to have been 'a pretty agile man' to kick Doyle on the chest while he was standing up. To this suggestion Thrustle merely replied, 'Yes'.

Marshall Hall decided not to call Doyle as a witness, which of course meant that he could not be cross-examined by the prosecution, explaining in his closing speech that Doyle had gone voluntarily to the police, asked to make a statement, adhered to that statement before the magistrates, had nothing to add to it and that the statement constituted his defence to the charges. The relevant part of that statement, which covered the time from when Doyle spotted Needham and Thrustle until he and Miss Wilford left the cricket field, reads as follows:

We had been stood there a few minutes when I noticed two men laid down in the field, close to the gate. I could see what their idea was, and naturally it made me a little bit wild. As I was not frightened of them I jumped over the gate to them. When I jumped over they suddenly jumped up.

I then walked up to them and said to them 'What sort of beastly idea is this you're playing? Chaps of your age ought to have more sense.' The stiffest (sic) man of the two said 'What do you mean? Get out. Take that,' and he bashed my hat down over my eyes, and brought his knee up into my stomach. He brought me to my knees.

Both men then started to kick me. I was on my knees. As I could not get up I brought a knife out to frighten them. They said 'Right', and made their efforts more vigorous. I struck out and seemed to hit them once or twice. It seemed to take no effect, till one of them stood back a few paces and said, 'The little . . . has got me.'

They then both ran away to the other side of the cricket pavilion. I was laid on the ground, a little while, expecting them to come back. I then got over the gate and they didn't come. Doris and I then walked along to where lights were, towards the War Memorial, and thought I would be safe.

In her evidence Miss Wilford corroborated the version of events given by Doyle to the extent consistent with her being some distance from the struggle which took place. In his closing speech Marshall Hall referred to the 'figure of Bishop flitting across the story' and suggested that the second man, whom Doyle said he saw with Thrustle after the killing, might have been him.

Summing up, Sir George Branson told the jury that the whole case turned on the facts and that if they accepted Thrustle's evidence it was a case of deliberate murder. On the other hand the judge said that if they thought Doyle was being attacked by 'two bullies' and that he was justified in using force against them to save his own life or to save himself from great bodily harm, then he was entitled to be acquitted. Not surprisingly in the light of the judge's summing up which was very critical of Thrustle, the jury, which was described by *The Doncaster Gazette* as being 'as fair as possible a sample of Yorkshire justice tempered with mercy' found Doyle not guilty of both murder and manslaughter.

One question which the accounts of the inquest and the trial do little to answer is why, in the first place, Doyle was carrying a knife. The only explanation for this was provided by Miss Wilford at the inquest, who told the coroner that she and Doyle had been watched on a number of occasions before 6 December and that several times when they had been out together Doyle had had the knife in a sheath attached to his belt. After his acquittal Doyle returned by train to Doncaster and was given a hero's welcome at the station. On Saturday 1 August 1925 James Doyle and Doris May Wilford were married at Doncaster Register Office.

Road accidents

Cases of murder and manslaughter involving cricketers are fortunately rare but, by the nature of their vocation, they travel a lot by road and they have been no more immune than other sections of the community from involvement in accidents. One of the first cricketers to be killed in a road accident was George Street, the Sussex wicket-keeper, who played for England in one Test. On 24 April 1924, on his way home on his motor cycle, he tried to avoid a lorry at a crossroads, crashed into a wall and was killed instantly. Although such accidents are followed by an inquest, few result in a prosecution. One which did occur on 12 January 1935 and involved Vallance Jupp, the Sussex and Northants all-rounder.

Jupp was one of cricket's all-rounders in the full sense of that expression. Not only did he score 23,278 runs and take 1,658 wickets in a first-class career extending over thirty years, but he was both captain and secretary of Northamptonshire, for a time simultaneously, and in Northants' years of famine, as Robertson-Glasgow put it, 'others flickered; Jupp shone steadily'. Starting as a professional with Sussex, he became an amateur and moved to Northants when he was offered the secretaryship after the 1921 season. He was unlucky not to have played in more than eight Tests, but for business reasons he had to refuse an invitation to tour Australia in 1920–1.

Jupp was captain of Northants from June 1927 until the end of the 1931 season and in 1932 had a particularly successful season, scoring more runs and taking more wickets than any other Northants' player, and achieving the double of 1,000 runs and 100 wickets. He gave up the secretaryship after the 1932 season and in the following year, at the age of 42, did the double for the tenth and last time. He missed the whole of the 1934 season due to illness, which was a major contributory factor in Northants' reverting to bottom of the championship, a position they occupied seven times in the 1930s.

On the night of Saturday 12 January 1935, some four months before the start of the next cricket season, Jupp left the George Row Club in Northampton shortly before half past eleven. He drove his 12 horse-power Vauxhall along the main road leading towards Brixworth, which is about 6 miles from Northampton and was approaching the turning leading to the village of Pitsford when he overtook an 18 horse-power Talbot driven by a Pitsford resident, Houison Craufurd, in which Craufurd's wife and a stockbroker called Colin Armstrong were passengers. Before Jupp could regain the left-hand side of the road, his car collided with a BSA motor cycle ridden by 19-year-old Charles Barrett and on which Wilfred Moisey, a friend of the same age, was the pillion passenger. Jupp, Barrett and Moisey were all injured – Moisey so seriously that he died in hospital less than four hours after the crash.

Jupp was committed for trial by the Northampton Divisional Bench for the manslaughter of Moisey and, on 24 January, the case opened at Northamptonshire Assizes before Mr Justice Humphreys. Reginald Vaughan appeared for the prosecution, while Jupp was defended by Norman Birkett KC[11] and Arthur Ward, whose instructing solicitors were Ray and Vials. George Vials, who dealt with the case, was himself a good all-round athlete and captained Northants for three seasons before the Great War, including 1912 when Northants were second in the table, a position they did not reach again until 1957 when Vials was president of the club.

Vaughan outlined the circumstances of the accident and called Craufurd, the driver of the car which Jupp had overtaken, as his first witness. His evidence was damaging to Jupp's case and he said that he did not see any attempt by Jupp to get the Vauxhall back to the correct side of the road and that he realised, before it occurred, that there was going to be an accident and he therefore stopped his car some 80 yards from the point of impact, before the accident happened. Craufurd's passenger, Armstrong, also gave evidence to much the same effect and both his and Craufurd's evidence stood up well to Birkett's cross-examination. Barrett, who was a clicker[12] and was brought into court in a wheelchair, said in his evidence that he was travelling at about 25 miles an hour when he saw two cars a considerable distance away, the one overtaking the other. Too late he realised that the overtaking car was not going to change course or reduce speed and, although he braked and tried to get on to the grass verge, he was unable to avoid a collision.

While the prosecution never alleged that Jupp had been drinking, the defence had no choice but to admit that his car had been on the wrong side of the road when the accident occurred. Jupp, who described himself in the witness-box as an electrical contractor and sports outfitter, told how when he was overtaking Craufurd he pulled at the ring and cord of his blind

[11] Later Lord Birkett.
[12] Shoemaker who cuts out leather.

attachment and the ring slipped out of his hand.[13] Jupp stated, 'I did not continue my efforts to pull down the blind because I was in a skid. . . . When I felt the skid I had to release the cord and I was blinded by the lights at the rear.' Jupp estimated his speed at about 40 miles an hour, which was consistent with the estimate given by Craufurd. In answer to questions from his counsel, Jupp then described how, having got out of the first skid, he had got into another which he had not been able to control before the collision.

Birkett called four witnesses to refute the police's contention that the road was not frosty or slippery and also called Stephen Schillizzi, the president of Northants CCC, who testified that Jupp had a very good general reputation and was an extremely careful and very thoughtful driver. In his final address Birkett returned to the question of the skids over which Jupp had no control and which had forced him, against his will, to remain on the wrong side of the road, thus leading to the accident, but Sir Travers Humphreys' summing up cannot have encouraged Birkett or his client. The judge said that, according to Jupp, the tragedy was the sort of thing that might be expected at any time when there was a slippery road, even when someone was driving carefully and properly. He added, 'I hope that is not correct. If it is correct then the sooner we go back to the old days of a man waving a red flag in front of each motor car the better, because it is too horribly dangerous, apparently otherwise.' He also suggested to the jury that even if Jupp had skidded, as seemed probable, that did not exonerate him. Humphreys added that Birkett had maintained that the whole question was skid or no skid, but 'I am not sure that appeals to me.'

Sir Travers told the jury that there were three verdicts open to them, which were first not guilty, secondly guilty of manslaughter and thirdly not guilty of manslaughter but guilty of dangerous driving. After an absence of 35 minutes the jury found Jupp guilty of manslaughter. The judge said that, in spite of Jupp's admirable character, he found it incon-

[13] By pulling the ring a blind would have been pulled up covering the rear window, thus eliminating the dazzle from the driver's mirror caused by the lights of a following car.

sistent with his public duty to deal with the matter by way of a fine and sentenced Jupp to nine months' imprisonment and ordered that he be disqualified from holding a driving licence for two years.

Not surprisingly, Jupp did not play for Northants in 1935, but in 1936 he played in sixteen matches and took 53 wickets for the county and again played fairly regularly in 1937. In 1938, he played in only four matches and finally retired from the first-class game at the age of 47. He lived for another twenty-two years until, on 9 July 1960, he collapsed and died in his garden at Spratton, which is about three miles from where the accident had taken place twenty-five years earlier.

Although Jupp was clearly badly at fault on that January night in 1935, he was probably unlucky not to have been convicted of the lesser offence of dangerous driving. But he is remembered as a fine all-round cricketer (only Wilfred Rhodes and George Hirst having done the double more often), who for most of his career was playing for one of the weakest sides in the championship. Geoffrey Cuthbertson, who captained Northants in 1936 and 1937, has written of him:

> I was told by certain people when I took over the captaincy of Northants that he would be a trouble for me to handle. Nothing could have been further from the truth. Juppie gave me his wholehearted support both on and off the cricket field. His business interests did not permit his playing too often, but when he did so he was a great asset.

Robertson-Glasgow ends his portrait of Jupp with a sentence which its subject might well have been satisfied should serve as his epitaph: 'No tougher cricketer has played in our times; but under the rock, I have not found a kinder man.'

The following year, 1936, was a particularly bad year for accidents involving cricketers and on 26 August Reginald Northway of Northants was killed in an accident in which his team-mate, A. H. ('Fred') Bakewell, was so badly injured that it ended his cricket career. Northants could ill afford to lose the services of such a talented cricketer as Bakewell who, in his final innings in first-class cricket, scored 241 not out against the champion county, Derbyshire. Less than a week later, on 2 September, when returning home from Gloucestershire's last match of the season in which Walter Hammond scored 317, Dallas Page, Gloucestershire's captain, was killed when, after swerving to avoid a motor cyclist, his car hit a wall. At the subsequent inquest the jury added a rider to their verdict that the motor cyclist had made an error of judgment, which amounted to negligence but not criminal negligence.

In 1937 one of the greatest Australian fast bowlers was the victim of a freakish accident on 22 July. Ted McDonald, christened not Edward but Edgar, and Jack Gregory were the famous pair of Australian fast bowlers who dominated the 1921 series against England. McDonald took twenty-seven wickets in the five Tests in which no less than thirty Englishmen appeared in a vain attempt to turn the tide. McDonald's international career was cut short when he joined Nelson in the Lancashire League and qualified for Lancashire. In the seasons of 1924 to 1931 he took 1,053 wickets for Lancashire and helped them to win the championship four times in eight years. After he retired from playing for Lancashire he ran the Raikes Hall Hotel in Blackpool and resumed playing league cricket. Indeed he was due to have played in a match the day after he was killed.

Shortly after one o'clock in the morning on Thursday 22 July 1937, McDonald was driving along the Blackrod by-pass towards Manchester when the off side of his car caught the off side of a car being driven in the opposite direction by James Murray of Salford. It seems that McDonald was too near the centre of the road and his car knocked the back mudguard off Murray's car and the impact caused McDonald's car to crash through some railings and down a bank into a field. Miraculously neither Murray nor McDonald was hurt, although both cars were badly damaged. The police were sent for and Police Constable Steele arrived on the scene. While he, Murray and McDonald were discussing the accident, another car approached them and this struck and killed McDonald; Murray and PC Steele jumped clear just in time on to the footpath. The third car was driven by George Foster, a typewriter dealer, of Manchester and he was charged with manslaughter and, alternatively, with dangerous driving and other lesser driving offences.

The case was heard on 5 August at Bolton County Police Court by the local magistrates under the chairmanship of Colonel H. M. Hardcastle; Foster was defended by Dennis Gerrard,[14] a barrister, and Henry Fazackerley, a partner in a Preston firm of solicitors, prosecuted on behalf of the police. The prosecution maintained that Foster's speed at the time of the accident had been much more than the 25 to 30 miles an hour that he claimed, as McDonald's body was thrown 24 feet from the point of impact and his right shoe was found 163 feet away. The defence contended that, after the first accident, Murray's car had been left in a dangerous position and that PC Steele, by flashing his torch to warn Foster of the accident, had confused rather than helped him, as a van flashing its lights had been approaching from the opposite direction at the same time. After a lengthy retirement the bench considered that no prima facie case of manslaughter had been made out and that the other charges had not been proved. The summonses were therefore dismissed and Foster was discharged.

On 6 September 1959 another overseas Test cricketer was fatally injured in a road accident, which occurred in the early hours of the morning. Three West Indian Test players, Tom Dewdney, a fast bowler who played in nine Tests, Garfield Sobers and O. G. ('Collie') Smith, were travelling to London to play in a charity match when, in the early hours of the morning, their car was in a collision with a cattle lorry near Darlaston in Staffordshire. All three were injured, Smith fatally, as he died in hospital four days later. Sobers was driving at the time and it seems that fatigue may have induced a moment's loss of concentration, something of which virtually every driver is at some time guilty, but usually without such tragic consequences. After the accident Sobers himself could remember little of it, except for 'the blinding blaze' of the headlights of the oncoming lorry, which had caused him to lose his sense of direction. On 11 November he was fined £10 at Stone Magistrates' Court for careless driving and his licence was endorsed and suspended for a month.

[14] Later Sir Dennis Gerrard.

Smith was an exuberant cricketer of great promise, who had scored four hundreds in the twenty-six Tests in which he appeared, including a century on his first appearances against both England and Australia. At the time of his death he was a popular and successful professional with Burnley in the Lancashire League and his popularity in his own country was evidenced by the 60,000 people who attended his funeral in Jamaica. Fortunately, Sobers and Dewdney were not seriously injured and Sobers, who was devastated by the death of his close friend, went on to become one of the game's greatest all-rounders, possibly the greatest. He was also a fine ambassador for the game, once described by Colin Cowdrey as 'the fairest sportsman ever to play with or against' and in 1975 he was knighted by the Queen in Barbados in recognition of his services to the game of cricket.

II

NEVER ON SUNDAY

The Boxgrove case

Most of the early references to cricket in law cases occur in those which relate to the illegal playing of cricket, especially on Sundays, and the location of the 'offences' in these cases reflects the cradle of the game as having been in Kent, Surrey and Sussex. The two earliest cases were heard in the Consistory Court of the Sussex diocese of Chichester and concern games played in two villages, which are both within five miles of Chichester. The first case, which was heard on Saturday 4 May 1611, resulted in a fine of one shilling being imposed on Richard Latter and Bartholomew Wyatt of Sidlesham for playing cricket instead of attending church on Easter Sunday, 24 March. Eleven years later a more fully documented case concerns two games of cricket played on Sundays 28 April and 5 May 1622 in the churchyard of Boxgrove, which is about six miles northeast of Sidlesham. The reference is contained in the Easter presentments of the Chichester Archdeaconry for 1622 and was discovered by Doctor Hilda Johnstone when editing a book of these. A presentment is a formal complaint of an offence made by the parish authorities to the bishop or archdeacon and the Boxgrove one, which has often been reproduced or quoted, reads as follows:

> BOXGRAVE. I present Raphe West, Edward Hartley, Richard Slaughter, William Martin, Richard Martin junior, together with others in their company whose names I have no notice of, for playing at cricket in the churchyard on Sunday, the fifte of May, after sufficient warning given to the contrary, for three speciall reasons: first, for that it is contrary to the 7th article; secondly, for that they use to breake the church-windowes with the ball; and thirdly, for that a little childe had like to have her braynes beaten out with a cricket batt.

And also I present Richard Martin senior and Thomas West the old churchwardens for defending and mayntayning them in it.

Wee present Anthony Ward, servant to Mr. Earle, our minister, and Edward Hartley, for playing at cricket in evening prayer tyme on Sunday the xxviij th of Aprill.

Item wee present Henry Hasted and his wife for incontinency before marriage, shee being with childe by him before they were married.

The item regarding the Hasted family is usually omitted but it seemed to add a bit of local colour and perhaps also an insight on the vicar's sense of priority.

In this case it was the vicar, rather than the churchwardens, who made the presentment relating to 5 May as the old churchwardens had been involved in the offence complained of. Incidentally, the 1622 Easter presentments for the Boxgrave Deanry (sic) make entertaining reading as a wide variety of matters in other parishes were brought to the attention of the ecclesiastical authorities. Most of these were reporting people for not receiving communion or for not attending church, although there was apparently only one such offender at Eartham as everyone there was reported as having received communion 'except Goodwife Martin, who lyeth in'. At Birdham, Nicholas Wingham, the miller, was presented 'for grinding on Easter Sunday last past with his windmill', while Earnley had trouble with Margaret Knight and Gartrude (sic) Warner 'for chiding and brawling and using many uncivill and undecent words . . . while the minister was catechizing the young communicants upon Easter Day last'.

The Boxgrove presentment was the subject of a detailed study[1] in 1972, its 350th anniversary, and I am indebted to that study for further information concerning the case. The mention of the 7th article is not a reference to the seventh commandment, which forbids adultery, nor to the seventh of the Thirty Nine Articles of Religion, which concerns the Old Testament, but to one of the Visitation Articles which provided incumbents and churchwardens with guidelines for preparing

[1] *The Cricket Match at Boxgrove in 1622* by Timothy J. McCann and Peter M. Wilkinson, Sussex Archaeological Collection, volume CX.

presentments. The articles applicable in 1622 do not appear to have survived but those administered in 1628 contain a section entitled 'Articles concerning the Church, the Ornaments, sacred utensils, and possessions of the same' and the seventh article in that section exhorts that churchyards should not be 'prophaned' by any 'use to quarrell, fight, play or make meetings, banquets, Church-ales[2] there . . .'.

The reference to breaking the church windows is self-explanatory, but I would not have thought, as the 1972 study concluded, that it necessarily suggested that some sort of hard ball was used; a soft ball hit hard can break windows, as I know to my cost! As to a little child risking having 'her braynes beaten out with a cricket batt', the generally accepted explanation is that in 1622 a batsman was allowed to hit the ball twice in order to avoid being caught and possibly allowed to hit it twice whether or not there was a risk of his dismissal. In a game played on a makeshift pitch and without boundaries, one can therefore understand how the fielding side and even spectators could be at risk. As mentioned in the chapter entitled 'Sudden Death' where this topic is discussed, in 1624 a player was killed in circumstances which also seem to support the theory that the ball could be hit twice.

The Boxgrove presentment having been made, the persons named appeared before the Consistory Court in Chichester Cathedral. The record of the court shows that the hearing took place on Monday 22 July when the various 'defend-ants' appeared in open court, publicly confessed their sins by individually reciting their offences and their repentance and were then severally dismissed by the bishop of Chichester with a pious admonition ('cum pia monicione eum dismisit'). Finally, it seems that each man had to pay one shilling for the court's expenses which meant that, bearing in mind that they probably lost a day's wages in attending court, they all suffered a significant financial penalty as well as a spiritual one.

---

[2] Church-ales were gatherings of parishioners following afternoon church when the people amused themselves and drank ale and at which collections were usually made for church purposes.

Four Kent cases

While in 1622 it was the vicar who made the presentment, seven years later it was the incumbent who was presented. In 1629 Henry Cuffin, a curate of Ruckinge, which is near Ashford in Kent, was presented in the Archdeacon's Court for playing cricket on many Sundays in the summer of 1628. It was alleged that 'after he had read divine service at evening prayer, in the afternoon [he] did immediately go and play at Cricketts in very unseemly manner with boys, and other very mean and base persons of our parish, to the great scandal of his ministerie and the offence of such as saw him play the game.' Cuffin admitted that he had played cricket with some of his parishioners, but denied that there was anything mean or base about them averring, on the contrary, that they were 'persons of repute and fashion'.

This case has been cited as evidence that, in its early days, cricket was played not only by the 'lower orders' but also by the 'quality' but I do not know what, if any, punishment was imposed on the erring cleric.

The next case too is not fully documented but does have an interesting background. In 1618 King James I was travelling through Lancashire when a petition was presented to him complaining about the acts of the puritan magistrates and ministers, who were trying to suppress the people's Sunday games. The king expressed sympathy and, after consulting the bishop of Chester, issued a proclamation known as the 'Book of Sports'. This recited that the king's subjects 'were debarred from Lawful Recreation upon Sundays after Evening Prayers ended and upon Holy days' and stated that one of the effects of this was that 'this prohibition barreth the common and meaner sort of people from using such exercises as may make their bodies more able for Warre'. The proclamation stated that no lawful recreation should be barred 'such as dancing . . . Archery, leaping Vaulting or any other such harmless Recreation, nor from having May-Games Whitson Ales, and Morris dances and the setting up of May poles'. James directed that all clergy should read the Book of Sports in parish churches but many puritan clergy refused to comply with what they regarded as profanity and James withdrew his command.

In 1633 James' successor, Charles I, reissued the order,

perhaps unwisely, although, because of the Sunday Observance Act of 1625 and the terms of the Book of Sports itself, the circumstances in which even the permitted games could be played on Sunday were very limited. The 1625 Act, which remained in force until after the Second World War, prohibited any meetings or assemblies of people on Sunday 'outside their owns Parishes . . . for any sports or pastimes whatsoever', while the Book of Sports made it clear that, even within their own parishes, people were forbidden to take part in the permitted recreations on Sunday unless they had previously attended church. Nevertheless many puritan clergy again refused to obey the king's order, while one priest read the Ten Commandments as well as the Book of Sports and ended by saying, 'Dearly beloved, ye have heard the commandments of God and man. Obey which you please.'

One of the clergy who refused to publish the Book of Sports was the Reverend Thomas Wilson, the vicar of Otham near Maidstone. As a result of his refusal Wilson was suspended from office in 1635 and later moved to Maidstone, of which he became vicar in 1643. Writing of a period before Wilson's suspension, the Reverend George Swinnock, Wilson's biographer, wrote[3] that 'Maidstone was formerly a very prophane Town, insomuch that I have seen Morrice dancing, Cudgel playing, Stool-ball, Crickets and many other sports openly and publicly on the Lords Day.' According to Swinnock these 'vain sinful customes of sports were reformed' before Wilson, who was clearly of a puritanical disposition, moved to Maidstone. However, the reform can not have been entirely effective as in 1640 Wilson charged some cricketers in an ecclesiastical court in Maidstone with playing cricket on a Sunday, breaking a window and endangering the life of a child on the common. The accused were found guilty on the first two counts but not, it seems, on the third and at least they had played their game on the common and not in the churchyard.

The next reference to the unlawful playing of cricket also involves Maidstone but as the location of the assizes where the case in question was to have been tried, not where the offending game was played. Among the indictments of the Kent Assizes held at Maidstone on 27 July 1652 and which

[3] *The Life and Death of Mr Tho. Wilson, Minister of Maidstone*, published 1672.

are now filed at the Public Record Office are two relating to the playing of cricket at Cranbrook, which is some 14 miles from Maidstone. The first alleged that on 17 May 1652 (which was a Monday), and on various other days between 17 May and 6 July 1652, John Rabson esquire, Thomas Basden clothier and John Reade husbandman all of Cranbrook together, with other persons unknown to the jurors, 'unlawfully and unjustly did play at a certain unlawful game called crickett' in a field at Cranbrook called Bullfield which belonged to Jehosaphat Starr, a yeoman of Cranbrook. The second indictment was similar and charged Stephen Osburne clothier, Thomas Ward barber, Thomas Basden clothier, John Reade husbandman and Isaac Walter the younger labourer, all of Cranbrook, with playing cricket on the same field on 20 May 1652 (which was a Wednesday) and also between 20 May and 6 July 1652. In both indictments the offence was alleged to be 'against the form of statute . . . and against the public peace'.

Thus there were apparently two separate games or series of games which, however large Bullfield was, must have been played on different days because Basden and Reade played in both of them. The strong implication in the indictments is that cricket itself was alleged to be an unlawful game, rather than merely playing it on a particular day or in a particular place, but this may be attributable to the indictments being badly drafted. In any event, neither indictment was proceeded with as they were found not to be 'true bills'.

The last of the four Kent cases again concerns playing cricket on a Sunday, in this instance at Eltham in 1654. Information concerning the incident, however, is limited to a short entry in the churchwardens' and overseers' book for Eltham for 1654. The relevant entry reads 'An accompt of all such moneys as hath been received for misdemeanours of whom and how disposed of Cricket players on ye Lord's Day'. It then names the guilty men who were Francis Clayford, Edward Layton, John Poole, William Fox, William Starbrock and widow Roode's son and indicated that two shillings was received from each. The tribunal in this case, if a court at all, was clearly an ecclesiastical one like the 1622 and 1640 cases, but no court is mentioned. It may be, therefore, that the churchwardens had, or assumed, certain powers of summary justice and that the seven miscreants were fined

on the spot. Although, it cost them each twice as much as the
Boxgrove offenders it seems that they did not have to confess
their sins publicly, be admonished by the bishop or lose a day's
pay.

A Surrey case

Like those of the Eltham case, details of the case in Surrey
are tantalisingly brief. The Surrey Quarter Sessions Roll for
May 1671 states that a certain Edward Bound late of Shere
was presented for playing unlawful games, commonly known
as cricket, on Sunday 16 April 1671 and on other Sundays both
before and after, in contempt of the laws of England, as a bad
example to others and against the peace. It also recorded that
Bound was exonerated under the General Pardon Act. Whether or
not this was due to the more relaxed attitude regarding activities
on Sundays following the Restoration, or to some other reason,
history does not relate, but it is worth noting, although probably
coincidental, that of the cases so far dealt with in this chapter,
'convictions' were secured in the cases brought by the ecclesiastical authorities, while there were 'acquittals' in the cases
brought by the civil authorities.

Later cases

Prosecutions for playing cricket on Sundays continued during
the eighteenth and nineteenth centuries and certainly in the late
eighteenth century the activity still provoked strong feelings, as
is evident from a short report in *The Times* of 24 September
1789:

> The writer of this paragraph has lately been a visitor to
> Southampton and was much concerned to see on a Sunday
> evening cricket matches permitted by the side of the public
> road. On expressing his surprise at the indecency of the act,
> as well as the supineness of the clergy and magistrates, he
> was told that this was the constant practice every Sunday.

The writer urged the local magistrates to follow 'the exemplary
conduct of their Sovereign, by discountenancing every appearance of vice'. However, the next actual prosecution which I have
come across took place almost 150 years after the presentment

at the Surrey Quarter Sessions in 1671. On 20 November 1817
several people were convicted before a magistrate at Larlingford
for playing cricket on Old Buckenham Green in Norfolk. Four
years later the issue of the *Morning Post* of 3 September 1821
reported that, on 31 August John Francis, John Standley, James
Toms, Thomas Wilson and John Ellis were convicted before the
mayor and magistrates of Dover for playing on the Sabbath.
They were fined 3s. 4d. each, which the first three paid, but,
the report stated, 'Wilson and Ellis, in default of distress,[4] will
be placed in the stocks for three hours.' In the following year
The Weekly Dispatch of 2 June 1822 contained the following
brief report: 'Last week ten young men of Whatlode Drove paid
the fine for playing cricket on the Lord's Day.' There is no
indication how much the fine was. Perhaps 3s. 4d, a sixth of a
pound and probably about £5 in current terms, was a standard
or prescribed amount.

The convictions in the last three cases, none of which
would appear to have been other than 'knock-up' games, are
surprising when it is remembered that the 1625 Act limited
unlawful sporting activities to those outside the participants'
own parish. That this provision did not fall into disrepute was
evidenced in the House of Commons on 15 August 1843 in
an answer given by the Attorney General to a question asked
by Lord John Manners[5] 'with respect to the recreations of the
working classes'. Lord John said it appeared that some young
men, who were playing cricket recently on a Sunday evening
'after the hours of divine service' at Hurley Common[6] in Berkshire, were brought before a magistrate and fined 15 shillings
each, which is about £25 in current terms. The men had asked
for time to raise the money, as they were only earning 7 or 8
shillings a week but were told that they must go to gaol unless
the money was paid at once. In fact some 'charitable persons'
paid the fines for the men who were set free. Lord John asked
the Attorney 'whether it was illegal for poor people to play at
cricket or any other manly game on Sunday after the hours of

---

[4] The legal seizing of a chattel in order to satisfy a debt out of the
proceeds of its sale.
[5] Later the seventh Duke of Rutland.
[6] Hansard says Burley, but I believe it should be Hurley.

divine service . . . ?' In his reply Sir Frederick Pollock said that the questioner had not stated whether the men had been in their own parish or not, but if they had been in their own parish 'they were not violating the law, but otherwise . . . they came within the meaning of the statute relating to persons assembling out of their own parish for purposes not justified by law'.

In late Victorian times prosecutions are known to have been instituted in a variety of places: Leicester in 1885, Dublin in 1894 and Sydney, New South Wales in 1897. The last is particularly interesting in that twenty-eight cricketers were charged under the Sunday Observance Act of 1625 'with forming a concourse out of their own parishes on the Lord's Day for the sport of cricket'. Thus, on the other side of the world, the authorities applied an Act of Parliament passed in 1625 – more than 150 years before the first white settlement in Australia and when the very existence of the country was unknown.

It is hardly surprising, that with the combination of the Sunday Observance legislation and the strict formality of the Victorian Sunday, organised games of cricket on Sundays did not become at all common until after the Great War and that, even then, they initially provoked a lot of opposition. This led to the members of some clubs, who wanted to play on Sundays, forming a separate club with a different name which was related to but separate from the main club. The main club thus remained untainted by Sunday play and members who disapproved of it could continue belonging to the club with a clear conscience. Even as late as 1937 Sunday cricket was common only in the south of England, if Sir Home Gordon is to be believed. Gordon was a copious cricket writer and for many years wrote the 'In the Pavilion' article in *The Cricketer*. His work is notable less for its accuracy than for its convoluted prose style, of which his reference to Sunday cricket in the chapter on club cricket in 'M.C.C. 1787–1937' is an example.

One post-War innovation is the multiplicity of Sunday club cricket. Some may remember how long ago those playing for the Thespids furtively carried their cricket bags to some remote field to encounter a rather conscience-stricken scratch side. Now many clubs, both peregrinatory and domiciled, exist more for Sabbatarian games than others, while amateurs engaged in county cricket utilize the seventh day in attempting to rattle up long scores. This feature, however, is almost entirely confined to the South. The first Sunday game ever played in Durham took place only last year, though at Ampleforth and other Roman Catholic schools it has long been a feature.

Since 1945 Sunday cricket has been commonplace, although most clubs still put out more sides on a Saturday and league games are generally played on that day rather than Sundays. In 1966 Rothmans International Cavaliers started playing 40-over matches, which were televised, and in 1969 the John Player League (now the Refuge Assurance League) started and one-day Sunday cricket now generally attracts larger crowds than the traditional three or four day game. Somehow I doubt if most modern professionals, as they engage in the remunerative and rather artificial form of cricket on Sundays, realise that 370 years earlier their conduct would have risked them having publicly to repent of their sins before the bishop.

III

FINANCIAL ALLSORTS

Virtually all cases which reach the courts have financial implications for the parties even if sometimes, as for example in criminal cases where a custodial sentence is imposed, the financial effects are incidental. In some types of case, such as gaming, theft and fraud, the subject matter of the case itself is of a financial nature and it is cases in that category which are dealt with in this chapter. The cases cover a period of over three hundred years and most of the early ones concern gaming.

Some gaming cases

The first case arose out of a wager on a cricket match which was played at Coxheath on 29 May 1646. The report of the case is contained in a partly illegible Latin manuscript, a translation of which is held in the borough records of Maidstone, which is about three miles from Coxheath. The match was between Samuel Filmer and Thomas Harlackenden on the one side and Walter Francklyn, Richard Marsh, William Cooper and Robert Sanders on the other. On the day before the match one Nicholas Hunt and a William Wood struck a bet on the match, with Robert Brooks acting as stakeholder. Hunt deposited 1s. and Wood deposited 4½d. with Brooks on the basis that if Filmer and Harlackenden won, Wood would deliver twelve candles to Hunt, while if they lost, Hunt would make up the 1s. to 3s. and this sum would be paid to Wood. The respective stakes seem to indicate that Filmer and Harlackenden were the favourites and, in the event, they won the match, but Wood, having failed to deliver the candles by 6 June, was sued by Hunt.

The manuscript does not reveal whether or not Hunt's claim was successful, but he was represented in the case by his attorney, James Sarys, who would, presumably, have advised Hunt against bringing the claim had it been one in which the court was, for any reason, disqualified from making an award consistent with the enforceability of the bet.

The next case was reported in 1719 in the 9 May and 4 July issues of *The Weekly Journal or Saturday Post*. The earlier issue reported that in the week ending 2 May 1719 a 'Tryal' was held at the Guildhall before the Lord Chief Justice, Sir John Pratt, where the Men of Kent sued the Men of London for £60[1] played for at cricket. After a long hearing, when nearly £200 had been spent on the case, 'My Lord, not understanding the Game' ordered the two teams to play it again and they accordingly assembled at Lamb's Conduit Fields near Islington on 4 May but, as one of the players was taken ill, the game was postponed. The issue of the 4 July reports that when the match did eventually take place the Londoners batted first and scored 30 but the Men of Kent's team of four were 'bowled out after they had made nine and lost the Match'. The game was played for a guinea a man on each side and thus, as is not unknown today, the cost of litigation exceeded the amount at stake and the chief beneficiaries were members of the legal profession.

The issue in the next three cases all arose out of the Gaming Act 1710 which was passed, as it says in the preamble to the Act, 'for the better preventing of excessive and deceitful Gaming' and made wagers on games for stakes of more than £10 illegal. It is not evident why the statute was apparently not considered in the 1719 case; perhaps it was, but it is not mentioned in *The Weekly Journal* which, unlike the sources from which I have derived my accounts of the next three gaming cases, is not a law report.

The first of these cases was *Jeffreys* v. *Walter* which came before the King's Bench Court in 1748. The facts of this case, of which only a half-page account appears in the law reports, are rather difficult to unravel but it seems that 'certain persons unknown to the defendant, who styled themselves of

---

[1] In cases before 1825 it is impossible to equate the sums of money involved with an amount in current terms as there were no indices and the value of money fluctuated quite sharply both up and down in the eighteenth and early nineteenth centuries. However, as a guide, to multiply sums involved by 25 will give a rough idea of their current values.

the County of Kent, played against certain other persons who styled themselves All England, at a certain game called cricket' and Jeffreys won 25 guineas from someone called Parsons 'on a bet upon tick' on that game and a further 25 guineas on another game played between the same teams, making a total of £52 10s. Jeffreys then agreed to pay to Parsons £447 10s. which, when added to the amount of the two bets, made a total of £500, on terms that Parsons would give Jeffreys a bond under which he was bound to pay Jeffreys an annuity of £100 during their joint lives 'at the four usual feasts' i.e. Lady Day (25 March), Midsummer Day (24 June), Michaelmas Day (29 September) and Christmas Day. For some reason not disclosed in the report, the defendant Walter gave Jeffreys a bond as collateral security for Parsons' bond and it was Walter's bond which Jeffreys sought to enforce. Jeffreys argued first that cricket was not a game within the meaning of Section 1 of the 1710 Act, which referred to 'cards, dice, tables, tennis, bowls, or other game or games whatsoever' and secondly that Walter's bond was not given in respect of a gaming debt, whether or not Parsons' bond had been so given. For Walter 'it was insisted' that cricket was a game within the meaning of the Act and 'a manly game, and not bad in itself' but that the game had been ill used by an illegal bet of more than £10 having been made on it. The court did not give judgment but stood the case over for further argument but the report does state that 'the Court inclined to give judgement' for Walter that cricket was a game and that his bond was void, which presumably would have meant that Parsons' bond was also void. There is no further report of the case and probably it was either dropped by Jeffreys or settled out of court.

In December 1812 the *Sporting Magazine* reported that a 'Mr Price, formerly of Southover and lately occupier of Montpelier Gardens, Walworth, obtained a conditional verdict of £30' against the treasurer of an unnamed cricket club for the use of Price's ground and for dinners provided for members of the cricket club in question. This was, however, a straightforward action for payment of goods and services and the next cricket case concerning gaming was in 1825. This was the case of *Walpole v. Saunders*, which was an appeal from the verdict of Serjeant Onslow at Hertford Assizes. The appeal was heard on 12 November 1825 by Chief Justice Abbott[2] and Judges Bayley and Holroyd.

Walpole had sued Saunders, who was the stakeholder, to recover £2 15s. (currently about £65), which was the amount of a bet on an eleven-a-side cricket match at 5s. a head. Onslow had found for the plaintiff and awarded him £2 15s. damages. Saunders' counsel moved to stay the judgment on the ground that, a wager on a cricket match being illegal, Onslow should not have tried the case. Abbott, giving the unanimous judgment of the higher court, said that the objection should have been taken at the original hearing and if the judge had thought it proper to try the cause, 'though frivolous', the court saw no reason for disturbing the verdict. Perhaps surprisingly, Abbott added 'this is not a cause within 9 Anne c 14[3] and I see no objection to the verdict'. From the facts as given in the report, the bet seems to me within the scope of the Act and, if so, I find it surprising that a decision wrong in law should have been regarded as within the proper exercise of Serjeant Onslow's discretion and allowed to stand.

Eight years later another case concerning the game of cricket and involving the 1710 Act came before the Court of the Exchequer being an appeal from Chief Justice Denman's[4] decision at the 1833 Warwick spring assizes to direct a nonsuit, which was an order made when a plaintiff failed to make out a cause of action to the satisfaction of the court.

The facts were that in 1832 a game of cricket had been arranged on the following terms:

The Birmingham Union Club agree to play at Warwick on Monday next, October the 8th, a match at cricket for twenty sovereigns a side with the Warwick club. A deposit of £5 is placed in the hands of Mr Terrill, on behalf of the Warwick club. Wickets to be pitched at ten; to begin at half past ten, or forfeit the deposit. Wickets to be struck at half past five, unless the game is finished before. To be allowed to change three men according to the list sent this morning.

J. COOKES
H. TERRILL

---

[2] Later Lord Tenterden.
[3] The Gaming Act 1710.
[4] Later Lord Denman.

A deposit of £5 is placed in Mr Terrill's hands on behalf of the Birmingham club.

On 8 October two umpires were appointed and a further £15 was deposited by each club with Terrill as stakeholder. In the case of the Birmingham club the deposit was made by one Hodson as agent for the club. The game was played and when wickets were struck on the first day Warwick led by 16 runs with nine first innings wickets standing and the outlook was therefore fairly bleak for Birmingham, but 'no objection was then made to any of the players'. The following morning, however, before play started, Birmingham objected to one of the Warwick side, stating that he belonged to another club and refused to continue with the game. Nevertheless wickets were pitched and the Warwick umpire called 'play', but Birmingham refused to 'play out the match' and Hodson gave Terrill notice not to pay the £20 to the Warwick club but to return it to him. Nevertheless, Terrill, having wisely first obtained an indemnity from the Warwick club, paid the full £40 over to them. Hodson sued for the recovery of Birmingham's £20 (currently worth about £600) and it was this action that was nonsuited by Denman at the Warwick Assizes the following spring.

There was no Dickensian delay in the appeal coming up as it was heard on 28 May 1833 and judgment was given two days later. On behalf of Terrill it was argued that Hodson was not entitled to recover the £20 as the contract was not illegal because it was outside the scope of section 1 of the 1710 Act, which dealt with forms of security given for bets won and lost and not with the bets themselves and also that it was not caught by section 2. Among the reasons put forward for the bet escaping section 2 was that cricket was not one of the games covered by that section, as opposed to section 1, the games mentioned in the two sections consisting 'of two distinct descriptions'. Whereas section 1 referred to 'gaming, or playing at cards, dice, tables, tennis, bowls, or other game or games whatsoever', section 2 referred only to 'cards, dice, tables or any other game or games whatsoever'. For Terrill it was contended that the latter section omitted games of skill and that the words 'other game or games whatsoever' must be construed as referring only to games of the same type as those specifically mentioned in section 2. It seems that this argument did not impress the judges as they 'were proceeding to give judgement, when a doubt suggested itself whether the money could be considered "as lost at any time or sitting" within the words' of section 2 and they asked Mr Humfrey, counsel for Hodson, to address them on this point. Humfrey pointed out that the Act did not say on one day but 'at any time or sitting' and maintained that the words covered the circumstances of a cricket match where the money was lost at one time, namely when the match was concluded. The judges then appeared to have had enough, as Humfrey 'was then stopped by the Court'. Giving the main judgment, Bayley B. said that the words of section 2 had in many cases been held to be as comprehensive as those of section 1 and therefore covered cricket and, as to the words 'at one time or sitting', they meant no more than in 'one transaction'. Accordingly the four judges unanimously held that Hodson was entitled to the return of the £20. Bayley was, however, careful to point out that the court had not sought to resolve the dispute as to whether the money had been properly won and lost, taking it for granted that the £20 had been lost but that Terrill, having been directed not to pay it over, had wrongly done so. Taking a lead from Sir John Bayley and at a distance of 250 years, I would not seek to reinterpret the scope of games covered by sections 1 and 2 but I do find it surprising that, with the omission of tennis and bowls, the scope of section 2 was generally considered to be as all-embracing as that of section 1.

Two years after *Hodson* v. *Terrill* the Gaming Act 1835 was passed. This altered the law as previously governed by the 1710 Act so that instead of all securities, including cheques, given in respect of bets being void these were instead deemed to have been given for an illegal consideration. The practical effect of this change was that after 1835 someone to whom a security had been negotiated without notice of the illegality of the original consideration could sue on that security in the courts, although a wager was still unenforceable as between the original parties. Nevertheless, betting remained an important part of the cricket scene until the late nineteenth century and from 1774 until 1884 the laws of cricket contained provisions regulating the settlement of bets and also one prohibiting umpires from betting. Probably because most bets, although not criminal acts, were unenforceable in the courts, and in that sense unlawful, there do not appear to be any more cases in the law reports concerning bets on cricket matches. However, Charles Box's book *The English Game of Cricket* does contain a short account of one such case, which took place in 1855.

In the year 1855 George Williams sued Thomas Mills, in the Woodstock County Court for £2, he (Mills) having kept the sum as holder of the stakes of £1 each. The deposit was for a single wicket match, which did not come off, owing to the non-attendance of the defendant, who still kept the stakes. It was shown that the parties agreed to meet at nine in the morning, when the plaintiff attended, but the defendant did not appear. His Honour (J. B. Parry, Esq.) said he was of opinion that, as the plaintiff omitted to pitch his wicket and get someone to bowl to him, he could not claim the stake. Each to pay his own costs.

Presumably the court entertained this claim as the amount of the bet did not exceed £10. The decision, which effectively meant that the bet was won by Mills, seems hard on Williams and it looks as if he might have won the case had he, like the Warwick club twenty-two years earlier, gone through the motions of trying to play the game.

A bankruptcy

Ten years before *Williams* v. *Mills* a case arose which, although it did not concern betting, did concern a subject which is sometimes the result of excessive gambling. Bankruptcy was, particularly in the first half of the nineteenth century, fairly common and after their discharge former bankrupts sometimes ran successful businesses and became respected members of society and I suspect that several cricketers in the early and middle years of the game, not to mention its later stages, became bankrupt. One of these was Alfred Mynn, 'The Lion of Kent', who lived from 1807 to 1861 and was a great all-rounder with a career spanning over thirty years, whom A. A. Thomson describes in *Barclays World of Cricket* as like W.

G. Grace, 'in his age . . . a national institution'. In any event on 20 August 1845, after taking 11 MCC wickets in a game at Bath, Mynn was served with a warrant claiming about £130 owing by him to a creditor in London. On 9 September Mynn was examined at the Bankruptcy Court in Exeter and 'in answer to a question, the insolvent stated that he did not get anything by playing cricket', a statement which, as Patrick Morrah says in his biography of Mynn, 'does not altogether carry conviction'.

Mynn had made arrangements for the money owed to be paid by instalments of £15 and it was because the first instalment, which had been due on 25 July, was not paid that Mynn found himself, not for the first time in 1845, imprisoned for debt. On this occasion Mynn explained that the £15 had not been paid because his brother-in-law George Powell, who had undertaken to pay the money on Mynn's behalf, had fallen ill. This explanation was accepted by the court and Mynn was freed from what, as far as is known, was his last spell of imprisonment. By 15 September Mynn was again playing cricket, this time at Brighton for the Gentlemen against the Players, where he took two of the three Players' wickets to fall before the match was abandoned owing to rain.

The Shilton case
The cricketer involved in the next case was also declared bankrupt and imprisoned for debt during his playing career and, in addition, was convicted and imprisoned for theft by false pretences. John Shilton was born in Yorkshire in 1861. He made his first-class debut for the North against the South in 1884, when the only wicket which he took was that of W. R. Gilbert who, as described later in this chapter, was also to serve a spell in prison. In 1885 Shilton joined Warwickshire on the basis that he had been born in the county, in support of which he produced the birth certificate of a first cousin, also called John Shilton, who was born in Coventry.[5]

Shilton was a slow left-arm bowler who appeared in only 24 first-class matches, but would have played in more had Warwickshire become a first-class county before 1894. Shilton's

[5] This and much of the other information on the Shilton case is obtained from Robert Brooke's fascinating *John Edward Shilton's Book*, 1984.

financial affairs were never soundly based and in 1887 he filed his own petition in bankruptcy, which revealed a deficiency of £614 14s. 3d., some £27,000 in current terms. In 1895, ten days before he was due to take his benefit in the game against Yorkshire, Shilton was imprisoned for debt. His release was arranged in time for him to play in his benefit match but, as he was still an undischarged bankrupt, counsel's opinion had to be taken before the benefit money could be distributed.

Later in the same year Shilton fell ill with asthma, a disease from which he perennially suffered, and his doctor advised a sea voyage to South Africa. A Shilton Convalescent Fund was set up which raised enough money for him to make the voyage and the following September, after his health had improved, he joined Western Province as a professional. However, by this time Shilton was getting into financial difficulties again and he had already given a Cape Town hotelier a post-dated cheque for £20, which was dishonoured.

On 20 November 1896 Shilton went into a shop in Cape Town, to which he already owed £4 6s. and chose three watches and various other items the cost of which, with the money already owed, totalled £45 9s. He gave the shop a cheque for £50 and received £4 11s. change, but inquiries subsequently revealed that the cheque was worthless. After leaving the first shop, Shilton went up the street to another where he ordered watches and jewellery costing £52 17s. 4d. for which he gave another cheque. Shilton said he wanted to take the goods with him and told the shop assistant that the manager had authorised this, but in fact the manager had told Shilton that he could not take the goods and, on realising this, the assistant ran into the street after Shilton, who at first denied he had the goods but, on returning to the shop, produced them. The police were called, as they had also been by the first shop, and Shilton was arrested and charged with theft by false pretences.

During the case, which lasted for three sessions, evidence was given of various ill-contrived attempts by Shilton during the previous five months to put himself in funds. As Brooke puts it in his book, 'Shilton's guilt was incontestable. His actions, hopeless and inept, were those of a desperate, and sick, man.' Shilton was convicted and sentenced to twelve months' hard labour, which he served in a prison near Cape Town. Apparently during his sentence he was, on one occasion, smuggled out of gaol to play cricket for the warders' team against a side from the De Beers Mining Company and Shilton, with 38 runs and several wickets, was primarily responsible for the warders' team winning. After his release from prison, Shilton returned to England where he died on 27 September 1899. His obituary notice in *Wisden* touches on the three main aspects of his career, all of which are brought out in Robert Brooke's account of his life, namely, that he was 'one of the players who did most to bring the Warwickshire eleven to the front', that 'he had his faults' and that he 'was personally quite a character'.

The lady cricketers

Four years before Shilton was imprisoned in South Africa, a case had been heard in London which was concerned not with a first-class cricketer, nor even with men's cricket but with a team of women cricketers. By 1892 women's cricket had been played for well over a hundred years and as early as 1745 the *Reading Mercury* published a short account of a game which had taken place in June of that year 'between eleven maids of Bramley and eleven maids of Hambleton, dressed all in white'. However, the only recorded professional women players were two teams known as the Red XI and the Blue XI which were raised in 1889–90. After they were raised the following advertisement appeared in several periodicals of the day:

> With the object of providing the suitability of the National Game as a pastime for the fair sex in preference to Lawn Tennis and other less scientific games, the English Cricket and Athletic Association Ltd have organised two complete elevens of female players under the title of THE ORIGINAL ENGLISH LADY CRICKETERS.

The ladies of OELC took their profession seriously and were coached indoors at Wandsworth and outdoors at Balham among others by Alec and George Hearne of Kent and Maurice Read of Surrey. The girls were forbidden to use their real names and were accompanied by a 'matron' wherever they went. They were provided with uniforms, which included a dicky on which the letters OELC were embroidered, and were given either 6d. or 1s. a day expenses in addition to their pay. From the case referred to below it seems that the girls were paid £1 15s. a week each, of which the current value is about £75. Especially when it is considered they were almost certainly only paid during the summer, this is hardly a fortune.

The OELC's first match was played at Liverpool on Easter Monday 1890 before a crowd of 15,000 and during that summer they toured the country playing at several well-known grounds, including Headingley. Incidentally, the fact that there were only twenty-two ladies from which to make up the teams speaks volumes for their resilience in the face of injury and illness, although it is recorded that on one occasion Daisy Stanley, the captain of the Blues, did not bat as she was 'very unwell'. All went satisfactorily in 1890 and at the beginning of 1891 twenty-two young ladies were engaged by a company called the Lady Cricketer's Association Limited to play cricket in various parts of the country. As *The Times* put it, 'whether it was the dexterity with which the ladies played or whether it was in consequence of their personal attractions' they were at first a great success but gradually their attraction faded and in July the secretary of the teams, one W. Matthews who had originally helped to recruit the girls, said there was no more money and that the teams would have to return to London.

A meeting was then held in London at which it was said that the agreement was at an end, that E. Mitchell (or Michel), 'daddy' to the ladies, would no longer act in that capacity and that Mitchell's paternal duties would be assumed by Henry Wood. Wood, who was present at the meeting, said that he would take all the girls over on the same terms and conditions as previously, which involved paying Agnes Rowney £1 15s. a week. Miss Rowney, and presumably her team mates, did receive some money but 'only in driblets and as it was impossible to play cricket without food the team broke up'. Miss Rowney therefore sued Wood for arrears of salary and compensation in lieu of notice.

The case was heard by the assistant judge Mr Roxburgh and a jury at the Lord Mayor's Court on 1 February 1892 and both parties were represented by counsel. Wood's defence was that it was not he but Mitchell who was liable and that he had never agreed to pay the girls' salaries but had lent Mitchell £150, for which Mitchell had given him a bill of exchange. According to Wood, the £150 had been to enable Mitchell to carry on with the OELC's English tour until a colonial tour to Australia or South Africa could be arranged.

The jury found in favour of Miss Rowney and awarded her £11 15s. plus costs. However the money was not forthcoming and Miss Rowney had to return to the Lord Mayor's Court on 15 March to try to enforce payment. Wood said he was an agent but was not doing any business, that his wife paid the rent of their house at Kew and that he could not really afford even to pay for the journey to and from the City. He complained that the case had been decided against him on perjured evidence and that he had no means to pay, but nevertheless the court ordered him to pay 8s. a month. History does not relate whether Miss Rowney received her money, but the Original English Lady Cricketers disbanded and for the time being professional women's cricket was at an end and, so far, has not resumed.

Balls and bats

In 1898 an action was brought in the High Court against John Wisden & Co., which following John Wisden's death as a bachelor in 1884 had been bought by his manager Henry Luff. Wisdens were sued, not in their capacity as proprietors of *The Cricketers' Almanack*, but as manufacturers and sellers of cricket balls. The plaintiffs were Duke & Sons, one of the oldest and most prestigious makers of cricket balls. Dukes made various grades of balls, including their number one or 'best' which retailed at 7s. 6d. each and their number four which retailed at 5s. each. In 1987 similar quality cricket balls cost much the same in real terms, about £18 and £12.

Initially, as far as cricket equipment was concerned, Wisdens was solely a retail operation and they sold balls manufactured by other firms at their shop and showroom in Cranbourn Street near Leicester Square. By the early 1880s Wisdens were getting their manufacturers, probably including Dukes, to make cricket balls for them and they then sold them as 'Wisden's Cricket Balls'. In 1894, under Luff's direction, Wisdens started manufacturing cricket balls as well as selling them and thus became a competitor of Dukes and anxious to promote the sale of their own balls rather than those of Dukes and their other rivals.

In 1896 James Phillips, who was a well-known umpire and did more than anyone else to stamp out throwing in first-class cricket at the end of the nineteenth century, warned Dukes that Wisdens were selling Dukes' number four balls at their shop as number one balls and charging 7s. 6d. instead of 5s. each for them. Dukes made inquiries which showed that not only had Wisdens supplied and charged for the number four balls as if they were number one balls but had extolled the merits of their own balls and said that Dukes' balls, although they wore well, were too hard. Consequently Dukes arranged for one Henry Edgar to ask for a Dukes' number one ball at Wisdens' shop. Edgar did this and was served by Luff himself, who sold Edgar a number four ball making out that it was a number one ball and charging 7s. 6d. for it.

Dukes therefore decided to institute proceedings against Wisdens and sought an injunction to restrain them from representing that Dukes' inferior balls were in fact their best and from publishing defamatory statements concerning Dukes' business. The case came up before the Lord Chief Justice, Lord Russell of Killowen, and a Middlesex Special Jury on 7 February 1898. Both firms were represented by leading and junior counsel, Wisdens' junior being Alfred Lyttelton. Lyttelton was awarded blues in five games at Cambridge and played four times for England against Australia as a wicket-keeper. His Test career is chiefly remembered because in the Oval Test in 1884 all members of the England team bowled, including Lyttelton, who finished off the Australian innings, which totalled 551, by taking 4 wickets for 19 runs with his lobs, his only wickets in first-class cricket.

In their case against Wisdens, Dukes called evidence which showed what Wisdens had been doing and that their actions had damaged Dukes financially. In spite of the fact that it was shown to have been a regular practice to offer Dukes' inferior balls as superior ones, Wisdens maintained they had really thought the Dukes' balls which they had sold were their best quality ones. Leading counsel for Wisdens, Alfred Lawrence,[6] said that immediately Wisdens had discovered their

---

[6] Later Lord Trevethin and Lord Chief Justice.

mistake they had taken steps to prevent its repetition and added that Wisdens would give an undertaking as to their future conduct and would pay the costs of the action. Robert Wallace for Dukes replied that their primary object was not to obtain damages and that they would agree to Wisdens' proposal. Accordingly the jury was not required to reach a verdict and judgment was entered for Dukes for £2 plus costs. Perhaps, however, Wisdens had the last laugh as in 1920 Duke & Son were acquired by John Wisden & Co.

Ninety years after *Dukes* v. *Wisdens* the problem of cricket equipment being sold under a false description still existed and this was ventilated in a piece in the *Daily Mail* headed 'Scandal of the forged English cricket bats' on 15 January 1988 and also in an article in the April issue of *The Cricketer International* entitled 'Bat Tricks of the East'. In essence the problem was – and probably still is – that, particularly in India and Pakistan, bats manufactured by cheap unskilled labour, often out of inferior materials, are made up to look as if they were a product of one of the well-known English manufacturers. It is very difficult in such cases for the English manufacturers to obtain any redress against those who make the counterfeit bats, as the costs of pursuing a successful action in India or Pakistan are prohibitive and the chance of ultimate success, certainly in financial terms, very small. However, in March 1987 a case did come up in the Bromley Magistrates Court concerning the sale of some counterfeit bats, which had been bought at an auction held in Beckenham fifteen months earlier.

On 11 December 1985 the treasurer of Locksbottom Cricket Club, which plays in the SCS Business Systems League, heard that twelve new Gunn & Moore bats were coming up at an auction the following day. Roger Tolman, a club member, agreed to go to the sale and bid for the bats on behalf of the club. The bats were in three lots of four and were described in the catalogues as GM cricket bats, GM being the insignia of Gunn & Moore, who also mark the spines of their bats with blue and green stripes. Tolman inspected the bats as best he could, as they were bound together with the blades facing inwards, but he could see the blue and green stripes and also the GM logo and the word 'Imperial', which is one of Gunn & Moore's trademarks. He accordingly bid for the bats and bought all three lots for a total of £49, about one seventh of what twelve new Gunn & Moore Imperial bats would have cost in the shops. It was only when he got home and undid the bats that Tolman discovered they were not Gunn & Moore bats at all but bats made of inferior wood marked 'Gain More' – an appropriate name perhaps – and that the blue and green stripes were the reverse of the Gunn & Moore colours.

The next day Tolman contacted Gunn & Moore and went to see Stanley Lowy their chief executive and Martyn Baine, their national sales officer at Gunn & Moore's offices in Forest Hill. Tolman told them what had happened and Lowy said that the bats had not been manufactured by Gunn & Moore and that the twelve bought by Tolman were in fact only a small fraction of about 1,000 bats, which had been bought from the Customs and Excise by some market traders who were selling them in small parcels at local auctions. It is believed that these bats had originally been seized by the Customs because some of them concealed drugs and, if this is so, it would not be the first time that bats had been used for this purpose. On 30 July 1983 Surget Chawla was sentenced to seven years' imprisonment at Aylesbury Crown Court for smuggling £190,000 worth of heroin, which was hidden in four cricket bats which were in his wife's luggage. Swaran Chawla was also given a prison sentence, two years, suspended for two years.

To return to the Gain More bats, Tolman said he would be willing to give evidence if a prosecution was brought against the vendors of the bats and, with the help of the Bromley Trading Standards Office, a prosecution was brought under the 1968 Trade Descriptions Act against Robert Perry and Reginald Barton, the traders who put the bats into the auction. They were charged on two counts, first with giving a false description of the bats in the auctioneer's catalogues and secondly with supplying a bat with a false trade description, in both cases giving an indication that the bats were manufactured by Gunn & Moore when they were not. The case came up on 27 March 1987 and Perry and Barton conducted their own defence. Both Tolman and Lowy gave evidence and were questioned by Perry and Barton, who maintained that they had never heard of Gunn & Moore and that they believed the bats must be all right as they had been bought from HM Customs and Excise. In the event they were found guilty on the first count and conditionally discharged for one year, but not guilty on the second. The costs of the case were paid out of public funds and no compensation was offered either to Tolman or to Gunn & Moore.

For Locksbottom Cricket Club, if not for Gunn & Moore, the story had a happy ending. First, Lowy presented Tolman with the real Gunn & Moore Imperial bat, which he had taken to court as an example of the genuine article, and secondly, the club made good use of the twelve Gain More products. Nine were sold to club members as souvenirs or for their children to play with in the garden, one was given as a 'joke' prize in the raffle at the club's dinner dance and one was auto-graphed by the Kent and Locksbottom teams at a match held to mark Locksbottom's fortieth anniversary. The twelfth was bought by Tolman, who had it made into a trophy which is awarded annually 'to the Locksbottom player who has made the worst error to do with cricket on or off the field'. This is presented at the annual 'stag' dinner when the recipient, as Tolman put it, has 'to drink several pints of beer from a suit-ably inscribed china receptacle, not normally used for holding ale' – the Locksbottom version of the Oxonian sconce!

Theft

A less subtle method of enrichment than selling inferior crick-et balls or counterfeit bats is straightforward theft, and for a cricketer one of its most easily achievable forms is stealing money from another player's clothes in the dressing room. One of the earliest practitioners of this form of theft was Walter Raleigh Gilbert, who played for Middlesex and Gloucestershire between 1873 and 1886. Gilbert had excellent connections in the game, he was a cousin of W. G. Grace and married a Miss Lillywhite of the famous cricketing family. He was a good enough cricketer to score 205 not out for The Eleven of England against Cambridge University in 1876 and to be included in a well-known picture of twenty-one 'Famous Cricketers – 1880'. He was also secretary of the United XI, which had a game against the Australians at Chichester in June 1882 and, as such, was sued by Charlie Howard, a Sussex professional, who had played for the United XI. Howard had been recruited at the last minute as the United XI were three short and, in fact, they played the match with only ten men. After the game Gilbert offered Howard £5 for his services but this was refused as Howard said that playing against the Australians always commanded a higher fee than ordinary county games. On 23 August, Howard's claim was heard in the Chichester County Court, where it was revealed that Gilbert had been paid £120 for recruiting the United XI, while Howard admitted in cross-examination that he had been paid only £6 for playing for Sussex against the Australians in 1880. No evidence was called for Gilbert and the judge, while regretting the absence of evidence of what was the usual fee, awarded Howard £6.

In the next three years, although Gilbert's cricket flourished, his financial affairs did not and, as *The Cheltenham Mercury* succinctly put it, he had been 'unfortunate with regard to his pecuniary affairs, which underwent liquidation'. This was probably the cause of him turning professional at the start of the 1886 season, but he was to play in only one first-class match in that capacity. This was for Gloucestershire on 26, 27 and 28 April against Surrey at the Oval, when he scored only 3 and 0 but did take 3 Surrey wickets for 30 runs. In addition to being a professional with Gloucestershire, Gilbert played for the East Gloucestershire Cricket Club, whose ground was at Charlton Park, Cheltenham. In the early part of the 1886 season, as in the previous two years, money had been disappearing from the pockets of the clothes left in the dressing room and the secretary of the club, Captain Harry Willes, notified the police and it was arranged that on Saturday 5 June, the second day of the match against Stroud, Sergeant James Woolford would go to the ground and secrete himself above the dressing room. In addition, marked gold and silver coins were placed in the pockets of Captain Willes' clothes and also in those of another member, William Piers, before their clothes were hung up in the dressing room. At about ten past twelve Sergeant Woolford saw Gilbert enter the dressing room and take a half-sovereign from Willes' waistcoat and put it into his own trouser pocket. Sergeant Woolford then saw Gilbert go to where Piers' clothes were hanging and search the coat and waistcoat before leaving the dressing room.

At lunch time, when Gilbert came back into the dressing room, Sergeant Woolford asked Willes whether he had lost anything. After searching his pockets, Willes said he had lost a half-sovereign and a shilling. Woolford then told Gilbert what he had seen and asked him where the stolen money was and Gilbert produced the marked half-sovereign from his pocket. Willes then told Gilbert he was sorry, but the thefts had been going on for some time, to which Gilbert replied, 'I can assure you I never did it before this season and, if you will forgive me, I will leave the country and go to Australia.'

Gilbert was brought up at Cheltenham Police Court on the following Monday, 7 June, on two charges, one of stealing 11s. from Captain Willes and one of stealing 10s. from Piers, in total worth something over £40 in current terms. Willes asked that, as Gilbert had pleaded guilty, the bench should deal leniently with his case and John Waghorne, the solicitor who defended Gilbert, made a strong plea for mercy, saying that Gilbert had been suffering from erysipelas[7] and had resorted to drink to try and drown his troubles. Waghorne also said that Gilbert would never again be able to hold up his head in England and that his only chance of retrieving his character was to go abroad, which to a man like Gilbert meant transportation. The magistrates, however, took the view that a fine was not sufficient punishment and Gilbert was sentenced to 28 days' hard labour in Gloucester gaol. On his release Gilbert did emigrate, although not to Australia, but to Canada. It seems that he did 'retrieve his character' there, playing cricket and working in the Land Titles Office in Calgary where he died, at the age of 70, in 1924.

The thief need not always be one of the players as, for example, at Lord's when at the start of the 1912 cricket season small sums of money started disappearing from cricketers' clothes left in the dressing room. This prompted the pavilion attendant, Philip Need, to put some marked coins in the pocket of an item of clothing and shortly afterwards Alfred William Noyes, a 23-year-old telephone operator at Lord's, was seen to enter the dressing room and take a marked half-crown. He was charged with stealing 2s. 6d. (currently worth about £4) and appeared in Marylebone Magistrates' Court on 24 May 1912. In his defence Noyes said that money left lying about in the dressing room was a great temptation to someone receiving 'a starvation wage' and that a barman at Lord's, who was alleged to have

[7] An inflammatory infection of the skin.

stolen £12, had been allowed to go free. This line of defence, however, proved counterproductive as the magistrate, Paul Taylor, said that the treatment of the barman illustrated the mistake of allowing people who committed crimes to go unpunished and sentenced Noyes to six weeks' imprisonment with hard labour, suggesting that his conviction should be made known to other employees at Lord's.

In the early 1960s a young professional on the staff of a first-class county stole £2 from a fellow player's jacket in a 2nd XI match. He was caught because, as money had disappeared before, the two stolen notes were marked ones. He was fined £20 for this and similar offences which he asked to be taken into account, but fortunately his counsel's fears that he had 'lost all further prospects of cricket' proved unfounded as, after a short gap in his career, he went on to play in over 250 first-class games.

More unfortunate than the victims of dressing-room pilfering were the South Africans, Cuan McCarthy and John Waite. McCarthy was a fast bowler who won a blue at Cambridge in 1952 and played in fifteen Tests for South Africa. Waite was the leading wicket-keeper batsman of his day, who toured England three times and played in fifty Tests for South Africa between 1951 and 1965, in which he scored 2,405 runs, including four centuries, and shared in 141 dismissals. During the South Africans' 1951 tour of England, McCarthy and Waite were staying at the Park Lane Hotel in Piccadilly when their suitcases were stolen. The culprit was Vincent Fullard, a 27-year-old electrician who had done a spell in Borstal, and he was sentenced to six months' imprisonment at Bow Street Magistrates' Court. Fullard was probably lucky not to have been caught red-handed by McCarthy as, in addition to his cricket blue, he was also awarded one for boxing.

False pretences

To return to 1898, at about the time that he was appearing for Wisdens as junior counsel in the case brought by Dukes, Alfred Lyttelton took a pupil in his chambers. He was Pelham ('Plum') Warner, who was later to captain Middlesex and England and in 1937 was knighted for his services to cricket. One of the teams of which Warner was appointed captain was the 1911–12 side to

Australia and, apart from the captain, this team contained two amateurs, namely J. W. H. T. Douglas who captained Essex and Warwickshire's captain, F. R. Foster. In later years they were both to feature in cases involving obtaining money by false pretences, Douglas in 1924 and Foster in 1950, the vital difference between the two cases being that Douglas was the 'prosecutor', while Foster was the defendant.

Douglas captained Essex from 1911 to 1928 and England in eighteen of the twenty-three Tests in which he played. In addition he won an England amateur cap at soccer and an Olympic gold medal at boxing, winning the middleweight title in 1908. During his first-class career he scored 24,531 runs, took 1,893 wickets and achieved the double five times. He was a fast-medium bowler but a slow and dour batsman, *Wisden* describing him as 'possessed of exceptional defensive skill and inexhaustible patience' and 'very hard to dismiss'. He was given the nickname 'Johnny Won't Hit Today' and once himself defined an optimist as 'a man who batting with Johnny Douglas, backs up for a run'. Douglas and his father were drowned on 19 December 1930 when the SS *Oberon*, on which they were returning from a business trip to Finland, collided with the SS *Arcturus* in thick fog.

On Saturday 23 August 1924 Douglas was at Leyton for the first day of the match against Northants when he was given a telephone message from a man who gave the name of Hill. In court Douglas stated that, 'years ago I played cricket with a man named Hill, and when the speaker asked if I could help him I answered that I would. He said that one of his motor lorries had broken down near the cricket ground, and would I advance one of his men £2 to pay for the repairs. I said that I would.' However, Douglas' suspicions were aroused and he informed the police who intervened when, an hour later, a man approached Douglas to collect the £2. The man, who called himself Kerry but whose real names were Holman Arthur Menday, said he had driven the lorry from Southampton but when Detective Sergeant Rogers asked him which way he had come he could not answer. He was then arrested and taken to the police station where he admitted that his story was 'all lies'.

On 1 September Menday was prosecuted for attempting to obtain £2 by false pretences from Douglas and also for obtaining

£2 by fraud from Captain T. Jameson, presumably the amateur who played for Hampshire in the 1920s. In a statement, Menday said that he had met a man named Shephard who had induced him to join in frauds and that, with the help of a young woman, although they had no success with Sir William Plender,[8] they had extracted £1 from F. E. Lacey,[9] the Secretary of MCC, £1 10s. from a Mr Thomas and £2 each from Lord Swaythling, Colonel White and Captain Jameson. Sergeant Rogers stated that Menday, who was aged 39, came from a good family but in 1911 had been convicted of stealing a dividend warrant. He subsequently joined the army where he became an officer and, after leaving the army in 1920, had been employed in two posts, 'his departure from the second leading to the discovery that £150 worth of stamps were missing', a lot of stamps when one considers that 24,000 letters could be posted for £150 in 1924. Sergeant Rogers said that Menday's downfall was due to drink and gambling and he was sentenced to three months' imprisonment with hard labour.

In the days when Douglas was their captain, Essex was generally one of the less successful counties and also one of the poorer ones. In order to raise money for the county an Essex County Cricket Supporters Club was formed which ran a Derby sweep, open only to members of the Supporters Club. In 1923 it was drawn to the attention of the City Police that a lottery scheme, which might be illegal, was being run by the Supporters Club in consequence of which Detective Inspector Wagstaff decided to become a member. On 30 April 1924 a circular relating to the 1924 Derby sweep was sent to members including Wagstaff, whereupon the Attorney General's fiat having been obtained, it was decided to prosecute. Thus on 9 October 1924, while Menday was still serving his sentence for trying to defraud the Essex captain, Edward Press, one of the officials of the Supporters Club appeared at the Guildhall on two charges. These were first, publishing circulars, etc., on which the printer's name did not appear and secondly, on the information of Inspector Wagstaff, publishing a scheme for the sale of tickets in an unauthorised lottery.

[8] Senior partner of Deloitte & Co., later Lord Plender.
[9] Later Sir Francis Lacey. He was knighted when he retired in 1926; cricket's first knight.

The prosecution made it clear that complete information regarding the lottery had been placed at the disposal of the police by Press and that his good faith was not being questioned. Nevertheless, Alderman Neal considered that the case was caught by the Lottery Acts, notwithstanding that only members of the Supporters Club were circulated and that they did not 'buy' tickets but paid a 'subscription' to the club and were then 'given' tickets in the sweep. The Alderman decided that, although the lottery was run for an excellent cause, there had been a technical infringement of the law and that he was therefore bound to convict the defendant as 'a rogue and vagabond'. The smallest possible fine of £1 was imposed on Press, who also had to bear 1 guinea costs on each summons. This reversal clearly did not do Essex's finances any good, as in March 1925 the club reported that 1924 had produced a loss of £369 and the committee warned that, if the necessary support was not forthcoming, it would recommend that the club should be wound up. Fortunately a more optimistic note was struck at the annual general meeting two weeks later, but Essex had more difficult days ahead before, finally, winning the County Championship for the first time in 1979.

Like Essex, Warwickshire was not one of the leading counties and before 1911 had never finished higher than fifth in the table. In that year, however, his first as captain, Frank Rowbotham Foster led Warwickshire to the county championship when in 1910 they had finished fourteenth out of the sixteen counties then competing. Unlike Douglas, whose first-class cricket career extended over thirty years, Foster's lasted under seven as a motor cycle accident in 1915, when he was only 27, put paid to his hopes of resuming his first-class career after the Great War. In that time, however, Foster achieved more than most men in a full cricketing career. In addition to leading his county to the championship in 1911, Foster toured Australia with the MCC in the winter of 1911–12 when he and Sydney Barnes were largely responsible for England winning four of the five Tests. Foster headed the bowling averages, taking 32 wickets in the series with his left-arm fast-medium bowling, Barnes took 34 wickets at a slightly higher cost and the next most successful bowler was Douglas with 15 wickets. In 1911 and 1914 Foster performed the double and in the latter season he scored 305 not out for Warwickshire against Worcestershire in four hours and twenty minutes.

Foster, who was not related to the Worcestershire brotherhood, was an immensely talented natural cricketer and an inspiring captain who was justly described in a retrospective article in the 1976 *Wisden* as 'a prince of the golden age'. On the other hand he was an eccentric character whose mother left a lot of money on trust for him which, as Foster's counsel put it in 1950, 'flowed from him like water in a brook' and meant that he was never forced to seek work. The tragedy of Foster's life was that his finest hours were the four years before the Great War and, although after 1914 he had his moments, for the last forty-four years of his life it was mainly downhill. In 1930 he published a lively book entitled *Cricketing Memories*, although character-istically a promised sequel did not appear, and in 1932, as one of the first exponents of leg theory, he was consulted by D. R. Jardine before the 'bodyline' tour.

In August 1950 Foster was remanded in custody in Southend on a charge of stealing a car. Opposing bail, Detective Inspector Todd said that Foster should have appeared in court on the preceding Friday and that there were nine other charges, all of fraud, to be preferred. Foster said he could explain it all as he had to go to Lord's to tell the MCC about a fast left-arm bowler he had discovered, 'even faster than myself'. According to a letter written by Foster, this bowler was a 20-year-old called Ron Bumstead and Foster wrote that there would be 'a hell of a row' if he was not picked for the 1950–51 side to Australia. Bumstead was not selected, indeed no one of that name has ever played first-class cricket in England. No doubt Foster, who wrote in the same letter that he would bet 5s. that England won the series 5–0, would have attributed England's losing it 4–1 to Bumstead's absence from the team.

On 26 September 1950 Foster appeared at Southend Quar-ter Sessions and pleaded guilty to twelve charges of obtaining money by false pretences, mostly relating to worthless cheques given to car hire firms, and to obtaining credit by fraud. The sums involved totalled £115 9s. 6d., which is currently worth about £1,300. In Foster's defence, George Pollock[10] said that after his accident in 1915 Foster had become 'surrounded by friends or, as they might sometimes be described, spongers.

And as he became further and further from his triumphs so his associates deteriorated in quality.' Pollock added that all the debts had now been paid by the trustees of Foster's mother's estate and also read a psychiatrist's report which said that Foster was suffering from senile dementia. The recorder put Foster on probation for a year on condition that he went to a home in Northamptonshire. Foster, 'grey bearded but upright', bowed to the recorder and consented to the condition which had been imposed. The case was a sad postscript to Foster's short but glittering years in the first-class game and he died in May 1958 at the age of 69 in St Andrew's Hospital, Northampton.

In May 1959 a less serious case of obtaining money by false pretences was heard at Hove Juvenile Court. A boy had collected a large number of free fixture cards from the Sussex County ground at Hove and then sold them at a penny each, telling the buyers that if they produced the card at a Hove restaurant they would be entitled to a free cup of coffee. A number of people went to the restaurant and asked for their coffee and consequently the boy was summonsed on two charges of obtaining money by false pretences. He admitted the offences and was conditionally discharged. What, I wonder, has become of this enterprising lad? Has he perhaps used his talents legitimately and become a successful and respected businessman?

Fraud and deception

A generation after the Foster case three more Test cricketers were involved in cases involving fraud and deception, the three in question being Michael Brearley, who was an innocent party, and Younis Ahmed and Terry Jenner, who were guilty ones. Brearley scored over 25,000 runs, including a triple century, in his first-class career but he is chiefly remembered as a magnificent captain of Cambridge University, Middlesex and especially England. He captained his country thirty-one times, and under his captaincy England won eighteen Tests and lost only four. In 1981 Brearley was brought back as captain against Australia after the second Test, when England were one down in the series. Assisted by three incredible performances by Ian Botham, freed from the burden of captaincy, and ably assisted

10 Later Sir George Pollock QC.

by Bob Willis, Brearley led England to victory in the next three Tests, which enabled England to retain the Ashes.

During the time that Brearley was captaining England he was persuaded by a firm called Quantock Stamps to invest £3,755 in buying stamps. Quantock Stamps was set up by Robin Houghton, an ex-army major, who wrote to Brearley 'while you have been winning the Ashes I have assembled a collection on your behalf'. Houghton ran the stamp investment service from his house in Somerset which was called Toad Hall, and induced eighteen people to invest a total of more than £100,000 in stamps. Apart from Brearley, the other seventeen included Houghton's own stepbrother and retired naval and RAF officers. However, Houghton's customers never saw the stamps, but only photocopies which enabled Houghton to sell the same stamps to more than one person. Police investigation also revealed that even the real stamps were not worth what Houghton had charged for them. At Bristol Crown Court on 9 February 1984 Houghton was found guilty on eight charges of fraud and deception and sentenced to eighteen months' imprisonment, twelve of which were suspended.

Younis Ahmed played in two Tests for Pakistan in 1969–70 and also played for Karachi, South Australia and three English first-class counties, Surrey, Worcester and Glamorgan. At his best he was a fine free-scoring left-hand batsman and in a first-class career extending from 1962 to 1986 he scored 25,388 runs including 44 centuries, one less than Brearley. He sued Surrey for wrongful dismissal and hence qualifies for an appearance elsewhere in this book, he was fired by Worcester in 1983 for placing a bet on his own county to lose a John Player League game, which in the event was washed out, and he left Glamorgan in 1986, as *Wisden* puts it, 'before the season ended'. The last departure may not have been unconnected with a fine of £750 imposed on him by a Cardiff court in that year after he had pleaded guilty to two charges of obtaining goods and services by deception. In March 1985 Younis had been implicated with his girlfriend in using a bogus credit card to defraud British Telecom and to incur a bill of £254 at the Crest Hotel, Cardiff.

Jenner was a leg-spin bowler and lower-order batsman who played in nine Tests for Australia between 1970 and 1975, four of them against England. He was never selected to tour England, but in 1972–3 toured the West Indies and in the final Test of that series he took five wickets for 90 runs on a good batting wicket. His highest Test score was 74, made against England at Adelaide in the 1974–5 series, when he was largely responsible for Australia making 304 after being 84 for 5. Jenner also shared the Australian's fondness for a flutter and in his case, unfortunately, this was carried to excess and proved his undoing.

In 1986, ten years after he retired from first-class cricket, Jenner was given a three-year suspended sentence for embezzlement and falsifying documents. His passion for gambling had resulted in his getting into debt and he stole A.$4,000 from his employer, an Adelaide car sales company, in the vain hope of the big win which would enable him to pay his debts. At his trial the managing director of another car sales company gave evidence for Jenner and subsequently employed him as a car salesman. Within three weeks, however, Jenner was stealing from his new employer. In January 1988 he was charged on three counts of embezzlement and, when he appeared in Adelaide Central Criminal Court on 30 September, he confessed to ten more incidents, making the total sum involved A.$10,045. Jenner pleaded guilty and the court was told that he was a sick man, who had taken money paid to him for cars and used it in search of the betting coup that would solve his problems. Sentencing Jenner to six and a half years' imprisonment, Judge John Greaves said he hoped that the appropriate treatment could be provided for Jenner during his imprisonment so that he would not slip back again after his release, which could come when Jenner would be eligible for parole in 1991.

Blackmail

Apart from those involving physical violence, blackmail is one of the nastiest ways of extracting money from someone. Blackmail is, however, a much less effective weapon when the potential victim has nothing to hide and it proved ineffective when tried on Christopher Martin-Jenkins in September 1982. Martin-Jenkins is the BBC's cricket correspondent and the editorial director of *The Cricketer International*, of which he was then editor. He was also a good enough cricketer to score 99 at

Lord's in 1963, when captaining Marlborough in the annual match against Rugby.

On the night of 3 September, the day before the Nat West Bank final, Martin-Jenkins' briefcase, containing cheques, credit cards and tape recordings of interviews, was taken from his car near Lord's. On Sunday 5 September Martin-Jenkins' wife received a telephone call from a man who said that his friend had found the case and would destroy the contents unless a reward was paid. On the following day the man spoke to Martin-Jenkins and asked for £50 but agreed to accept £40 and he arranged to meet the man at Victoria station. Martin-Jenkins went to Victoria, where he met a man who handed over the stolen items in a holdall and was arrested by the police.

The caller turned out to be Maurice Connell, a 26-year-old from Hornsey, who already had three previous convictions for dishonesty and drug offences. Connell appeared at the Old Bailey some nine months later, where he pleaded guilty to blackmail but, in mitigation, said that he had not intended to profit from his offence but was acting on behalf of someone called 'Belfast Johnny', whom he had met in a pub and to whom he was going to hand over the £40. Connell was unable to give any further details about Belfast Johnny and the judge said that, in his opinion, it was most unlikely that Connell had ever met such a man. After reports had been obtained, Connell was sentenced to fifteen months' imprisonment with three months of a previous suspended sentence for drug offences activated, making a total of eighteen months.

Connell appealed on the grounds that the judge had refused to believe his story about Belfast Johnny, on which his plea for mitigation had been based, without hearing any evidence about it. In October 1983 the Court of Appeal held that there was 'a limit to the extent to which a judge need have his credulity stretched' and that a court was not bound to accept the truth of facts contained in a plea for mitigation, in the absence of hearing evidence on those facts. Connell's counsel also emphasised that the blackmail was 'of a comparatively trivial nature, carried out in an extremely amateurish fashion, coupled with a fairly modest demand for money'. It also emerged at the appeal that, since Connell had been sentenced, his wife had died in tragic circumstances, having been on a life support machine following a car accident. Taking all this into account, and mainly on compassionate grounds, the court reduced the sentence by six months, thus reducing the total sentence to a year.

An expensive meal

The last case in this chapter arose out of a visit to a restaurant in September 1984 by members of the Havering-atte-Bower Cricket Club and the visit in turn arose out of a company which sold burglar alarms going into liquidation. Vernon Jackson was employed by Roboco Security Systems Limited to sell burglar alarms and when Roboco went into liquidation a company cheque in favour of Jackson for £273 60p. was dishonoured. Jackson was, understandably, aggrieved and reckoned that Robin Bamford, who had been a director of Roboco, should pay the money. Bamford said that he had left Roboco before it went into liquidation and that he had nothing to do with Jackson's grievance. By September 1984 when the Havering-atte-Bower CC were on tour in Devon, Bamford was running a seafood restaurant called The House of Prawns in Stokeinteignhead.

Jackson decided to get his own back on Bamford by taking the whole team to The House of Prawns and telling them that he would pay the bill. They enjoyed an excellent meal with wine and Jackson had 'the biggest lobster he [Bamford] could find'. The bill came to £250 and Jackson refused to pay it and, as the bill amounted to some £20 less than Roboco's dishonoured cheque, he decided to make up the difference by punching a hole in the ceiling of the restaurant's lavatory. At Teignmouth Magistrates Court on 22 May 1985 Jackson, who admitted the damage charge, was fined £30 and given a one-year conditional discharge for dishonestly intending to evade payment of the bill for the meal. He was also ordered to pay £113 35p. costs. Apparently the cricket club paid the bill for the meal and after the case, when he heard this, Jackson paid the club back because, as he said, they had nothing to do with it and that he had 'just used them to get the case to court'. In that respect at least he was successful.

IV

TAXES AND WILLS

Income Tax

For well over a hundred years cricketers have enjoyed benefits, usually towards the end of their playing careers, and these have been an important source of revenue to the recipients. Until the abolition of amateur status in 1962 only professionals had benefits, although some amateurs had complimentary matches or benefits described by some other euphemism and W. G. Grace was given three testimonials which, according to *Wisden*, raised a total of £8,835, although in his excellent biography *The Great Cricketer* A. A. Thomson writes that 'the total handed over to W. G. was £9,073 6s. 5d.' In either case an enormous sum worth, in current terms, well over £400,000.

Traditionally a player's benefit comprised the proceeds of gate money at a selected home match, of collections taken at that match and of any other subscriptions by members and well-wishers. A hundred years ago, A. G. Steel wrote that 'if a man is a favourite with the crowd, it means a good round sum in his pocket, sufficient to keep him to the end of his days, or else set him up in a small way of business' and he added that 'a well-known man in a good county' could expect £500 or £600, over £20,000 in current terms.

In 1920 the Kent Committee granted James Seymour a benefit and he took this in the match against Hampshire played in Canterbury week. Seymour played for Kent from 1902 to 1926, scoring 26,828 runs for them, including 53 centuries. He was a key member of the strong Kent sides in the years either side of the Great War and, although he never won an England cap, he played in a Test Trial and was a county batsman of the first rank. In his benefit match he was run out for a duck in the first innings, but scored 74 in the second innings, which was the highest score in the match after Frank Woolley's 80. More important, Kent won the match by 165 runs and *Wisden* describes Seymour as having 'a very good benefit'.

Seymour's benefit, in fact, raised £1,492 8s. 7d. of which £939 16s. 11d. represented gate money. The money was invested and held in trust by Kent for Seymour until 1923 when the proceeds of the investments and certain other money were paid to Seymour. He received a total of £1,914 14s. 5d., currently worth about £39,000. Thereupon the Inland Revenue assessed Seymour to tax on the gate money on the basis that it was 'part of the profits or emoluments' accruing to him as a professional cricketer employed by Kent. The General Commissioners considered the sum to be a gift and consequently not taxable, which decision was affirmed by Mr Justice Rowlatt on appeal. The Revenue again appealed and, by a majority, the Court of Appeal reversed Sir Sidney Rowlatt's decision and held the sum taxable. With the active support of the chairman of Kent, Lord Harris, Seymour appealed to the House of Lords and, as an important point of principle was involved, most of the costs of the appeal, which amounted to £511 13s. 4d., were guaranteed by the MCC and eleven of the first-class counties.

Seymour was represented by Sir John Simon KC[1] and Walter Monckton[2], who in 1910 had kept wicket for Harrow in Fowler's Match and was president of MCC in 1956. In May 1927, by a majority of four to one, the House of Lords overturned the Court of Appeal's decision and reinstated that of Mr Justice Rowlatt, holding that Seymour was not assessable 'in as much as it was a personal gift, and not a profit or perquisite arising from his employment within Schedule E rule 1 of the Income Tax Act 1918'.

Less than a month after the House of Lords gave judgment in Seymour's case another similar case came before Mr Justice Rowlatt. This concerned the Surrey cricketer, Andrew Ducat, whose benefit match against Middlesex was played at the Oval on the 11, 13 and 14 August 1923. Ducat played for Surrey from 1906 to 1931 and scored over 23,000 runs for them, including 52 centuries. He won one England cap – in the ill-fated 1921 series – but also played for England six times at

[1] Later Viscount Simon, who in his career held office as Home Secretary, Foreign Secretary, Chancellor of the Exchequer and Lord Chancellor.
[2] Later Viscount Monckton, confidant of Edward VIII during the abdication crisis, post-war Cabinet minister and chairman of the Midland Bank.

football and led Aston Villa to victory in the 1920 Cup Final. In his benefit match Ducat scored 75, after Hobbs and Sandham had put on 244 for the first wicket. (Ducat later died at Lord's from heart failure on 23 July 1942 while batting for the Surrey Home Guard against the Sussex Home Guard. The game was thereupon abandoned and *Wisden* shows Ducat's score as 'Pte. A. Ducat not out ... 29'.) The total receipts of Ducat's benefit were £1,600 17s. 8d. (currently worth about £32,000) of which £881 14s. 5d. comprised the gate receipts. As in Seymour's case, it was only the latter element on which the Revenue claimed tax. However, in view of the similarity with Seymour's case, counsel for the Crown asked the court to dismiss the appeal with costs, which it did.

Since 1927 Seymour's case has, to an extent rightly, been regarded as establishing the principle that the proceeds of benefits are tax free. In fact, in both Seymour's and Ducat's cases the Revenue sought to assess tax only on that part of the total receipts which represented gate money and which was, therefore, received by the county club and passed on to the beneficiary. The £552 11s. 8d. which represented the proceeds of subscriptions in Seymour's case was conceded by the Revenue not to be assessable, as this was made up of gifts to Seymour from members of the public and was not income which was taxable as such.

Since the early 1960s the tradition of a beneficiary having a specific home match from which he took the gate money has gradually been abandoned and replaced by highly organised campaigns covering a wide variety of sponsored events, specially produced goods, raffles and other devices for swelling the receipts of the modern benefit, which enable players to raise substantial sums – £153,906 in the case of Graham Gooch in 1985. This is a large sum, but allowing for inflation, it is only about the same in real terms as the £14,000 received by Cyril Washbrook, who took his benefit in the Lancashire v. Australians match in 1948. Not surprisingly, Washbrook entitled his autobiography *Cricket – the Silver Lining.* An approximately similar value in real terms can be ascribed to the £3,703 raised by George Hirst's benefit, which he took in the 1904 Roses Match. However, on the basis of the Seymour case, it would seem that even if the House of Lords had found in favour of the Revenue, virtually the entire proceeds of modern benefits would escape the Revenue's net as being personal gifts – provided always there was no contractual commitment between the player and his county that he would be entitled to a benefit.

Seymour's case can be contrasted with that of *Moorhouse (Inspector of Taxes)* v. *Dooland* which was heard by the Court of Appeal in November 1954. The Dooland in question was Bruce Dooland, the leg break and googly bowler who played in three Tests for Australia in the 1946–7 and 1947–8 series but, when he was not chosen for Don Bradman's 1948 side, came to England on his own account. He played with great success, first in the Lancashire League and then from 1953 for Nottinghamshire for five years in two of which he performed the double of 1,000 runs and 100 wickets. The case concerned the time when Dooland was employed under a contract dated 27 August 1949 with the East Lancashire Cricket Club.

The contract contained a clause which stated, 'Collections shall be made for any meritorious performance by the professional with bat or ball in any Lancashire League or Worsley cup match.' In 1951 collections were made for Dooland on eleven occasions and these produced a total of £48 15s. – currently worth only about £500 – upon which Dooland was assessed to tax. Dooland appealed against the assessment and his appeal was allowed by the General Commissioners and their decision was affirmed by Mr Justice Harman in the High Court. The Revenue appealed to the Court of Appeal where the case was heard by the Master of the Rolls, Sir Raymond Evershed, and by Lords Justice Jenkins and Birkett.[3]

During the hearing the judges showed a marked lack of enthusiasm for the Revenue's case in pursuing Dooland for a mere £20 and the proceedings contained examples of rather ponderous judicial humour, as when Sir David Jenkins asked if they ever had collections for umpires and the Master of the Rolls suggested collections might be appropriate for rejecting more than four appeals. Sir Norman Birkett was well known for his love of cricket and was one of the finest after-dinner speakers on cricket there has ever been and both he and the Master of the Rolls said in their judgments that they had reached

---

[3] Later Lords Evershed, Jenkins and Birkett.

their conclusions with regret. However, in the best tradition of judicial impartiality, the unanimous decision of the court was that the £48 15s. was taxable as, although a voluntary payment, Dooland was entitled to it under the terms of his contract of employment. The court distinguished *Seymour* v. *Reed* on the ground that Seymour's contract did not contain any right in any circumstance to a benefit, whereas Dooland's gave him the right to receive the voluntary payments. One of the consequences of the decisions in the two cases is that it is not the practice of cricketers to try and have a provision for a benefit or testimonial included in their contracts with the counties, thus making life slightly easier for county committees.

Other taxes

Other forms of tax gave rise to litigation but these involved clubs rather than individual cricketers. Thus in 1922 the court held that a certain proportion of the subscriptions paid by members of the Essex CCC was paid for admission to see home matches and was therefore subject to entertainment tax. This caused problems for cricket clubs and the government policy was castigated by Francis Lacey, Secretary of MCC, who accused it of 'the commercial stupidity of killing the golden egg-laying goose'. In fact it was not until 1953 that cricket was finally made exempt from the tax, which had first been introduced in 1916.

Having escaped the net of entertainment tax, twenty years later county clubs found themselves liable to value added tax, which is of much wider application and will probably prove a permanent feature of the taxation scene. On 15 March 1973 the Commissioners of Customs and Excise wrote to the Club Cricket Conference stating that the Conference was liable to register as a taxable person for VAT, as the Conference supplied services to its members in the course of a business by virtue of the fact that it was providing 'facilities' which were available to members. The Conference is an association, originally formed in 1915 to keep the organisation of club cricket together in the Great War, the main object of which is 'to foster amateur cricket'. Over 2,000 clubs, mainly in the south-east of England, are members and they pay an annual subscription for which the Conference provides a wide range of services, including a fixtures bureau, an umpires' panel and answers to inquiries about the laws of cricket.

The Conference appealed against the decision of the Commissioners and maintained that it was not liable to register for VAT as it was not providing 'facilities' but was providing 'advantages' for its members. The London VAT Tribunal, which heard the appeal on 29 and 31 May 1973, considered that 'facilities' and 'advantages' were not mutually exclusive and that, notwithstanding the facilities might be advantageous to members, the Conference was supplying services in the course of a business to a value of more than £5,000 a year which, in 1973, was the qualifying figure for registration. The Conference's appeal was therefore dismissed.

Another service – or facility – which the Conference provides is help to clubs seeking remission from rates and advice about valuations. Rating assessments on cricket clubs have provoked several appeals and, although the amounts involved were usually small, some of the cases are interesting for the reason behind the decision and the sidelight thrown on the affairs of the club concerned.

The late 1950s, when money was worth about eight times its current value, saw five appeals which covered a wide range of clubs, although it is unlikely that any of them was ever a member of the Conference. In December 1956 Wearmouth Colliery Cricket Club appealed against the refusal of the Sunderland County Borough Council to grant relief from rates. The club claimed relief on the ground either that its main object was 'the advancement of social welfare' or because the spectators were only charged for admission 'on special occasions'. The recorder dismissed the appeal holding that the main objects were not concerned with social welfare, as if they were almost every sports club in the country would be exempt, and that cricket matches were not special occasions but the 'modus vivendi of the club' and thus precisely the opposite of 'special'. In the next case, *Hyde Borough Council* v. *Wilkes*, it was decided in 1958 that land given to trustees to be used and enjoyed 'by the inhabitants of Flowery Field within Hyde' primarily as a cricket ground was assessable at £25 and not exempt as being dedicated to the public because, among other reasons, the inhabitants of Flowery Field were only a section of the public. In May 1959, an appeal by Heaton CC, a member of the Bolton Amateur League, was successful to the extent of reducing the valuation officer's assessment from £80 to £72 as 'league grounds were the urban parallel of village clubs and could look for only limited support'.

A rung or two up the ladder in September of the same year the Warwickshire county ground at Edgbaston was assessed at £3,200, which was nearer the valuation officer's assessment of £4,250 than the club's suggestion of £600, while higher up still, in December 1959 the tribunal announced its verdict in the case of *MCC* v. *Morley*, after a four-day hearing, on what the proper assessment was for Lord's. The evidence gives a lot of background information about MCC and its finances at that time, including the facts that the annual subscription had remained at £3 for a hundred years until it was increased to £4 in 1947 and that, having lost £10,831 on its catering operations in 1956, MCC had in January 1957 placed the catering in the hands of Ring and Brymer from whom the club received £5,121 in 1957. In the event the tribunal held that Lord's must be valued for use as a cricket ground, which was its only practicable use, and the assessment, which had been £5,000 in 1956, was increased to £9,000, almost exactly half-way between the £15,000 claimed by the valuation officer and the £3,500 suggested by MCC.

Wills

Many cricket enthusiasts have left 'cricket legacies' in their wills but some have made wills which caused problems of interpretation after their deaths. In July 1926 John Hornsby, an MCC member who played for Middlesex in 1893, died and in the following May an application was made to Mr Justice Eve to ascertain whether an allocation could be made to the Cricketers' Fund Friendly Society out of Hornsby's residuary estate. Sir Harry Eve ordered that a scheme should be prepared for the application of the bequest and in March 1928 a scheme was approved by the court and 'the Hornsby Professional Cricketers Fund' registered as a charity. Under the terms of the scheme grants and other benefits could be made to 'professional cricketers or their wives, widows (until remarriage), children or other dependants', provided that such persons were 'in necessitous circumstances'. In December 1987 the first issue of the *MCC Newsletter* drew members' attention to the charity (which at 31 May 1987 had investments amounting to £134,000), as one which made regular grants to former professional cricketers and recommended it as a candidate for donations and legacies.

On 22 November 1927, William Fletcher Moore Patten signed a will which, following his death in February 1928, gave rise to difficult problems involving the Settled Land Act 1925 and the rule against perpetuities. The Westminster Bank as executor took out a summons asking the court to determine various questions, including whether effect should be given to a legacy to the Sussex CCC. The relevant wording in the will itself was 'to the Sussex County Cricket Club: £300 of Funding Loan in trust to pay the interest yearly to the Nursery Fund'. This was a fund established by Sussex in 1908 for the purpose of coaching young cricketers to enable them to become professionals.

The rule against perpetuities in effect provides that a gift made in a will must vest absolutely in the beneficiary during the period of a life in being at the time of the testator's death plus 21 years. As the Nursery Fund was only entitled to the interest, the capital would never vest in it and the legacy was therefore invalid unless the Nursery Fund could be shown to be a charity, as the rule against perpetuities does not apply to charities. J. W. F. Beaumont,[4] the counsel for Sussex CCC, did his best, including arguing that the Nursery Fund was one for the 'supportation aid and help of young tradesmen handicraftsmen and persons decayed' within the meaning of the Charitable Uses Act 1601, part of which was still then in force. Mr Justice Romer[5] was not, however, impressed by this argument and held that the legacy was not charitable and was therefore invalid. Coincidentally, had Patten left the Funding Loan outright its proceeds would have almost have financed the Nursery Fund for one year, as its total expenditure in 1928, including wages, amounted to £305 8s. which, even when considered in terms of its current value of £6,500, is not an excessive sum to devote annually to the future professional cricketers of Sussex.

[4] Later Sir John Beaumont.
[5] Later Lord Romer.

V

STOPPING THE SEVENTY TOUR

The first South African cricket tour of England took place in 1894 and subsequently official South African sides visited England regularly, the twelfth tour being that made in 1960 under the captaincy of Jackie McGlew. The 1960 side was also the first to be involved in controversy arising out of the apartheid policy of the South African government. When the team arrived at Heathrow it was met by a group of hostile protesters, while the subsequent refusal of Reverend David Sheppard,[1] a former England captain, to play for the Duke of Norfolk's XI against the South Africans in their opening match aroused widespread publicity. The 1965 South African side was also the subject of anti-apartheid demonstrations but, as in 1960, these did not disrupt the tour; however the situation was soon to change.

In 1968–9 England were due to tour South Africa and when Tom Cartwright, the Warwickshire all-rounder, withdrew from the team through injury Basil D'Oliveira of Worcestershire, a Cape Coloured, was chosen to replace him. The South African government thereupon accused England of mixing sport and politics and told MCC that D'Oliveira would not be an acceptable member of the English team. The MCC responded by saying that if South Africa would not accept the team as selected the tour would be cancelled and that is what happened.

In the summer of 1969 Wilfred Isaacs, a South African Jew who had strong links with English cricket, brought a side to England to play sixteen matches. The side was a strong one and only one match was lost and that after a sporting declaration by the tourists' captain. From the start this tour, although not an official South African one, was subjected to demonstrations and harassment. The first match

[1] Later the Right Reverend David Sheppard, successively Bishop of Woolwich and Bishop of Liverpool.

against Essex was interrupted when about a dozen people ran on to the ground and sat on the pitch, most of them having to be removed by the police before the game could be resumed. Two days before the next match, which was against Oxford University, a 45-yard trench was dug across the square. This was repaired before the match was due to start, but the game itself was interrupted both when two demonstrators ran on to the ground and removed the wickets and, for about forty minutes, by an anti-apartheid 'sit-in' during the game. Nevertheless, at no time did the demonstrations and interruptions reach a level which forced any game to be abandoned, but throughout the tour the visitors were under pressure.

On 17 July 1969, while Wilfred Isaacs' XI were playing Surrey at the Oval, South Africa were playing Great Britain in a Davis Cup tennis match at Bristol. While one of the matches was in progress and the players were changing ends, two men and two women jumped on to the court and displayed anti-apartheid banners to the crowd. They refused an official's request to move and were lifted up and carried off the court by the police. The four, who were Peter Hain and three other Young Liberals, were then detained for three hours at Redlands police station but were not charged. On 19 July two more demonstrators disrupted play and a flour bomb was thrown on to the court, both of which caused short interruptions in the tennis.

In the following winter an official South African rugby team toured the British Isles and from the moment of their arrival in November 1969 until they left over two months later they were subjected to a persistent direct action campaign. The mainspring of this campaign was, of course, the opposition to apartheid and to the United Kingdom having any sporting links with South Africa, but the campaign really had a dual purpose. The first was to disrupt and, if possible, secure the abandonment of the rugby tour and the second was to persuade the Cricket Council that it should cancel the official South African tour which was due to take place the following summer. To try and achieve the second aim, a 'Stop The Seventy Tour' committee had been launched in September 1969 and the leader of STST was Peter Hain, who was one of the four who had interrupted the Davis Cup match at Bristol. Hain was a 19-year-old white

South African, who was an engineering student at the Imperial College of Science and Technology. The whole rugger tour was a nightmare for the Springboks, the games were constantly interrupted, on one occasion by drawing pins being scattered on the pitch, and the members of the team were subjected to harassment and abuse off the field. During the tour a number of police were injured, there were several arrests and some demonstrators were prosecuted and convicted. The games were, however, played.

On 27 November 1969 the Cricket Council confirmed the continuance of the following year's cricket tour and the battle lines of those in favour of and those against the tour were drawn up. On the night of 19–20 January 1970 there were co-ordinated attacks by anti-apartheid protesters on eleven cricket grounds, including Lord's, the Oval, Old Trafford and Headingley. Walls, sight screens and scoreboards were daubed with paint and at Cardiff a hole four feet square was dug in the pitch. Shortly after these incidents, it was announced that the tour would be shortened to one of twelve matches to be played on fairly defensible grounds. In addition to STST those against the tour were represented by the Fair Cricket Campaign under the chairmanship of the Bishop of Woolwich, while those in favour of the tour launched the 1970 Cricket Fund under the chairmanship of Colonel Charles Newman V.C. Nor was the controversy limited to the activists on either side. In April the Right Reverend Basil Guy, the Bishop of Gloucester, wrote in his Diocesan Letter that no good could come of the tour but people should address themselves to repairing the damage and 'we can, of course, pray for rain'. This provoked a letter to *The Times* from S.W.Wilson, who considered the bishop's suggestion 'a bit unfair, not least on the farmers in his Diocese, for as the bishop will recollect, the rain falls on the just and the unjust'.

On 14 May there was an emergency debate on the tour in the House of Commons and on 18 May the Cricket Council held a special and secret meeting at Lord's, which went on well into the night. On the following day the Cricket Council announced, contrary to general expectation, that the shortened tour would proceed as arranged. On 21 May James Callaghan,[2]

---

[2] Later Prime Minister and subsequently Baron Callaghan.

the Home Secretary, asked representatives of the Cricket Council to meet him and at that meeting requested that the tour should be cancelled 'on the grounds of broad public policy'. In the circumstances the Cricket Council decided that it had no alternative but to comply with the Home Secretary's request and on 22 May it was announced that the invitation to the South African touring team had been withdrawn. STST had succeeded in its object.

Also on 22 May Francis Bennion, a 48-year-old barrister, announced that he would launch a private prosecution for conspiracy against Hain, the chairman of STST. It was over two years before the case came up and when it did, at the Old Bailey on 24 July 1972, Hain was charged in the name of the Queen, who is the prosecutrix in all prosecutions both public and private. He was accused of conspiring with others first to disrupt the 1969–70 South African rugby tour, secondly to disrupt the 1969 Wilfred Isaacs cricket tour, thirdly to disrupt the Davis Cup match at Bristol in July 1969 and fourthly 'to prevent and cause to be cancelled' the 1970 South African cricket tour. Hain pleaded not guilty to all four charges.

The prosecution, which was brought by Bennion on behalf of an organisation called Freedom Under The Law Limited, was represented by Owen Stable QC, with Brian Potter as his junior counsel. Hain's counsel were Michael Sherrard QC and Brian Capstick, who were instructed by Larry Grant, the legal officer of the National Council of Civil Liberties. The presiding judge was Bernard Gillis QC and the jury of twelve comprised eleven men and one woman.

The first week of the trial was taken up with three and a half days of legal argument followed by the prosecution's opening speech, which took one and a half days. On 31 July the prosecution started calling its witnesses and these included Wilfred Isaacs and the captain of the 1969–70 Springbok rugby team, Dawe de Villiers, both of whom were cross-examined by defence counsel. Evidence was then given of the interruption of the Davis Cup match and further witnesses were called by the prosecution including Wilfred Wooller, a former Welsh rugger international and also a former captain and secretary of Glamorgan Country Cricket Club. On 3 August, against the advice of his counsel, Hain decided to conduct his own defence and it also transpired at this stage of the trial that the prosecution had decided not to call Bennion, although he had given evidence at the committal proceedings, and also that Hain was not going to go into the witness box.

Hain then called various witnesses including the Bishop of Stepney, the Most Reverend Trevor Huddleston, a well-known anti-apartheid campaigner. Hain sought to show that there was no agreement, or conspiracy, between him and other persons as alleged by the prosecution, just as the prosecution, relying in part on extracts from Hain's own book *Don't Play With Apartheid*, had sought to satisfy the jury that there was. After all the witnesses had been called, Stable made his closing speech for the prosecution and this was followed by Hain's final address on his own behalf, which lasted for two days. On Wednesday 16 August the judge started his summing up and this lasted until the Friday afternoon. On Monday 21 August, after deliberating for over seven hours, the jury delivered a majority verdict by ten votes to two on one of the four charges but said that they could not agree on any of the other three. The charge on which the jury had reached a verdict was that of disrupting the Davis Cup match at Bristol, on which they found Hain guilty. The prosecution then requested that the remaining three indictments should not remain on file and verdicts of not guilty were recorded on those counts.

The judge fined Hain £200 on the charge on which he had been convicted with the alternative, if it was not paid within three months, of three months' imprisonment and also ordered him to pay £50 towards the costs of his defence. In fact the £250 was met by the Hain Defence Fund. Hain subsequently appealed against his conviction, but this was rejected by the Court of Appeal on 22 October 1973 and Hain was ordered to pay a further £150 towards the costs of the appeal.

Twenty years have passed since the days of STST but the subject of sporting – and indeed other – links with South Africa is still one of bitter controversy. It is perhaps curious (or is it?) that two different but equally sincere groups of people dedicated to freedom and liberty could arrive at such diametrically opposed interpretations of which was the right cause to espouse of the two supported in 1970 by Freedom Under The Law and the National Council for Civil Liberties.

VI

TWO MURDERS

The Hylton case

In the first murder trial described in this chapter the accused was a fast bowler who played in six Tests for the West Indies. Of the many fast bowlers who have played such an important role in the history of West Indian cricket he is not, therefore, one of the most prominent, but Leslie George Hylton has a unique place in cricket history as the only Test cricketer to have been convicted of the crime of murder.

Hylton was born on 29 March 1905[1] and was the son of Ernest Hylton and Elizabeth Jackson. His mother died when he was two or three years old and Hylton grew up with one of his aunts, Maria Jackson, who died when he was about thirteen. He attended Calabar elementary school, which he left in 1917 or 1918, when he started work at the Temple of Fashion Printery. After that he was apprenticed in the tailoring trade and he then had several jobs until, in 1933, he started work with the banana section of the United Fruit Company as a wharf worker.

By this time Hylton had become quite a well-known cricketer, having played for Jamaica as a fast bowler and lower-order batsman since the 1926–7 season. In January 1935 Hylton was chosen for the first Test against R. E. S. Wyatt's England side and had bowling figures of 3 wickets for 8 runs in England's first innings of what was an extraordinary match. On a pitch affected by rain, only George Headley and Walter Hammond were able to cope with the conditions, and the West Indies scored 102 and 51 for six declared, while England, who won the match, responded with 81 for seven declared and 75 for six. Hylton also played in the remaining three Tests of the four-match series, which

---

[1] In *The Daily Gleaner*, which was the main source for the account of the Hylton case, Hylton is reported as having stated in court that he was born on 29 March 1904, but all the standard reference books give the year as 1905.

the West Indies won by two games to one, and he finished with thirteen wickets at just over 19 runs each.

Hylton represented Jamaica against Yorkshire when the county side toured there in 1936 and recorded his highest first-class score of 80 against the champion county in the last match of the tour. He was not a member of the side originally selected for the West Indies' 1939 tour of England, but joined the team following a public subscription in Jamaica. However, although he had a good match against Northants when he scored 55 and took seven for 104, he was not a success in the Tests. After taking only 3 wickets for 167 runs in the first two Tests Hylton was dropped for the third, which turned out to be the last match of the tour, as the last seven games were cancelled owing to the international situation. After the tour Hylton did not play in another first-class match, although he continued to play cricket until 1950 and was always a keen student of the game. On his return from the 1939 tour Hylton again changed jobs and became part of the Jamaican Civil Service as he joined the Rehabilitation Department, where he worked for the rest of his life. He worked under a rehabilitation officer and ultimately became a grade one foreman.

Some time in 1940 he first met Lurline Rose and a friendship grew between them, which gradually ripened into something more. Lurline was about nine years younger than Hylton and was one of a large family, five brothers being referred to during the course of her husband's trial. Her parents were Inspector Rose, the first coloured man to have been made an inspector of police in Jamaica and who died in about 1948, and his wife Constantia, who was to be a witness at Hylton's trial. When it became apparent that their daughter and Hylton might want to get married, Lurline's parents were unhappy about the prospect, owing primarily to Hylton's lack of education, his uncertain family background and the Roses' feeling that he was of an inferior social class. Hylton, however, was not deterred by Lurline's family's hostile reaction and in 1942, he proposed and was accepted. He subsequently had an interview with Lurline's father who told Hylton that before he could agree to the marriage he would have to investigate Hylton's background thoroughly, including finding out whether or not he had a police record. After some time the Roses' consent to the match was forthcoming and the couple were married on 6 October 1942. They must have looked an impressive couple as Hylton was 6 feet 2 inches tall and Lurline was only four inches shorter.

When they were first married the Hyltons lived in Kingston and in 1947 their son, Gary, was born. In the late 1940s the Hyltons moved house, before moving again in April 1951 when they went to live with Lurline's mother, by then a widow, who lived at 31 Arnold Road, St Andrew, which is just north of Kingston. This last move had been made in anticipation of Lurline going to the United States, with Hylton's agreement, in order to further her career as a dressmaker. Lurline was in the States for just over a year during which time she and Hylton corresponded regularly. She returned to Jamaica in May 1952 and the following April went back to the States, this time to take a course in French designing. It was also intended that, if the Hyltons could get permission from the US authorities to live permanently in America, her husband should go and join her there but, if not, she would return home in April 1954. As on her first visit, the Hyltons corresponded regularly during Lurline's absence.

On the morning of Saturday 17 April, while Hylton was out, a letter arrived at 31 Arnold Road addressed to him, which Mrs Rose put on the bureau in his bedroom. Hylton arrived back at two o'clock, opened the letter, and read it: his world was shattered. The letter, which was dated 15 April, was an anonymous one from the States and signed only 'An Old Friend'. It was fairly long and thoroughly unpleasant both in content and in tone and was later to be described by counsel as 'a dark thread running throughout the whole fabric and texture of this case'. The nub of it was that Lurline had gone to live in Brooklyn Avenue, New York, with someone called Roy Francis who 'boasts of his immoral life, especially when it happens to be another man's wife' and that Lurline had assumed Francis' name and that, like all Francis' women, she had 'to supply him with money'.

Hylton was, naturally enough, very upset by the letter which he showed to his mother-in-law and asked her what he should do about it. Mrs Rose pointed out that the letter was anonymous and might just be an attempt at blackmail and that Hylton should not come to any conclusion about its contents until he had heard what Lurline had to say. Hylton then rang two of his brothers-in-law, Philip and Gilbert Rose, who came round to Arnold Road and, after discussing the matter with them and Mrs Rose, Hylton decided to send a cable to his wife, which he did shortly before four o'clock.

Hylton's cable read: 'Cancel arrangements re school. Come home immediately. Do not ask questions.' About two hours later a telephone call was received from Lurline, who asked Hylton what all the fuss was about. Hylton told Lurline about the letter, asked her some questions and said that he was expecting her home immediately. Lurline did not take steps to return at once to Jamaica, but two days later, on Easter Monday 19 April, she wrote quite a long letter to her husband which she sent to him by airmail.

Although the letter amounted to a denial of the allegations made against her, it was neither conciliatory nor particularly affectionate in tone, starting 'Lo Leslie' and ending 'Cheerio, Luris'. In the letter Lurline claimed that she had known Francis since 1929, that he was a friend of the Rose family and had been well liked by her father. She also suggested the anonymous letter might have been written either by Hazel Cruise or by Nellie Waddell, two sisters who were friends of Hylton and who 'must have had such a heck of a time with you that they now want to take you by trying to frame me'. Finally Lurline turned to the financial implications of Hylton's summons, writing, 'It never occurred to you that by ordering me home because you are still my husband I'm losing a lot of money.' Thus, although Lurline denied that there was anything improper in her relationship with Francis, the letter can have done little to reassure Hylton.

Early in the morning of the Tuesday, the day after Lurline had written the letter but before Hylton had received it, Hylton saw Edmund Wright, under whom he worked at the Rehabilitation Department, and explained the situation to him, without mentioning Francis' name, and was granted two days' leave so that he could 'fix up some papers'. On Thursday 22 April, his first day back at work, Hylton was telephoned by his mother-in-law to say that a cable had arrived from Lurline which read: 'Booked seat for flight 771 to arrive Sunday 2nd. Don't worry all will be well. Love from your wife.' This made Hylton feel much better and the following Wednesday, the 28th, he applied for and was granted thirteen days' leave starting on Monday 3 May.

Meanwhile in the evening after work on Friday 23 April, Hylton attended a meeting of the Jamaican Cycle Racing Association, of which he was a member. Mrs Rose let him in when he arrived back at 31 Arnold Road and, according to Hylton, he remarked on the Guntleys' house being all lit up and asked her if there was anything wrong, Mrs Rose replying that a thief had broken into it and stolen a radio. Hylton later maintained that his response to this was to tell Mrs Rose that on Monday he was going to buy some cartridges for his revolver, as there were always thieves lurking about at night, but Mrs Rose subsequently had no recollection of this conversation. What is certain is that Hylton kept a revolver at 31 Arnold Road, which was meant to be kept in the bureau drawer during the day and on the bedroom windowsill at night. Sometimes, however, the gun was left lying around the house and, especially as the Hyltons' son was about, Mrs Rose would put it away and on occasions telephone Hylton at work to remonstrate with him for being so careless. The following Thursday, 29 April, Hylton telephoned Bernard Cridland at Aguilar's Store and asked him if he could supply a few rounds of .32 calibre revolver ammunition and on Saturday 1 May, Hylton went to the shop and bought fifteen rounds for about 12s. The following day Lurline was due to arrive home in Jamaica.

On the Sunday Lurline arrived at Palisadoes airport where she was met by Hylton, by members of the Rose family and also by friends of the family. They all went to 31 Arnold Road where, after all the guests and relations had left, Hylton, Lurline and Mrs Rose were left sitting in the dining room. After a little desultory conversation Hylton said, 'I got a letter that hurt me for true, so I must have a talk with you,' to which his wife replied, 'Same thing over again?' Before Hylton could reply Mrs Rose suggested that they should go and talk things over in their bedroom, which they did. They both sat on the bed[2] and Hylton gave Lurline the anonymous letter to read. While reading it she said, as she had in the letter to Hylton of 19 April, that

---

[2] The narrative throughout reflects Hylton's version of events when other evidence is not available.

only Hazel Cruise or Nellie Waddell could have written it, and that she thought it might have been Hazel Cruise because she was 'fooling around' with Roy Francis, who had not paid her any attention. In response to various questions from her husband, Lurline described Francis as 'a casual acquaintance', a description hardly consistent with having known him since 1929, and denied that she had ever slept at his home or supported him with money.

After Hylton had finished his questions Lurline took his hand and said, 'Les, darling, don't you know that you are the one man I love? I married you. I love you. I have been true to you. I have been and always will be.' This made Hylton feel rather ashamed, as he was convinced of his wife's innocence and thought that he had been accusing her falsely. The couple then embraced and kissed each other and then, in the delicate language of *The Daily Gleaner*'s report, 'the matter was settled in true matrimonial form'. The couple were in the bedroom for about two and a half hours and remained at home for the rest of the day.

The next morning the Hyltons did not emerge from their bedroom until about eleven o'clock and in the afternoon Hylton went out to keep two appointments from which he returned at about seven o'clock. Neither Hylton nor his wife went out that evening and they went to bed at about ten o'clock. The next morning, Tuesday 4 May, Hylton went to the dentist and also paid some insurance premiums, returning to 31 Arnold Road shortly before midday. In the afternoon he carried out a cricket coaching engagement at Excelsior College and Hylton and his wife again spent the evening at home, still apparently on the best of terms. However, unbeknown to Hylton, some time during the day, Lurline had written a letter to Roy Francis.

On Wednesday 5 May Hylton stayed at home in the morning, during which his wife was visited by a friend, Mrs Ethline Robinson. In the afternoon Hylton fulfilled an engagement at the local army camp, returning home shortly after six o'clock when he went to his bedroom, changed into his shorts and went and sat on the verandah. While he was sitting there he saw the garden boy, Melvin Richards, pass about two yards from where he was sitting and he noticed that Richards was holding a letter addressed to Roy J. Francis with a Brooklyn

James Doyle
Doncaster Library Services and
Sheffield Newspapers

William Bestwick. The picture
which appeared in The Ilkeston
Pioneer on 1st February 1907.
Nottingham Evening Post

Doncaster Town Cricket Club's pavilion, which was within a few
yards of where Albert Needham (inset) was stabbed to death on
6th December 1924.
Doncaster Library Services and Sheffield Newspapers

Vallance Jupp
The Cricketer International

Ted McDonald's car after colliding with James Murray's car and crashing
through the railings and running down an embankment on 22nd July 1937.
Bolton Evening News

John Edward Shilton

W. R. Gilbert. A picture which appeared in the magazine 'Cricket' in 1886.

M.C.C.

The Original English Lady Cricketers. A photograph taken in May 1890, probably during a match. Two of the ladies in the front row are wearing pads, the one on the right apparently as wicket-keeper.

Miss N. Rheinberg, MBE

F.R. Foster, a picture probably taken in about 1929.

James Seymour. A photograph taken at Canterbury in 1920 during his benefit match.

David Frith

Thumbs-up and thumbs-down. Peter Hain's reaction to the Cricket Council's decision that the 1970 South African tour should proceed but only on the basis that it would be the last tour until non-white players were considered for selection.

The Press Association

Leslie Hylton (standing) in 1939.
The Cricketer International

Lord Constantine, who as plain Mr Learie Constantine was excluded from the Imperial Hotel in 1943, arriving to take his seat in the House of Lords in 1969.

The Cricketer International

address in what appeared to be his wife's handwriting. Seeing Lurline standing near the dining-room door and not wishing to involve Richards in a domestic matter, Hylton did not ask the boy to give him the letter or stop him going to post it but, about half an hour later, Hylton went to the local post office where he asked the post mistress, Amy Munroe, if she could help him to recover a letter addressed to Roy J. Francis which had been posted in the Arnold Road letter box. Miss Munroe told Hylton she was sorry but she could not help him, as once a letter had been posted it became the property of the Crown but she suggested the Postmaster General might be able to help. Hylton then returned home and after supper took his bicycle and went for a ride, still brooding on the problem of the letter and trying to decide whether to speak to Lurline about it that night or to wait until the following day, when he would know whether or not he had been able to retrieve the letter. Hylton arrived back at 31 Arnold Road at about half past ten, but he had still not decided which course to take.

On returning home he went into the bedroom, but his wife appeared to be asleep so, after changing into his pyjamas and going into the bathroom, he got into bed beside his wife. However, he could not get to sleep as he was still worrying about the letter and so, shortly after midnight, he turned on the light and woke up his wife in order to discuss the letter with her. At first Lurline denied that she had written any such letter but, when Hylton told her that he had already been to the post office and had made arrangements to recover the letter early the following morning, she said, 'I had written to him, so what? I should have followed my parents' advice and not married you. You are out of my class. What have you done to make me happy? You are a hindrance to me. Look at the likes of you! Roy is a better man than you. I love him. Just the sight of you makes me sick. I can't bear to touch you. I can't bear you to touch me. I am finished with you.' Hylton then asked her whether she was crazy and what was to happen to them and their son and, according to him, his wife then continued, 'You brute, after all these years I have wasted my life with you and now that I have found the man I love, you cannot stand in my way. He has given me joy that I have never known with you. I want to bear his children. Yes, I have slept with him. I have never felt like that before. My body belongs to him. I am Roy's, Roy's, Roy's,' and with these words Lurline pulled up her knee-length nightdress revealing the lower part of her body.

Hylton then told his wife that he was her husband and that she could never get rid of him, to which she replied, 'If you stand in my way I will shoot you,' and, grabbing the revolver from the windowsill, pointed it at Hylton and pulled the trigger, which clicked. Lurline and Hylton then wrestled and he got control of the gun. Then, according to Hylton, he felt dizzy and did not know what was happening but suddenly saw blood all over the place and realised that he had shot his wife. Hylton said he was alarmed and frightened and, deciding to end his own life, loaded two cartridges into the gun. He said that one of these was accidentally discharged while he was raising the gun and that he then leant his head against the bed and pulled the trigger and that the gun went off but he was not hit by the other shot.

Meanwhile the sound of a shot had awoken Mrs Rose and, as she lay in bed trying 'to take in the circumstances', she heard another shot and a third one as she got up and went down the passage to the Hyltons' room. On reaching the bedroom she pushed open the door and called out 'Leslie what are you doing there?' He did not reply but Lurline said, 'Don't come Mummy he is going to kill you.' Mrs Rose then ran outside, screamed and called out to Richards, the garden boy, at the same time hearing further shots. Hylton had no recollection of Mrs Rose coming to the bedroom door, but it was common ground that, after the shooting, Hylton came out of the bedroom with the gun still in his hand, where he saw Mrs Rose and told her that he had shot Lurline.

Hylton then went to the dining room, where he telephoned Wright, his boss at work, Mary Rose, the wife of Lurline's brother, Philip, and the police to tell them that he had shot his wife. The first person to arrive on the scene was Corporal Carlton Roache, who was on duty in a police car and was called on the car radio and told to go to 31 Arnold Road. Roache arrived there at 12.40 a.m., where Hylton said to him, 'My name is Leslie Hylton. I shot my wife, Lurline Hylton. She is in the bedroom. Come along with me to the bedroom.' Roache went to the bedroom door where he saw Lurline, who was gravely wounded but still alive, and he therefore went back to the dining room and telephoned for an ambulance. Within five minutes, however, Gertrude Swaby, a friend of the Hyltons who lived nearby and was a sister tutor at Kingston Public Hospital, had arrived with her brother, Archdeacon Swaby. Miss Swaby did what she could for Lurline but the end was clearly near and at about one o'clock she died.

Meanwhile several more people had arrived at the house, including Lurline's brothers Philip and Manley accompanied by their wives, another nurse, a doctor and more police, including Superintendent Frank Forbes, who was in charge of the police in the St Andrew district. Forbes gave instructions for Hylton to be taken to the Cross Road Police Station where he was arrested, charged with the murder of his wife and cautioned. When he was cautioned Hylton said, 'I am sorry . . . I guess I lost control of myself.' At Hylton's request, the police also got in touch with his solicitor who was Noel – known as 'Crab' – Nethersole, a good all-round cricketer, who played for Oxfordshire while at Oxford as a Rhodes Scholar, subsequently captained Jamaica and served on the West Indies Board of Control for fifteen years.

Hylton's trial opened on Friday 8 October 1954 and was held at the Home Circuit Court in Kingston before Mr Justice MacGregor and an all-male jury. Harvey Da Costa[3] and Louis Fox appeared for the prosecution, while Nethersole instructed Vivian Blake and Ramon Alberga to represent Hylton. The case lasted nine days about two of which were taken up with Hylton's own evidence, his cross-examination by the prosecution and subsequent re-examination by his own counsel. Except for Roy Francis, everyone who had played a part in the events of the night of 5–6 May and of those leading up to it gave evidence, as well as various other people such as a ballistics' expert and the doctors who examined Lurline's body.

Various witnesses gave evidence about those of the events narrated above in which they had been involved and, in addition, the evidence disclosed some important matters to which reference has not so far been made. First, the contents of the letter which Hylton saw Richards taking to the post. Hylton was, of course, bluffing when he told Lurline that he had made

---

[3] Later QC and Attorney General of Jamaica.

arrangements to recover the letter from the post office, but the bluff worked and, in the event, Hylton's suspicions proved to have been well founded. The letter, which was read out by the judge on the first day of the trial, was a long letter, written on 4 May, and its opening words, which contrast starkly with the opening words of her letter to Hylton on 19 April, show that Francis was more than the 'casual acquaintance' which Lurline had claimed. 'My Beloved,' the letter begins, 'Here I am again. [The letter shows later that Lurline had also written to Francis on 3 May, the day after her return from New York.] Do I miss even hearing your voice? It's now I'm realising even more than I did before just how much I love you.' The letter also gives Mrs Robinson's address as 'my address for our correspondence' and in the letter Lurline says she is 'going to force my man's hand as soon as I can' and, near the end of the letter, perhaps with the contents of the anonymous letter in mind, she writes, 'Remember honey not to flirt around and kiss up the girls.' Had Lurline realised that her husband would probably not have been able to recover the letter from the post office she could have pretended that its contents were not compromising and, even if Hylton had not been convinced, it is most unlikely that she would have been shot.

Secondly, evidence was given by Doctor Vernon Lindo that seven bullets had entered Lurline's body. This meant not only had Hylton reloaded the revolver, as he had no option but to admit in court, but that one of the bullets with which he said he had intended to end his own life had hit Lurline. A third point, which came out during the trial and was important in relation to Hylton's appeal, was that although the police, in the person of Corporal Roache, arrived at 31 Arnold Road no later than 12.40 a.m. it was not for another hour and twenty minutes that Hylton was cautioned.

In his closing address for the defence Blake virtually admitted that Lurline had 'met her death at the hands of the accused' and that the issue in the case was whether the offence was murder or manslaughter. The question the jury would have to ask themselves, Blake said, was whether the provocation was such as would cause a reasonable man to lose his self-control and drive him into such a passion as to make him use the revolver to kill his wife. Blake was followed by Da Costa, the counsel for the prosecution, who laid great stress on the fact that Lurline had been hit by seven bullets, which must have involved Hylton in first firing all six rounds and then breaking the revolver to reload it, getting the cartridges from the bureau, inserting them into the gun and firing it again, a course of action which, he maintained, was 'out of all proportion to the provocation'.

In his summing up the judge started by reminding the jury that for them to convict it was necessary for the prosecution to prove the prisoner's guilt beyond reasonable doubt. He said, however, that if the jury were satisfied that Hylton had fired the shots which killed Lurline – and Hylton had not admitted it in so many words – they must find him guilty either of murder or manslaughter. The judge dealt at length with the issue of provocation and said that, if the offence was to be reduced to one of manslaughter, the mode of resentment shown must bear a reasonable relation to the provocation and directed the jury that mere words, even embracing a confession of adultery, could not constitute provocation of a sort which could reduce murder to manslaughter. He also told the jury that Hylton's claim that Lurline had been shot as the result of an impulse which he could not control was not a defence, as that amounted to a plea of temporary insanity and there was no evidence to justify a verdict of guilty but insane, nor had the defence asked for such a verdict.

Mr Justice MacGregor then considered the question of the various statements made by the prisoner after the shooting, but before he was cautioned well over an hour after the police first arrived on the scene. He told the jury that Corporal Roache should have cautioned Hylton earlier and, if it appeared to him that any of the statements made by the prisoner before he was cautioned had not been made voluntarily, that it was his duty, as presiding judge, to rule out those statements, but if, as was the case, he was satisfied that they were voluntary statements, then it was up to the jury, if they were also satisfied, to pay attention to them. The judge then went through all the events leading up to the fatal night of the 5–6 May and of the night itself, both before and after the shooting, and went through the evidence given, including that given by Hylton himself. Finally the judge again referred to the question of provocation, before reminding the jury that, provided they were satisfied that Hylton fired the shots which killed Lurline, if they had reasonable doubt whether the crime was murder or manslaughter their verdict must be one of manslaughter.

After an hour and a half the jury returned, but only to say that they had not arrived at a verdict. The judge asked if there was anything he could do to assist them but the foreman said there was nothing that could clarify the position. The judge then asked them to go back and consider the matter further, emphasising that it made for 'great public inconvenience and expense if jurors cannot agree owing to the unwillingness of one or more of their number to listen to the arguments of the rest', but adding that if eventually they could not agree a verdict, they must say so. After a further hour and a quarter the jury returned, this time with a unanimous verdict of guilty on the charge of murder coupled with a strong recommendation for mercy. Hylton was asked if he had anything to say but he made no audible reply, the judge then donned the black cap and passed sentence of death. After telling the jury that they were excused jury service for a period of eight years, the judge concluded by saying that their recommendation for mercy would be forwarded to the Governor of Jamaica, Sir Hugh Foot.[4]

Hylton appealed against his conviction and on 10 January 1955 the Chief Justice of Jamaica, the Honourable John Carberry[5], delivered the judgment of the Jamaican Court of Appeal. The appeal raised several questions of law and fact and the court dealt first with the submission that the trial judge had wrongly exercised his discretion in admitting as evidence the statements made by Hylton after the shooting but before he was cautioned. Hylton's counsel had argued that the appellant had technically been in custody once Corporal Roache had arrived at 31 Arnold Road and that there had been a breach of the Judges' Rules in that Hylton had not been cautioned. However, the Court of Appeal held that Hylton had made the statements voluntarily and not in response to any questions by the police and that, therefore, Mr Justice MacGregor had correctly exercised his discretion to admit the statements.

The next point considered was the submission that the trial

---

[4] Later Baron Caradon.
[5] Later Sir John Carberry.

judge had not properly left the defence of provocation to the jury. Here the court held that, although Mr Justice MacGregor had at one stage said that mere words alone could not constitute a sufficient provocation, he had later qualified this by the words 'save in circumstances of a most extreme and exceptional character' and had also later referred to the alleged attempt by Lurline to shoot Hylton. Thus all the elements of provocation had been put to the jury, although somewhat disjointedly. The Court of Appeal also held that there was nothing wrong with the judge's address to the jury when, after first retiring, they had failed to reach a verdict, as it was 'the duty of a judge to try and persuade a jury to agree on their verdict, provided that no improper pressure was used in doing so'.

A number of other matters were raised on behalf of Hylton, among which were two which the Court of Appeal regarded as very important. These were first a reference by the trial judge in his summing up to the possibility that Hylton had shot Lurline not only to injure her but also, as there were two injuries to her groin and private parts, 'to inflict injury on any possible child she might be bearing for Francis' and secondly that the judge had allowed Hylton to be cross-examined about a document which itself was not admissible in evidence, namely the police register recording the theft of the Guntleys' radio. The Court of Appeal was of the opinion that these matters were of sufficient gravity to justify them in quashing the conviction and ordering a new trial, unless the proviso to section 16(1) of the Court of Appeal Law applied. This provided that 'the court may, notwithstanding that they are of opinion that the point raised in the appeal might be decided in favour of the appellant, dismiss the appeal if they consider that no substantial miscarriage of justice has actually occurred.' The court decided that the proviso applied in Hylton's case.

Finally the judgment dealt with 'the vital question of the appeal. Did the appellant's mode of resentment bear a reasonable relationship to the provocation he suffered?' The court considered the matter on the basis of the provocation as stated by Hylton, which 'consisted of a sudden confession of adultery, together with insulting and contemptuous language and an attempt to shoot him'. Even on this basis the Court of Appeal considered that Hylton's 'mode of resentment was

entirely disproportionate to the provocation he suffered' and
the court was satisfied that, even if there had been a perfect
summing up and the questions objected to had not been allowed
in cross-examination, 'a reasonable jury must have come to the
conclusion that the appellant was guilty of murder'. The court
added, on the question of the 'black-out' suffered by Hylton,
that 'an unusually excitable or pugnacious individual is not
entitled to rely on provocation which would not have led an
ordinary person to act as he did'. The appeal was therefore
dismissed and Hylton's conviction for murder and sentence to
death were affirmed.

Three days after the Court of Appeal's judgment was delivered, it was announced that Hylton's appeal would be taken
to the Judicial Committee of the Privy Council in England, a
forum available for appeals from British dominions and colonies
and which has been retained by Jamaica since independence.
In fact appeals in criminal cases can only be brought by leave
of the Committee itself, thus in Hylton's case the Committee
considered the cases of the Crown and of the defence in order to
decide whether or not to grant leave to appeal. Both the Crown
and the petitioner were represented by different counsel before
the Committee, as Derek Grant appeared for the Crown, while
Bernard Gillis QC, who seventeen years later was to be the
judge in the Hain case,[6] led for Hylton.

For the petitioner Grant said the trial judge had considered
that there was sufficient material in the defence of provocation
to leave it to the jury as an issue and it had never been suggested
by counsel for the Crown that there was no material for the
consideration by the jury on that issue. He contended that, for
the first time in the Court of Appeal, the point had been taken
that the mode of resentment was so out of proportion to the
provocation offered as to render it inevitable that the jury would
come to the conclusion that the offence of murder was proved.
Gillis submitted that the Court of Appeal had misdirected itself
when it came to that conclusion and had thus closed the door
against the defence of provocation. For the prosecution Grant
said that the Court of Appeal had been bound to consider the
degree and continuance of the violence and said also there was

[6] See the chapter entitled 'Stopping The Seventy Tour'.

evidence that the revolver did not operate very effectively and had to be fired with considerable deliberation. The Crown thus maintained that the Court of Appeal was entitled to come to the conclusion that the provocation was not sufficient to justify such a savage and continuous attack. On 21 April, after consultation, the Committee decided that the case was not one in which leave to appeal should be granted.

Hylton's appeal against his conviction had failed but it was still possible that the Governor of Jamaica would grant a reprieve in the light of the jury's recommendation for mercy and in response to a petition submitted on Hylton's behalf by his solicitor, Nethersole. However, on 6 May the petition was turned down and Hylton's execution date was fixed as Tuesday, 17 May. While in prison Hylton was received into the Roman Catholic faith and was reported to have slept well and to have looked forward to the weekly visits from his priest. Shortly before half past eight on the morning of 17 May 1955 Hylton was taken to the gallows at the St Catherine District Prison, wearing a white shirt and a light grey suit. He strode calmly to the gallows and indicated that he had reconciled himself to his fate. There was a large crowd waiting outside the prison to see the posting of the death certificate to show that Hylton had been hanged. After a coroner's inquest his body was buried in a 20-foot pit in the prison compound where the body of another murderer already lay. As Jeffrey Stollmeyer, who played Test cricket with Hylton in 1939 and later captained the West Indies wrote, 'It seemed a great shame that one so powerful and vital should have to pay the full penalty, but his temper had let him down for the last time.'[7]

The Carroll case

Twenty years after the Hylton case there took place in Bristol the murder of a young cricketer which, of the cases described in this book, stands alone in the absence of motive for the crime and the callous savagery with which it was committed. On page 134 of the 1973 *Wisden* there appear details of 'the remarkable batting feats in Rhodesia of a nineteen-year-old schoolboy Simon Kerr of St George's College, Salisbury'.

[7] *Everything Under The Sun* by Jeff Stollmeyer.

Playing for his school in 1972, in six innings Kerr scored five unbeaten centuries. In the following year Kerr paid his own fare to England and joined the Gloucestershire ground staff, living in the pavilion on the Bristol ground. In 1973 he played a few games for the Gloucestershire 2nd XI but without any success, scoring only 17 runs in four completed innings and failing to take a wicket.

On Friday 16 March 1974 Kerr went to a party at North Road, Bristol, given by two nurses in their flat, which was above a basement flat shared by Desmond Carroll, a 24-year-old aircraft machinist, and Paul Davis, who was away when the party was held. Kerr had too much to drink at the party, but was not offensive, and Carroll allowed Kerr, whom he had never met before, to go down to his flat so that he could sleep off the effects of the drink. The full horror of what happened next is vividly described in Carroll's own words which were quoted in *The Daily Telegraph*:

> He was under the bedclothes and he didn't see me come in. I got the knife from the cupboard. I saw the terrible fear on his face. I stabbed him in the back about three times.
>
> While I was stabbing him he was shouting for help. Nobody heard because of the noise of the party. I put a hand over his mouth to stop him shouting. I stabbed him in the heart three times and I stamped on the knife.
>
> He took about fifteen minutes to die. He was as hard as concrete. It's easy to get a knife out, but not to put it in. It was so pleasant I feel I could do it again. I have no regrets; I feel better now.

On 18 March Carroll was charged and on 3 October 1974 he was tried for Kerr's murder at Bristol Crown Court. Evidence was given that in the police car, after his arrest, Carroll said that there was nothing wrong with him, that he was glad that he had killed Kerr but that he could understand the police's point of view. Not surprisingly, Carroll was sentenced to life imprisonment.

Almost six months before Carroll came up for trial the Lord Chief Justice, Lord Widgery, with two other judges of the Queen's Bench Division sat on the case of *R.* v. *Bristol Coroner*, *ex parte Kerr,* which arose out of the refusal of an application by the Bristol coroner, following Kerr's murder. On 18 March, the day on which Carroll was charged, the coroner adjourned the inquest on Kerr's body in view of the prospective criminal proceedings. Subsequently Kerr's parents wished to take their son's body back to Rhodesia for burial and applied to the coroner for its release. The coroner refused in case a further examination was necessary in connection with the murder trial. At the time, although the prosecution were willing for the body to be released, the defence were not but they hoped to be able to agree to its release before too long.

Kerr's father, Wellesley Kerr, applied for an order of certiorari[8] to quash the order made by the coroner, on the ground either that the coroner had no power under the (Amendment) Act 1926 to detain the body or, if he had, he had no reasonable ground for exercising it. The court, while expressing great sympathy with the Kerr family, held unanimously that the coroner had the power and that, in this case, he had not exercised his discretion wrongly and that accordingly Kerr's father's application must be refused. One hopes that the body was not detained for long and that Simon Kerr now rests in peace in the beautiful country whence he came.

[8] An order made by a superior court to quash the decision of an inferior one on the ground of some irregularity.

VII

NO ROOM AT THE INN

Any one asked to name the important men in the history of West Indies cricket would almost certainly include Lord Constantine of Maravel and Nelson, although they would probably refer to him as Learie Constantine and not by the title conferred on him eighteen months before he died. Constantine's inclusion may seem strange as he was not knighted or subsequently ennobled for his services to the game of cricket and his first-class career record of 4,475 runs and 439 wickets – both at an average of between 20 and 25 – do not, on the face of it, suggest that he played the game outstandingly well. Like Gilbert Jessop, however, he commands a place in the hall of fame for the way in which he played and the memorable circumstances of his most famous performance.

Constantine was a black Trinidadian, whose ancestors were slaves on both his father's and his mother's side. His father, Lebrun Constantine, was a good cricketer who toured England with the West Indies in 1900 and 1906, before they had attained Test match status. Constantine himself was born in 1902 and he first played for Trinidad in the 1921–2 season and, after playing in only three first-class matches, was chosen to tour England in 1923 with Harold Austin's[1] side, when he made little impression except for his fielding, *Wisden* describing him as 'an amazingly good cover-point'.

In 1928 he toured again and, although he failed in the three Tests, he was successful on the tour as a whole, finishing second in the batting averages and top of the bowling averages with 1,381 runs and 107 wickets. However, it was his inspired fielding, hard-hitting batting and spectacular fast bowling which attracted the public's attention, rather than the number of runs he scored or wickets which he took. In particular he had a personal triumph against Middlesex when, in response to

[1] Later Sir Harold Austin.

Middlesex's total of 352, Constantine scored 86 in less than an hour to save the follow-on, then in Middlesex's second innings he took 7 for 57 and finally, batting at number seven, he came to his side's rescue by scoring 103 in an hour and enabled the West Indies to win by 3 wickets, when they had looked certain to be defeated.

After the 1928 tour Constantine joined Nelson in the Lancashire League, where the brand of cricket played eminently suited his talents, and in his ten seasons with them, Nelson won the League eight times. During this period he still played some first-class cricket and, in particular, he toured Australia in 1931–2 and played in the 1934–5 series against England in the West Indies. He was also a member of the 1939 West Indies side and in the third Test, having taken five English wickets for 75 runs, he scored 79 in quick time, 'surpassing', as *Wisden* puts it, 'Bradman in his amazing stroke play'.

Constantine remained in England during the war when he was employed by the Ministry of Labour as a welfare officer with West Indian and other coloured workers. He also played a lot of representative one-day matches and on 31 July 1943 he was due to play against Guildford for the British Empire XI and he had also been chosen for the Dominions XI, which was to play England at Lord's on 2 and 3 August. Constantine, therefore, booked a room for himself, his wife, Norma, and his daughter, Gloria, at the Imperial Hotel in Russell Square for the night of 30 July and the three following nights. When making the booking he paid a deposit of £2 and specifically ascertained that there would be no objection to him and his family on account of their colour.

When the Constantines arrived at the hotel it became apparent that, because of their colour, they were not welcome and Constantine was told that, in spite of having booked in for four nights, he could stay for one night only. Soon afterwards, Arnold Watson, a friend and colleague of Constantine's at the Ministry of Labour, arrived at the hotel and, on finding out what had happened, took the matter up with the manageress, Miss Margaret O'Sullivan, who told him, 'We won't have niggers in this hotel . . . because of the Americans.' But, as Constantine subsequently pointed out in cross-examination, even if the Imperial had a number of guests from the United States (where colour prejudice was then common), the hotel must have been aware of that when Constantine made his booking. Having crossed swords with Miss O'Sullivan, Watson saw that the hotel was unlikely to back down and, anxious to avoid a scene, advised the Constantines to leave, which they did. They went to the nearby Bedford Hotel, which was in the same ownership as the Imperial, where they were accommodated. In September 1943 the matter was raised in the House of Commons but by then Constantine had decided to take action against the Imperial and the matter was therefore sub judice.

Constantine had three possible causes of action against the Imperial. First, an action for slander in respect of the contemptuous and insulting words used by the hotel staff, secondly, an action for breach of contract for failing to honour the contractual obligation to accommodate Constantine, his wife and daughter when the hotel had agreed to do so and accepted a deposit, and thirdly, an action for breach of the hotel's common law duty as an inn to accommodate the Constantines. An action for slander, although it would possibly have yielded the highest damages, might have failed and, while a claim for breach of contract would certainly have succeeded, the damages could only have been nominal as the Constantines had been adequately accommodated nearby at no extra cost. Probably for these reasons and because of the wider implications for coloured people in Britain who were contributing to the war effort, it was decided to sue in respect of the hotel management's breach of its common law duty as an inn keeper. The case was heard on 19 and 21 June 1944 in an improvised air-raid shelter room in the law courts. Constantine was represented by Sir Patrick Hastings KC, one of the best-known and most brilliant advocates of his day, and Rose Heilbron,[2] while Gerald Slade KC[3] and Aiken Watson appeared for the hotel; the judge was Sir Norman Birkett, who in his days at the bar had often appeared in famous cases as Hastings' adversary.

Evidence was given for Constantine by Watson and by Charles Leatherbarrow, the manager of the Dominions XI who had been at the Imperial with the Constantines, and by Constantine him-

---

[2] Later Dame Rose Heilbron.
[3] Later Sir Gerald Slade.

self. Giving evidence for the defence, Miss O'Sullivan claimed that she had taken particular care not to be offensive and both she and the manager denied that the word 'nigger' had been used. However, the manageress cannot have done the hotel's case much good by her reply when Hastings asked her if she recognised Constantine, who was in court. 'I am not sure that that is the man,' Miss O'Sullivan replied. 'Why?' asked Sir Patrick. 'They all look alike to me, these negroes,' responded Miss O'Sullivan.

Giving judgment on 28 June, Birkett reviewed the facts of the case and made it clear that he preferred the evidence of Constantine and his witnesses to that of the hotel's witnesses. He described Miss O'Sullivan as 'a lamentable figure' whose evidence was 'unworthy of credence'. He held that the Imperial had refused to receive and lodge the Constantines and that it had not fulfilled its duty to do so by offering them accommodation at the Bedford. He also rejected Slade's contention that, as the claim was an action on the case, it was not maintainable unless damage was actually suffered and proved. Quoting from judgments in earlier cases, Birkett held that if a man had a right, as Constantine had, he must of necessity have a remedy if that right was violated. On the other hand, Birkett said that, having regard to the nature of the action and in the light of the authorities, he could not accede to Hastings' request for examplary or substantial damages in spite of the 'unjustifiable humiliation and distress' suffered by Constantine and awarded him nominal damages of five guineas.

The day after unwillingly spending the night at the Bedford instead of the Imperial, Constantine duly played in the match against Guildford and took it out on the Guildford batsmen dismissing seven of them for 37 runs – all clean bowled. He continued to play war-time cricket and played his last first-class match at Lord's in August 1945 for the Dominions against England. The Dominions were to have been captained by the Australian Lindsay Hassett, but he became ill and the other ten, who were all white, honoured Constantine by choosing him to captain the side. It was a wonderful match in which Martin Donnelly and Keith Miller scored hundreds for the Dominions and Walter Hammond scored one in each innings for England. Constantine scored 5 and 40, took a wicket and ran out Eddie Phillipson with a brilliant piece of fielding. More importantly he led his side to victory by 45 runs in a match in which over 1200 runs were scored and over 350 overs bowled in three days.

After the war Constantine played for three seasons in the Yorkshire League, was called to the bar by the Middle Temple in 1954 and, when he returned to Trinidad in 1957, was elected a member of the Trinidad Legislature and became Minister of Works and Transport. In 1961 he was appointed High Commissioner for Trinidad and Tobago in London, in 1962 he was knighted and in 1963 he was granted the freedom of the borough of Nelson. He subsequently became a member of the Race Relations Board and a governor of the BBC and in 1969 was made a life peer for his services as a member of those organisations. He died in London on 1 July 1971 and two months later Lady Constantine also died.

VIII

THE PACKER CASES

Between the wars and for seventeen years after the Second World War the pattern and structure of cricket throughout the world altered little. The same cannot be said of the period since 1962 as, starting with the abolition of amateur status and the introduction of the first one-day competition, the changes in the last twenty-five years have been many and far-reaching. However, most of the changes were initiated, willingly or unwillingly, by the established cricket authorities, but not those resulting from the Packer revolution which the authorities were virtually forced to accept in order to end the dispute with World Series Cricket.

As Sir Christopher Slade put it on 25 November 1977 in his judgment in the main case, 'Mr Packer is an Australian national, who has been engaged all his adult life in business activities of one kind or another.' To be more precise, Kerry Packer was the younger son of Sir Frank Packer from whom he inherited a newspaper, television and publishing empire. He was also keen on sport, both for its own sake and as a vehicle with which to make money. It was the latter consideration that was behind his initial approach to the Australian Cricket Board and subsequent setting up of WSC.

In 1975 Packer approached the ACB to try and acquire for his Channel Nine network exclusive rights to televise Tests in Australia for five years. After some delay this approach was rebuffed by the Board, which also tried to prevent Packer from acquiring the rights in Australia to the 1979 series against England. This left Packer feeling that he had been unfairly treated and very distrustful of the Board. It also acted as the catalyst, which was to set in motion the events which led to the cricket establishment appearing in the autumn of 1977 in a High Court case in London, which lasted for thirty-one days.

The history of the Packer affair has been fully narrated elsewhere and the sources, shown at the end of this book, list some of the publications in which detailed accounts of it can be found. My concern is only to give a full enough precis of what happened to set the accounts of the cases spawned by the affair in an intelligible context. Thus, following his rebuff by the ACB, Packer approached a number of top cricketers from Australia and other Test-playing countries, including South Africa, and signed up thirty-five of them, mainly on three-year contracts, to play a series of matches to be staged for television and starting in Australia in the 1977–8 season. General dissatisfaction among Test cricketers with the rewards available to them resulted in most of those approached accepting Packer's offer with what he described as 'frightening alacrity', and on 9 May 1977 an announcement of the signings was made. The thirty-five comprised eighteen Australians, including Dennis Lillee and the Chappell brothers, five South Africans including Graeme Pollock and Mike Procter, four from England including Tony Greig and John Snow and four each from Pakistan and the West Indies. It also transpired that the highly respected Richie Benaud had been recruited as Packer's 'cricket adviser' and that Greig, who was the current England captain, had done much of the recruiting of the non-Australian players.

The news threw the cricket world into confusion and it was split into two camps, more bitterly opposed to each other than on any issue since the proposed 1970 South African tour of England. Conduct of the cricket establishment's case was taken over by the International Cricket Conference and the Test and County Cricket Board and various discussions and negotiations, both official and unofficial, took place with Packer's company, J. P. Sport (soon to be renamed World Series Cricket), but these broke down. The failure to agree any compromise resulted in the ICC 'declaring war' on Packer and on 26 July 1977 the ICC issued the following statement:

At the meeting today, member countries gave long and earnest consideration to the effect of the Packer proposals on cricket at all levels and in all countries. They reaffirm the demands of the Test match playing countries, at their meeting on June 14th, that the whole structure of cricket, for which their governing bodies are responsible, could be severely damaged by the type of promotion proposed by Mr Packer and his associates.

Following the breakdown of negotiations with Mr Packer, when the Conference was unable to accede to his demand for exclusive TV rights in Australia, members of the ICC today unanimously resolved to ensure that it could honour its responsibilities to players at all levels. To do so they are determined to continue to promote international matches between countries and to oppose to the maximum extent the series of exhibition matches arranged to take place in Australia during the forthcoming Australian summer.

These matches will not rate as first class matches, nor appear in the official records. In order to give effect to these views the ICC passed unanimously a change in ICC rules relating to qualification for Test matches as follows: 'Notwithstanding anything hereinbefore contained, no player who after October 1st 1977 has played or made himself available to play in a match previously disapproved by the Conference, shall thereafter be eligible to play in any Test match, without the express consent of the Conference, to be given only on the application of the governing body for cricket of the country for which, but for this sub-rule, the player would be eligible to play.'

In addition to this new rule, the Conference passed unanimously a resolution disapproving certain matches. This read: 'It is hereby resolved that any match arranged, or to be arranged, by J. P. Sport (Pty) Limited, Mr Kerry Packer, Mr Richie Benaud or associated companies or persons, to take place in Australia or elsewhere between October 1st, 1977 and March 31st, 1979, is disapproved.'

The Conference also passed a guidance resolution as follows: 'For future guidance, the Conference records and minutes that matches are liable to be disapproved if so arranged, whether by reference to date or otherwise, as to have the probable result that invitations to play in such matches will conflict with invitations which have been or may be received, to play in first class matches subject to the jurisdiction of the governing bodies of foundation and full members of the Conference.

'The Conference strongly recommends that each member

country should pursue as soon as possible at first class level
and other domestic cricket activities the implementation of
decisions made with regard to Test matches.'

Two days later the Australian fast bowler, Jeff Thomson,
who was a member of the Australian side touring England,
announced that he was leaving the Packer camp and this was
followed on 31 July by the Warwickshire and West Indies batsman, Alvin Kallicharran, following suit. On 2 August Packer
announced in London that he regarded the restrictions that the
ICC and the TCCB were seeking to impose as unlawful and said
that he would be initiating proceedings to seek injunctions and
to recover damages against them. He also sought an injunction
against David Lord, who was Thomson's and Kallicharran's
manager, to stop him inducing players to break their contracts
with J. P. Sport. On 4 August the vacation judge, Sir Gordon
Slynn, refused to grant an injunction against ICC and TCCB,
both of which gave undertakings that no Packer player would
be banned before April 1978, but he did grant a seven-day
injunction against Lord restraining him from inducing players
to break their contracts with Packer. This, however, was only
the preliminary skirmish before the main battle, which was to
start in the Chancery Division of the High Court seven weeks
later.

A glittering array of legal talent appeared in court number
fifteen on Monday 26 September before Mr Justice Slade, a
scholar of both Eton and Oxford who had then been on the
bench for two years. Robert Alexander QC[1] and Andrew Morritt
QC appeared with two junior counsel for the plaintiffs, while the
defendants were represented by Michael Kempster QC,[2] who
had also two juniors.

In fact neither Packer, nor the ICC, nor the TCCB was a
party in the case. The plaintiffs were Greig, Snow and Procter,
as nominees of the cricketers signed up by Packer, and World
Series Cricket (the new name of J. P. Sport), while Douglas Insole
and Donald Carr appeared as representatives of the TCCB and
Hugh ('Tagge') Webster with Jack Bailey as representatives of the

[1] Later Lord Alexander.
[2] Later Sir Michael Kempster.

ICC, both bodies being unincorporated associations and thus having no legal 'personality'. All four defendants were officials of one or the other of the two bodies and they were all cricket blues who had played county cricket and, in the cases of Insole and Carr, played Test cricket as well.

In the proceedings the plaintiffs sought a declaration that the changes of rules by the ICC and the proposed changes by the TCCB were ultra vires and an unlawful restraint of trade. The three cricketers also claimed that the changes or proposed changes were void as denying them the freedom to practise their profession when, where and how they wished, while WSC claimed that the changes and proposed changes were an unlawful inducement to the players involved to break their contracts with it. In their turn the defendants alleged that the contracts between WSC and the players were void and that the ICC and the TCCB were both 'employers' associations' within the meaning of the Trade Union and Labour Relations Act 1974 and were therefore entitled to immunity from an action for inducing a breach of contract even if, which they denied, they would otherwise have been liable.

The case opened with a long address by Alexander on behalf of the plaintiffs, following which he called nine witnesses including Greig, Snow, Procter and Packer himself, who were cross-examined by defence counsel. All this lasted until the tenth day of the contest. Kempster then made his opening speech for the defendants and called twelve witnesses, including Insole, Bailey and Geoffrey Boycott, who was generally thought to have been one of the defence's most effective performers. They too were cross-examined by counsel for the plaintiffs and, except for the judgment, the case concluded with a long closing speech by Kempster for the defendants followed by an even longer one for the plaintiffs by Morritt, who spoke for over twelve hours. The judge then reserved judgment and said that he would deliver it later in the month.

On Friday 25 November, Sir Christopher took five and a half hours to deliver his judgment, which runs to 64 pages in the official law report where parts of it are summarised rather than given verbatim. The judgment first sets out the background and facts of the case and then examines the legal issues involved with great clarity and thoroughness. In it the judge said that in order to reach a decision he had to answer nine principal questions. These, with the answers which he gave and some of the reasons for those answers, were:

1.   Are the contracts between WSC and its players void? The defendants had submitted that the contracts were unduly restrictive and therefore void ab initio, having regard to their duration, the right to assign given to the promoter, the fact that the promoter was not bound to promote a tour at all and the absence of a provision entitling a player to terminate the contract. The judge rejected these submissions and held that the contracts were not void nor even voidable (i.e. terminable without penalty) at the option of the player concerned.

2. & 3.   Has WSC established that as at 3rd August 1977 (the date when the writ was issued) it had, subject to any protection afforded by the Trade Union and Labour Relations Act 1974, a good cause of action against the ICC (question 2) and the TCCB (question 3) for inducing a breach of contract? Sir Christopher held that there were five conditions which had to be satisfied in order for the answer to this question to be 'Yes'. They were direct or indirect interference by the defendants, intention to interfere, knowledge by the defendants of the contract, significant damage to the plaintiffs accruing or being likely to accrue and the defendants not being legally justified in their actions. The judge held that WSC had established a good cause of action against both the ICC and the TCCB, while making it clear that good faith on the part of the defendants was not a good defence.

4. & 5.   Subject to the provisions of the 1974 Act, are the new rules of the ICC (question 4) and the proposed new rules of the TCCB (question 5) void as being in restraint of trade? Here the judge found that, although none of the plaintiffs was a member of nor in contractual relationship with the ICC or the TCCB, those bodies were in a position to place a restraint on the players' freedom of employment,

who therefore had the status to proceed against the ICC and the TCCB. Sir Christopher also held that these two bodies had legitimate interests, which they were entitled to protect and said that there was 'much force' in Kempster's description of the WSC organisation as being 'parasitic'. Notwithstanding this, he held that the ICC and the TCCB had not shown the proposed ban to be reasonable and justifiable and that therefore the new rules were void as being in unreasonable restraint of trade.

6. & 7. Are the ICC (question 6) and the TCCB (question 7) employers' associations within the meaning of the 1974 Act? In order to qualify as an employers' association, a body had to show that it was an organisation consisting 'wholly or mainly of employers'. The judge held that this hurdle had not been surmounted in respect of either body and that therefore the answer to the question was 'No'. In the case of the TCCB he reached his conclusion on the narrow ground that the members who had associated themselves were not responsible to each other, but to the ICC as the TCCB's controlling body, and thus did not fall within the definition of an employers' association for the purposes of the 1974 Act.

8. If either or both the ICC and the TCCB were employers' associations, did that bar any cause of action by any of the plaintiffs which would otherwise exist? This question did not need an answer in view of the answers to questions six and seven.

9. In the light of the answers to the eight preceding questions, what relief (if any) should be given respectively to the three individual plaintiffs and to the WSC? In answer to this final and vital question, the judge granted Greig, Snow and Procter a declaration that all the changes of the rules of the ICC and its resolutions referred to and set out in the press statement of 26th July 1977 were ultra vires and void as being an unreasonable restraint of trade and also a declaration that the new or proposed new rules of the TCCB regarding the qualification and

registration of Test and county cricketers were ultra vires and void for the same reason. He also granted WSC similar declarations regarding the rules and also declarations that the new rules and proposed new rules were an unlawful inducement to the cricketers to break their contracts with WSC.

Sir Christopher concluded his judgment by making it clear that 'the defendants acted in good faith and in what they considered to be the best interests of cricket', but this can have done little to sugar what was a bitter pill. Packer's victory was complete or, as Insole succinctly put it, 'We were well and truly stuffed' and Packer's prediction, made when the story broke, that if the authorities did not co-operate they would 'walk straight into a meat mangler' had been fulfilled. So while Packer and his players had cause for celebration, the ICC and the TCCB had to go and lick their wounds and decide what to do next, in particular whether or not to appeal against the judgment in whole or in part. On 2 February 1978, it was announced that, although both the ICC and the TCCB felt they had reasonable grounds for an appeal, no appeal would be made and that the two organisations would share the costs of the case, which were estimated at £250,000.

Others much better qualified than I have considered the implications for cricket of Sir Christopher Slade's judgment and, in any event, well over ten years have now elapsed since November 1977 and the effect on cricket of the Packer affair is no longer speculation but historical fact. I would, however, offer two observations on the case from the legal, as opposed to the cricketing, point of view. First, for the lawyer it is not an important case: it does qualify for a mention in the relevant sections of legal textbooks, but largely in the footnotes, as the case did not really break any new ground but was decided by applying established principles and existing case law. Secondly, and this is the personal opinion of someone who did not attend and was not involved in the case, I believe that had the judge been asked to reach his decisions on the points at issue solely on the basis of the documents that would have been available to him had no witnesses been called, his findings would have been little, if any, different from those after thirty-one days of evidence and submissions by counsel. This does not, of course, mean that both sides were not right to adduce what arguments and evidence they could in their support, but the preparation and hearing of this evidence must have accounted for a large proportion of the substantial costs, which ultimately had to be borne by the average cricket follower and county member.

In addition to the main Packer case and the preliminary skirmish in August, there were three cases heard in the Australian courts arising out of the affair. There may well have been others, as writs and threats of proceedings were flying about at one stage, but many of these never came to court.

The first two of these three cases occurred while the main legal battle was being fought in London. One concerned whether or not WSC could use the Sydney Cricket Ground and the other the right of WSC to describe its matches as 'Tests'. On 25 July 1977 the SCG Trust announced that Packer's application to use the SCG during the 1977–8 season had been turned down because of the trustees' long-term contractual commitments to the New South Wales Cricket Association. Packer responded by saying that the decision had been made by 'a group of crusty old men sitting behind closed doors'. However, on 30 September, the trustees announced that they had reversed their earlier decision and accepted an offer from WSC to use the SCG for thirteen days in December and January. Whether this change of mind was occasioned by Packer's comments or by the A.$260,000 which he offered for the use of the ground I do not know, but the NSWCA expressed its disappointment at the decision, which it said would affect two first-grade matches and the annual boys' coaching classes. The Association decided to challenge the trustees' change of mind and the following month it took both WSC and the SCG trustees to court. On 18 November, exactly a week before Mr Justice Slade delivered his judgment in London, Mr Justice Helsham upheld the Association's claim that it had a legal right to first call on the ground and therefore also had the right to hold its matches and coaching classes on the dates arranged, which effectively excluded WSC from using the ground. Thus for the 1977–8 season WSC had to play on the Sydney Showground, but in 1978 Packer was allowed to use the SCG for seventeen days in the ensuing season.

The case concerning the WSC describing its matches as 'Tests'
was heard on 30 September, the same day as the SCG trustees
had announced the reversal of their original decision not to let
Packer use the SCG. The case arose out of a brochure which
had been inserted in *The Australian Women's Weekly*, which
caused the ACB, through its chairman Robert Parish who led
the Board's fight against Packer, to seek various injunctions as
the Board alleged that the brochure could mislead people into
believing that WSC's matches were Test matches organised by the
Board. Mr Justice St John, sitting in the Federal Court, granted
the application and ordered that WSC should be restrained from
saying or implying that any of its matches had any association
with the ACB or with the ICC, from referring to any of its
matches as 'Tests' or 'Super Tests' and from referring to
any of its teams as 'Australia' or 'The Australian Team'. In
the event the initials WSC were commonly used in the title of
Packer's sides, for example 'WSC Australia', and although the
games were sometimes known as 'Super Tests', no confusion
with official Test matches seems to have arisen.

A year after these injunctions had been granted Jeff Thomson,
whose defection from WSC had resulted in his agent David Lord
being sued in London, appeared as a defendant in the Sydney
Equity Court for attempting to defect back from the ACB to
Packer. In early October 1978, the Board issued the following
statement:

> It was announced last Friday, September 29, that World
> Series Cricket had entered into a three year contract with
> Mr. Jeff Thomson despite its awareness that Mr. Thomson
> had agreed to play only in matches controlled by the Board
> and state associations during the 1978–79 Australian season,
> and despite the publicity given to the fact that the Board had
> refused Mr. Thomson's request that he be released from his
> contractual obligations to the Board.
>
> The Board would naturally have preferred to resolve this
> matter without resort to the courts and, in order that Mr.
> Thomson's contractual obligations to the Board should be
> respected, the Board sought an assurance from World Series
> Cricket that it would not select Mr. Thomson to play cricket
> in any of its teams until after the conclusion of the Australian

cricket season on March 31, 1979. World Series Cricket had declined to give such an assurance.

The case lasted twelve days and Thomson was out of his element in the box and was not a good witness. On 3 November Mr Justice Kearney decided that Thomson was bound by the contract which he had signed with the Board and could not therefore play for WSC until April 1979, which would have prevented him going on WSC's tour to the West Indies. As it happened, the Board later decided to release Thomson from his contract before the tour began and he was thus able to go to the Caribbean after all. However, the case was an unhappy experience for Thomson, which was aggravated by his being fined A.$20 for speeding the day after judgment had been given against him.

In fact, by the time Thomson returned from the West Indies in 1979, peace between Packer and the ACB was near. On 24 April it was announced that the Board had granted Channel Nine exclusive television rights of its matches, including Test matches, for three years and on 30 May, in a further announcement, the Board gave details of a ten-year contract with one of Packer's companies to market the game in Australia. The contract did make significant concessions to the Board's views, but Packer got most of what he wanted and there was some disquiet at the ICC that the Board seemed to have given in over certain fundamental issues on which for two years it had refused to compromise. However, the misgivings were outweighed by a general sense of relief that the conflict had at last been settled and at the end of June the agreement between Packer and the Board was accepted by the ICC. The war was over but, as with all wars, things would never be the same again.

IX

RESTRAINTS AND DISMISSALS

The main issue of the Packer Case involved restraint of trade, namely whether the new rules, which the International Cricket Conference and the Test and County Control Board sought to introduce following the emergence of World Series Cricket, were void as being in restraint of trade. As recounted in the chapter on the Packer cases, the English courts decided that the rules were void as being an unreasonable restraint of trade. This, however, was not the first time that a court had considered the legality of a restriction which one of cricket's governing bodies had sought to impose on a player, as four years before the Packer case this had happened in South Africa.

SACBOC

Well before South African cricket was cast out into the wilderness in 1970 the various racial groups in that country had been represented by different organisations. The South African Cricket Association (SACA) governed the whites, the South African African Cricket Board (SAACB) represented the Africans and the South African Cricket Board of Control (SACBOC) handled the cricketers of mixed race, namely Indians, Asians and Coloureds. In 1969 Jack Cheetham, a former Springbok captain and president of SACA, declared that in future South African sides would be chosen on merit alone and announced that SACA would make a substantial grant 'for assisting the development and advancement of non-white cricket'. This initiative was spurned by SACBOC, led at that time by the militant Hassan Howa, whose guiding principle was 'no normal sport in an abnormal society'.

SACA continued to make efforts to bring SAACB and SACBOC into the fold, which was recognised as an essential first step if South Africa was ever to be re-admitted as a Test-playing country. In March 1973 a meeting of the three governing bodies was held but ultimately the parties could not agree and thus no real progress was made. In 1973–4, however, the South African government allowed Derrick Robins, an enthusiastic patron of cricket who played twice for Warwickshire in 1947, to take a multi-racial side to South Africa. The tourists were captained by Brian Close and among the players were the West Indian, John Shepherd, and the Pakistani, Younis Ahmed, both of whom had played Test cricket for their respective countries. The tour went very smoothly and was a great success and included seven first-class matches, one of which was a drawn game against a South African Invitation XI played at the Newlands ground in Cape Town in late November 1973. One of the spectators at that game was Sedick ('Dickie') Conrad, one of SACBOC's best cricketers.

Conrad tells in his article in *Cricket in Isolation*[1] how, when he returned home on 23 November, the first day of the match, he was telephoned by Howa, the president of SACBOC, and asked if he had been at Newlands. On Conrad admitting that he had been there, Howa told him he would be banned from future matches and said to him, 'You are not one of us any more.' Howa was as good as his word and on the following day, when Conrad went to the Primrose ground where he was meant to be playing, Howa walked into the dressing room and, as president of the Western Province Cricket Board, ordered Conrad to leave the ground, which he had no option but to do.

On 4 December Conrad appeared at a meeting of the Cape District Cricket Union where he was questioned by the executive about his visit to Newlands. Although he wanted to continue playing cricket under the auspices of SACBOC, Conrad said that given the chance he would go to Newlands again, which resulted in the Union banning him from playing in games under its control. Conrad challenged the Union's decision in the court, asking for the cancellation of his registration to be set aside. In giving judgment in favour of Conrad and awarding costs against the Union, the judge said that he was not 'prepared to enforce a rule purporting to confer an unfettered discretion to inflict indefinite and unlimited punishment upon members of an association'.

---

[1] *Cricket in Isolation: The Politics of Race and Cricket in South Africa*, edited by Andre Odendaal, 1977.

In the following season on 26 March 1975 Conrad and Edward Habane broke new ground by appearing at Newlands for the President's XI against another touring side run by Derrick Robins. The experiment was acclaimed in many quarters as a vital precedent for the future, although Syd Reddy, the secretary of SACBOC, was severely censured by his association for attending the match, but less than a year later SACA, SAACB and SACBOC set up a nine-man committee designed to bring about change in South African cricket. This resulted, in September 1977, in the fusion of the three organisations into a new body called the South African Cricket Union, but the merger did not meet with universal approval, as a sizeable faction of SACBOC under Howa, who was no longer its president, opposed the merger and in November 1977 set up a rival body called the South African Cricket Board. However, in spite of all that has been done in South Africa in the last twenty years to run cricket on an integrated basis, the return of South Africa to the Test-match arena looks as far away as ever, as political considerations now take precedence over sporting ones and a political regime in South Africa which meets with the approval of all Test-playing countries looks a long way off.

Lillee and Hughes

Both Dennis Lillee and Kim Hughes were magnificent cricketers, who played for Western Australia and represented their country in seventy Tests, but there the similarity ends. Lillee, who was five years older than Hughes, was tall, dark and heavily moustached and one of the greatest fast bowlers the game has known, while Hughes was a talented fair-haired right-handed batsman, who captained Australia in twenty-eight of his seventy Tests. Lillee finished his Test career with what was then the record haul of 355 wickets, 167 of them against England, while Hughes scored 4,415 runs, including nine centuries, in his Test career.

On 27–30 January 1984, less than four weeks after he had made his final appearance for Australia, Lillee was captaining Western Australia at Brisbane in a Sheffield Shield match against Queensland. *Wisden* describes this game as 'an undistinguished match, in which much time was lost through rain [and which] will be chiefly remembered for heated altercations between Lillee, captaining Western Australia, and the umpires'. This was by no means the first clash which the temperamental and tempestuous Lillee had 'enjoyed' with umpires but it was, I believe, the only one which reached the courts.

The dispute between Lillee and the umpires arose as Lillee instructed drinks to be brought on to the field after the umpires, John King and Col Timmins, had ruled that drinks should not be taken because the pre-lunch session of play had been shortened by rain. The umpires reported Lillee but their complaint was dismissed by a committee of Lillee's team-mates, who felt that his lack of knowledge regarding the umpires' ruling had led him to order the drinks. The umpires appealed to Bob Merriman, the co-ordinator of the Australian Cricket Board's cricket committee who, on 2 February, upheld the appeal and suspended Lillee from all cricket until 1 March.

Lillee contended that the correct procedures had not been followed in reaching the decision to ban him and, on Saturday 4 February, he served a court order on the Western Australian Cricket Association and on the ACB, the effect of which was to render Merriman's ban inoperative until 7.30 p.m. on Tuesday, 7 February, by which time the court would have had time to consider the case. Taking advantage of the suspension of his suspension, Lillee played for his club, Melville, against Southern Districts on the Saturday afternoon.

On Monday, 6 February, the case was heard by Mr Justice Brinsden in the Supreme Court of Western Australia. On behalf of Lillee it was argued that he had not committed an offence under the code of behaviour, that he had misinterpreted the rules and that an adjournment of the appeal in order to hear evidence of a material witness had been wrongly refused. For the WACA, it was stated that the umpires had given a specific direction, that Lillee had disputed their decision and that he had acted 'in a provocative and disapproving manner'. Brinsden reserved judgment and on the following day dismissed Lillee's claim to have his suspension lifted, saying that, right or wrong, an umpire's decision must be obeyed, as otherwise the game of cricket would become unplayable.

The effect of the suspension was that Lillee could not play for Western Australia in their Sheffield Shield matches against

Tasmania and New South Wales, but that he would be available for the final, which started on 9 March, if Western Australia reached it. In the event Western Australia did reach the final and Lillee led his team against Queensland, who had never won the Sheffield Shield and were led by his Test-match bowling partner, Jeff Thomson. Queensland batted first and scored 431 for seven declared, in reply to which Western Australia were all out for 363, of which Lillee contributed 18. In their second innings Queensland were all out for 154, which left Western Australia to score 223 to win. They made the runs with four wickets in hand and, although in the match Lillee only took two wickets for 150 runs, he had the satisfaction of seeing Western Australia win the Sheffield Shield for the ninth time.

Lillee's Test career ended on 6 January 1984 in a blaze of glory with eight wickets for 153 runs against Pakistan. Hughes also played in his last Test in 1984, in December, but he scored nought in each innings and the only reason he did not play in more Tests than Lillee was his failure to be selected for the next match. For Hughes 1983–4 was a disastrous season. He started it as Australia's captain, but after the West Indies had won the first two Tests comfortably he resigned from the captaincy, issuing a statement which said that 'the constant criticism, speculation and innuendo by former players and a section of the media over the past four or five years have finally taken their toll'.

Hughes' failure as a batsman in the third and fourth Tests not only led to him being dropped for the fifth, but was instrumental in him not being chosen as a member of Allan Border's side to tour England the following summer. Although Hughes at first determined to get back into the Australian team, his disillusionment with the politics of Australian cricket made him decide to join a 'rebel' Australian tour to South Africa, which had been arranged with the South African Cricket Union. On 15 May 1985 Hughes signed an agreement with SACU in which he agreed to take part in two tours of South Africa, the first from 1 November 1985 to 31 March 1986 and the second from 1 October 1986 to 31 March 1987. This resulted in the ACB's instituting proceedings against Hughes and the other players who had signed, seeking to restrain them from performing their agreements with SACU. The basis of these actions was that the Board maintained that the respondents had undertaken not to play cricket except in matches controlled by the Board. The actions were settled at the last minute on terms which, as far as Hughes was concerned, allowed him to participate in the South African tours without being in breach of any contract between himself and the ACB. Under the deed of settlement, however, Hughes accepted the lawfulness of bans imposed on him by the Board from playing state cricket before 1 October 1987 and international cricket before 1 October 1988. The deed made no reference to playing cricket at club level.

On 4 November 1985, before the tourists had played their first game, the Cricket Council, which was an autonomous body established under the auspices of the WACA, amended one of its rules so that anyone who took part in an unapproved cricket match without the Council's consent was 'automatically disqualified until reinstated by the Cricket Council'. The effect of this amended rule was to ban Hughes indefinitely from playing club cricket. Hughes considered that this unlawfully deprived him of his right to earn his living as a cricketer in the country and state of his choice and he therefore sought relief in the courts. The respondents in the proceedings were, among others, the WACA and the Cricket Council and they were attacked by Hughes on a wide front.

Hughes sought a declaration that the Council's amended rule was in breach of the Trade Practices Act 1974 and he also brought common law actions alleging breach of the Western Australian Equal Opportunities Act, bad faith and bias, restraint of trade, conspiracy and breach of the right to work. The case was heard in the Federal Court by Mr Justice Toohey, who described Hughes' case as 'indeed complex, both as to fact and law' and the hearing lasted twenty-one days. Among the people who gave evidence was Hughes himself, who told the court that he had first heard of the proposed South African tour while playing for Australia in Sharjah in 1985, but had been told that if he leaked the information about it he would 'end up on the bottom of Sydney harbour in cement boots'.

In a judgment almost as long as that in the main Packer case (which was cited several times), Mr Justice Toohey dealt with all the issues raised by Hughes and made it clear that the court was not concerned with the propriety of playing cricket in South Africa, but only in applying the relevant legal principles to the facts of the case. The judge decided that Hughes' claim failed on the grounds of the Equal Opportunities Act, bad faith and bias, breach of the right to work and conspiracy. He concluded, however, that the Cricket Council's amended rule was a breach of the Trade Practices Act and that its operation constituted an unreasonable restraint of trade in relation to Hughes and was therefore void and unenforceable.

As Hughes had not really suffered financially by being disqualified from playing club cricket, because of his commitment to the South African tours, the judge awarded Hughes only minimal damages of A.$250. He also decided that, as the amended rule was void, Hughes was entitled to a declaration against all the respondents, the effect of which was to allow him to resume playing cricket for his club, Subiaco Floreat, and to resume playing district cricket generally. The court later also decided that the respondents should pay three-quarters of Hughes' legal costs, which one newspaper estimated at A.$275,000. On this basis and with its own legal costs, they could have had a bill of about A.$500,000. When the court made its decision about the costs Hughes, who was in Cape Town leading the second 'rebel' tour, said that he was pleased for himself but sad that the money needed to pay the legal fees would not be available to develop cricket in Australia.

Partly in the light of the amount of legal costs generated by the case, there is one other interesting fact that emerged from Mr Justice Toohey's judgment. On 3 February 1986 at a meeting of the Cricket Council under the heading 'Players undertaking unofficial tours of South Africa', a resolution was proposed that Hughes and three other players should be reinstated so that they could participate in certain competitions and allowed to fulfil their obligations to their district clubs. This resolution was lost by seven votes to eight and it subsequently transpired that the delegate from South Perth CC, Charles Bull, had voted against the motion contrary to the instructions from his club. No satisfactory explanation was given during the case of how this misunderstanding had arisen but, as the judge remarked, had the resolution been passed, Hughes 'would not have been disqualified from playing for his club. This might have had the further consequence that this long and costly piece of litigation could have been avoided.'

Bedi and Younis

For over twenty years from 1961 Bishan Bedi was a popular first-class cricketer, his coloured turban making him instantly recognisable, especially on English grounds. He was an ortho-dox slow left-arm bowler, who took 266 wickets in 67 Tests for India and from 1972 to 1977 played for Northants. During those six years Bedi took over 400 wickets for the county at an average of under 21, but after the 1977 season Northants announced that Bedi's contract would not be renewed. Bedi decided to sue the county club for unfair dismissal which is a statutory right given to employees, subject to certain qualifying conditions, and is independent of, and need not also involve, a breach of contract. Thus, in Bedi's case there was no breach of contract, because the county honoured its contractual obli-gations, but decided not to enter into a new contract after Bedi's existing contract ended. Although his contract did not end until March 1978, Bedi's claim was filed in December 1977 while he was captaining the Indian side in Australia.

On 19 June Bedford Industrial Tribunal ruled that, although his petition had been filed while his contract was still current, Bedi's claim could proceed. The tribunal also considered the question of whether Bedi could be regarded as having been in continuous employment with Northants for at least twenty-six weeks in the year, which was one of the qualifying conditions for a claim for unfair dismissal, although the period was later increased in stages to two years. For Bedi it was argued that his contract amounted to one of continuous service, although he played for Northants for less than twenty-six weeks in a year. For the club Stuart McKinnon[2] contended that Bedi was only employed for the cricket season and he drew an analogy with Father Christmas whom, McKinnon said, 'cannot be regarded as employed throughout the year'. After hearing legal arguments from both sides, the tribunal came down in favour of Bedi, deciding that he had been in continuous employment with Northants for twenty-six weeks.

Having decided that it had jurisdiction to hear Bedi's claim, the tribunal then took the rest of the 19th, the whole of the 20th

---

[2] Later Sir Stuart McKinnon.

and part of the 21st June to consider its merits. For Northants, McKinnon said that, from being a star, Bedi had become 'no better than ordinary' and that he had been bowling too much, both summer and winter, could not bat and was a liability in the field. In addition, the Northants' secretary, Kenneth Turner, said that the county's financial problems and the need to build a new and younger team necessitated getting rid of Bedi, who was the club's most expensive player. For Bedi, whose action was financed by the Cricketers' Association, it was claimed that no warning had been given by the county and that, on the other hand, Bedi had been led to believe that he would be with Northants indefinitely. Bedi also disputed that his bowling was no better than ordinary, emphasised that cricket was a team game and said that his performances had been adversely affected by the county bowling him 'when a medium pace bowler should have been on with green top wickets'.

On 22 June, the third day of the hearing, it was announced that the tribunal had unanimously rejected Bedi's claim and that its reasons would be given later. On 20 July in a reserved judgment, the tribunal said that its decision had been based solely on the merits of the case and that Bedi's contract had not been renewed because the club considered his performance no longer matched his status as a Test star. The tribunal added that, although it would have made no difference to its decision, it would have been fairer had Bedi been given a chance to defend himself before the Northants' committee. Not surprisingly, the outcome of the case was regarded as 'good for cricket' by the Northants' secretary, while Bedi said that it would be regretted by professional cricketers throughout England. However, the Cricketers' Association must have been relieved that the case seemed to have established that county cricketers had the right to sue for unfair dismissal if their contracts were not renewed, even though they actually played for their counties for less than twenty-six weeks a year.

Younis Ahmed, who also features in the 'Financial Allsorts' chapter, made his first-class debut in Pakistan at the age of 14 and until 1968 was known as Mohammad Younis. He played twice for Pakistan in 1969–70 but in 1973, after touring South Africa, he was banned for life from playing for his country and most of his first-class cricket was played in England and Wales, where he assisted Surrey, Worcester and Glamorgan. His longest connection was with Surrey for whom he scored over 14,000 runs, including nineteen centuries, between 1965 and 1978. In 1978 Roger Knight took over the captaincy of Surrey from John Edrich and one of his first moves was to dispense with the services of three experienced players, including Younis.

Younis moved to Worcester, but decided to sue Surrey for unfair dismissal and his case was heard by a London industrial tribunal on 16 July 1979, less than a week after Worcester had awarded him his county cap. The chairman of the tribunal was Jack Rumbold,[3] a New Zealander, who had won a blue for Oxford in 1946. Perhaps not surprisingly, he failed to retain his place in the strong 1947 Oxford side, for Rumbold was an opening batsman and his top score in fourteen completed first-class innings was 25.

As in Bedi's case, before it could decide if the dismissal had been unfair, the tribunal had to consider whether it had jurisdiction to hear the claim. For Younis it was argued that, although his contract ran only from April to September 1977, his employment with Surrey had continued throughout the winter of 1977–8 when he had been coaching and playing cricket in Rhodesia and that, therefore, Younis had been in continuous employment for at least twenty-six weeks. Among the reasons given for this were that Younis remained registered as a Surrey player with the TCCB until 31 December 1977 and that certain obligations in his agreement remained in force after the end of the English cricket season.

McKinnon, who a year earlier had represented Northants in the Bedi case, was Surrey's counsel and he argued that if Younis' contentions were right it was necessary to show that an arrangement existed between Younis and the county club for him still to be considered as employed by Surrey after September. McKinnon added: 'There is no evidence whatsoever that there is any general arrangement or custom, whether in county cricket generally or with Surrey County Cricket Club, whereby in a situation such as this a player is regarded as continuing in the employment of a county cricket club during the winter.' After hearing submissions from both

[3] Later Sir Jack Rumbold.

sides, Rumbold adjourned the hearing to consider the point. Four weeks later the tribunal reconvened and announced that it was not qualified to hear Younis' claim because he had been in continuous employment with Surrey for less than twenty-six weeks, there being no question that registration with the TCCB had anything to do with the terms of his employment. Younis' departure, however, seems to have benefited both his old county and his new one. In 1979 Surrey moved up the championship table from sixteenth to third while Worcester improved their position from fifteenth to second, Younis finishing top of the Worcester batting averages with 1,508 runs, including a century against Surrey.

On the face of it, the tribunals' decisions in the Younis and Bedi cases seem inconsistent. In the latter case, the chairman ruled that Bedi had been in continuous employment for twenty-six weeks, although he played for Northants for less than that period in any one year, while in Younis' case the tribunal reached the opposite conclusion. It may be that the two decisions were indeed inconsistent and that, therefore, one of them was wrong. However, the answer may lie in the different wording of the two contracts, as Bedi's contract clearly covered the whole year and not merely the cricket season, while Younis' contract apparently ran only from April to September.

The groundsman and the steward

Northants was again involved in an unfair dismissal case at Bedford Industrial Tribunal, which was the venue for a claim by the county club's former groundsman, 54-year-old Leslie Bentley, following his dismissal in August 1982. This case lasted even longer than Bedi's, as it ran for five days from 26 to 30 April 1983. Turner, who was again the chief witness for the county, claimed that Bentley 'did not have the experience, knowledge or ability to do the job' and that he did not even carry out the basic duties of a groundsman, such as putting up signs and painting seats. Turner also claimed that, although Northants had risen from bottom to thirteenth in the pitch quality table drawn up by the TCCB, this was not attributable to Bentley's efforts but largely to the improvement of outside grounds which Bentley did not help to prepare.

Bentley gave evidence on the third day of the hearing and

described in detail the programme which he had followed in order to improve both the wickets and the practice area at Northampton. On the fourth day of the hearing two Northants' Test players, Peter Willey and Wayne Larkins, gave evidence for Bentley. Willey claimed that Bentley had improved the match wickets, had made the Northampton outfield one of the best in the championship and that by 1982 the practice wickets were some of the best he had known since he had been with the county. Willey's views were endorsed by Larkins, who agreed with Willey about the improvements for which Bentley had been responsible. On the last day of the hearing Jim Watts, who had captained Northants from 1978 to 1980, said that although he agreed with the committee's decision to give Bentley an ultimatum to improve the wickets, he had been upset by the decision to sack him. On 25 May, while Willey and Larkins were playing for Northants against Yorkshire at Bradford, the tribunal announced its decision. This was: 'It was the unanimous decision that the employer (Northants) honestly believed on reasonable grounds that the applicant (Bentley) was incapable or incompetent and that in all other respects when dealing with the applicant against [the] backcloth of that belief the employer acted reasonably.' Northants had won the second battle of Bedford.

Apart from the county clubs and the northern league sides, few cricket clubs have paid employees, or at least employees the terms of whose contracts of employment would qualify them to make a claim for unfair dismissal. Uxbridge Cricket Club, which is the MCC's junior by only two years and whose ground is used by Middlesex for some of its matches, was an exception. The claim against Uxbridge CC was brought by Geoffrey and Sylvia Simmonds and heard at a London industrial tribunal in November 1984, following their dismissal the previous August. The Simmondses were employed in June 1984 as bar steward and caterer at Uxbridge CC and lived at the club premises in the two-bedroomed flat which went with the job. From the start difficulties arose and the committee contended that neither of the Simmondses was integrating properly with members of the club, that Simmonds was not getting on with the other staff and was allowing the club to be used by non-members and that Mrs Simmonds was not appearing often enough behind the bar.

Consequently, following an executive committee meeting on 2 July, a long letter was written to Simmonds seeking 'to identify and resolve some of the problem areas' and a week or so after receiving this letter the Simmondses replied to the chairman of the club, Roger Smith. This was an even longer letter in which the Simmondses responded point by point to the executive committee's letter and ended, Smith may have thought somewhat ironically, with the sentence: 'Assuring you of our full co-operation at all times.'

On 1 August a further meeting of the executive committee was held which, at Simmonds' request, he and his wife attended. There was a lot of discussion on the various difficulties which had arisen and the committee continued discussing the matter after the Simmondses had left the meeting. However, no decision to dismiss them was recorded in the minutes which did, however, contain the sentence: 'At this stage a vote was taken by the committee as to the next step forward and this was approved on a unanimous basis.' Unbeknown to the committee, however, four days before that meeting the Simmondses had joined the Associated Clerical Technical and Supervisory Staff section of the Transport and General Workers' Union. Following the committee meeting the Simmondses had two meetings with a union representative and, at the Simmondses' request, the district officer of the union subsequently wrote a letter to all the members of the executive committee. This letter, which was later described by the tribunal as 'extremely insulting and ill advised', alleged that the club, the executive committee and the members of that committee 'did not have a clue' and also suggested meeting the committee, rather than continuing 'with this clear indictment of your ineptitude'. On receipt of the letter of 14 August, Smith telephoned Simmonds, who was then in the club's bar, and it is on what was said during this conversation that the tribunal's decision primarily depended.

According to Smith, he asked Simmonds if the letter represented his views and Simmonds said that it did. Smith also maintained that, among other things, he told Simmonds that on 1 August the executive committee had decided to dismiss him and his wife and that the letter made it clear that the Simmondses' views meant that the committee's decision had been the right one. Smith said that Simmonds became very emotional and said he would not accept dismissal unless it was approved by the committee and also said that he would not vacate his flat. Simmonds' version of the conversation was that Smith said: 'I have just received a letter from the union. I am totally disgusted, you are sacked.' Simmonds also alleged that Smith went on to say: 'If you are not out of the premises by tonight I will come down and break the door of the flat and forcibly evict you and your family and throw you and all your furniture out on to the street. I won't have a union in this club.'

On the same evening the executive committee met and decided, in view of the unconstructive attitude adopted by the union, not to meet its officials to discuss the situation. The committee also realised that it would have to go through with the termination procedure and instructed the club's solicitors to write to the Simmondses telling them that their employment was terminated with effect from 30 September and asking them to vacate the flat. This was done on 21 August and two days later the Simmondses instituted proceedings against the club for wrongful dismissal, claiming that they had been dismissed because they were members of a trade union, which under the appropriate legislation is a circumstance where dismissal is automatically unfair and does not require the usual qualifying period of employment. The case was heard by the London (Central) Industrial Tribunal under the chairmanship of Lady Elizabeth Mitchell and opened on 19 November 1984.

Apart from the Simmondses themselves and Smith, among those who gave evidence were L. S. Cook, a member of the club, and a non-member friend of his called Brinton, both of whom had been in the bar when Simmonds received the telephone call from Smith on 14 August and who both supported Simmonds' version of the content and duration of the call. On the other hand, evidence was also given by Miss Jane Hamilton, who had helped behind the bar on a temporary basis for over four years and was herself a union member. She told the tribunal of staff problems and chaos when Simmonds was working at the club and of 'faultless' nights when he had time off.

The tribunal gave its unanimous decision in a 64-paragraph document on 31 January 1985. The tribunal did not accept the club's contention that a decision to dismiss the Simmondses because of their unsatisfactory performance had been taken on

1 August but not implemented until after 14 August, although it accepted that difficulties had arisen with the Simmondses even before they began work. The tribunal concluded that the Simmondses were dismissed on 14 August because of their membership of an independent trade union and that the dismissals were therefore unfair. The tribunal also noted that the Simmondses had asked for reinstatement, but it agreed with the club that this would not be practicable in view of the smallness of the club and of the ill feeling engendered by what had happened. This request and refusal, however, qualified the Simmondses for a special award of £10,000 each under the Employment Act of 1982. In total, under all heads, the Simmondses were awarded £27,901, of which Simmonds received £14,710 and his wife £13,191.

The amount of the awards was a nasty shock to the club, who had expected that if they lost the case they would have had to pay not more than about £4,000. After the case Smith commented: 'The club is more than a little dumbfounded as to how we end up with £28,000 for ten weeks' service.' The Simmondses, who had told the tribunal that they were looking for jobs in the licensing trade, were not, it seems, too much concerned with the financial aspect, as after the case Mrs Simmonds was reported to have said: 'We are not bothered how much money we have got. We are just so pleased to have cleared our names.' The club took counsel's opinion on the likelihood of a successful appeal, but were advised that an appeal could only be made on a point of law and that one would be unlikely to succeed.

X

PITCHES AND PAVILIONS

Three old cases

In the light of all the scholarly books and articles written about early references to cricket and the trenchant comments made by some writers on the work of others, I will not claim that the first case covered in this chapter is the oldest containing a reference to the game, but it is the oldest known to me. The case itself was heard in 1598 but the reference in it is to cricket having been played almost fifty years earlier.

The court records of Guildford for 1598 contain entries concerning a case relating to the alleged unlawful enclosure by John Parvish of a piece of land in the parish of Holy Trinity Guildford. The relevant extract is:

> John Derrick of Guldeforde aforesaid gente, one of the Queene's Majestie's coroners of the county of Surrey, beinge of the age of ffythy and nyne yeeres or thereaboute and voluntarily sworne and examined saith upon oath that hee hath known this parcell of land lately used as a garden and sometime in the occupation of John Parvish late of Guldeford aforesaid, Innholder deceased [and also that he] did knowe that the same lay waste and was used and occupied by the Inhabitants of Guldeford aforesaid to saw Timber and for Sawpitts and for making of fframes of Timber . . . . And also this deponent saith that hee beinge a Scholler in the ffree Schoole of Guldeford hee and diverse of his fellowes did runne and play there at Creckett and other Plaies And also that the same was used for the Baytinge of Beares in the said Towne until the said John Parvish did inclose the said parcell of land.

Although the reference to cricket is only incidental the case does show that the game was played in Guildford at some time during the period from about 1547 to 1553, when Derrick would have been a schoolboy.

On 4 February 1795, almost two hundred years after the Guildford case, the Court of Common Pleas heard an appeal by one Fitch against the dismissal of an action for trespass against three people called Rawling, Fitch and Chatteris. The reports of the case do not indicate whether or not the plaintiff was related to the defendant of the same name. The plaintiff alleged that the trespass had been committed by the defendants 'breaking and entering the plaintiff's close at Steeple Bumstead in Essex, playing there, with divers other persons to the plaintiff unknown, at a certain game called cricket, and other games, sports and pastimes'.

In the original action all three defendants had denied liability but Chatteris' plea had been slightly different from that of the other two defendants. Chatteris stated that there was 'an ancient and laudable custom', which allowed all the inhabitants for the time being of the parish to play lawful games, sports and pastimes in Fitch's close at all seasonable times of the year. Rawling and Fitch maintained the custom applied to all persons for the time being in the parish, whether or not they lived there. For the defendants, Serjeant Le Blanc[1] argued that the custom was good and, in support of his argument, cited *Abbot* v. *Weekly*, a 1665 case where a custom for the inhabitants of a village to dance in someone's close had been held to be a good one. He also maintained that, as far as such customs were concerned, there was no material difference between the inhabitants of a parish and the people who happened to be in the parish. For the plaintiff Serjeants Bond and Heywood contended that a custom embracing all the inhabitants of a place, who must include 'servants, visitors, women and children', was bad for uncertainty and also, that for a custom to be good, it had to be shown 'that the games were for the recreation and health of the inhabitants' and that it was not enough if 'they were merely for pleasure'. As regards the plea by Rawling and Fitch, counsel for the plaintiff maintained that a custom which applied to everyone in the parish, whether or not they lived there, must be void for generality. After Bond and Heywood had finished,

[1] Later Sir Simon Le Blanc.

Le Blanc was going to reply but was 'prevented by the court' and Sir Francis Buller, the Justice of Common Pleas, gave the main judgment.

After rejecting two technical points made on behalf of the plaintiff, Buller said that the real question was whether the customs as stated were good. He said that the pleadings showed that Chatteris had entered the close to play cricket and other games, sports and pastimes and what were sports and pastimes but recreations? He also said that, as regards the custom being one in favour of the inhabitants of the parish, he considered he had no authority to oppose *Abbot* v. *Weekly* and that the custom was reasonable and Chatteris' plea therefore good. He went on to reject, however, the contention that the custom could apply to anyone who happened to be in the parish as 'how that which may be claimed by all the inhabitants of England can be the subject of a custom I cannot conceive'.

The case of *Fitch* v. *Rawling, Fitch and Chatteris* is still mentioned, nearly two centuries later, in the current editions of legal textbooks as one of the authorities for the statement that a custom must be limited to the inhabitants of a district for which it is claimed and cannot extend to the general public or to people who happen to be in the place in question. Like *Abbot* v. *Weekly* it can also be cited to show that customary rights, although they affect the ownership of land, may be enjoyed by persons having no interest or estate in the land. Thus, although by no means the oldest cricket case to appear in the law reports, it is, I believe, the oldest which is still an authority for the law as it is today.

Another case which still merits a mention in legal textbooks was heard in 1891 by Sir Joseph Chitty, one of that rare breed – now surely extinct – who won blues for both cricket and rowing. Chitty kept wicket for Oxford in the 1848 and 1849 university matches, but in neither year did he assist in the dismissal of any of the Cambridge batsmen. He also rowed in two boat races and subsequently umpired the boat race for twenty-five years. The case which he heard in 1891 concerned the enclosing of a cricket ground on a common.

In the early 1880s the cricket ground on Barnes Common was continually being damaged and spoiled by horses and cattle and many of those using the ground wanted a fence put up to protect it. Eventually in 1884, at the expense of the ratepayers, the conservators of the common had a 3-foot-high fence erected and this consisted of wooden posts with a 2-inch iron bar at the top. The fence had two openings for pedestrians and at one place the iron bar, which was secured by a padlock, was removable to allow a sufficient opening for the passage of horses and cattle and also of a cricket roller. Part of the fence ran between the cricket ground and an approach road to The Laurels, where a lady called Jowers lived. History does not relate whether she was Mrs or Miss Jowers, but she was the only person to raise any objection to the fence.

Ms Jowers complained that the fence was an unauthorised enclosure of part of the common and wrote to the conservators about it. As the correspondence did not bring her satisfaction, she arranged for one of the wooden posts to be cut down in order to precipitate some action by the conservators. They responded by bringing proceedings against her in the name of their clerk, Ratcliff, seeking damages and an injunction to restrain her from damaging or removing any part of the fence. Mr Justice Chitty postponed giving judgment in the hope that negotiations between Ms Jowers and the conservators would produce a settlement, but the negotiations broke down.

In his judgment the judge said that the rights and powers of the conservators derived from a scheme set up pursuant to the Commons Acts of 1866 and 1876, which invested the conservators with certain powers of management over the common. The conservators were entitled to enclose a section of the common for the playing of cricket and other games, but only temporarily and in such a way that it did not adversely affect the rights of the commoners. In this case, the judge said, although the bar where the cattle and commonable beasts could cross the fence was usually kept padlocked, the conservators had never refused to unlock it for any of the commoners and had never been asked to do so by Ms Jowers. He also said that the requirement for the cricket ground only to be enclosed 'temporarily' did not mean only while cricket or other games were actually being played and that 'the proper formation of a cricket ground required a considerable period of time'. Mr Justice Chitty held that the conservators had not exceeded their powers by erecting and maintaining the fence and that Ms Jowers had no right to cut the post, which had never constituted an obstruction to the exercise of her commonable rights. He granted the conservators an injunction restraining her from the commission of further such acts and awarded the conservators £1 damages, but said that they must allow her access for commonable beasts at suitable times and seasons. Finally, he added, he was at a loss to understand what the defendant's object had been in embarking on the contest.

Whatever Ms Jowers's object was she secured for herself posthumous fame of a sort in that she is one of the great host of whose lives nothing is now known, except for the detail of one small episode which is recorded in the law reports. The case is still quoted as an authority on the law relating to commons in that where a power of temporarily enclosing a space to play cricket and other games is given, the rights of commoners must be subject to the reasonable exercise of the right to play the games in question, but the enclosure must not unreasonably interfere with rights of the commoners, to whom the conservators must allow access for commonable beasts at suitable times and seasons.

Two pavilions

A fence and a commonable beast precipitated another dispute about a cricket ground in May 1968 when Squadron-Leader Charles Robinson erected a fence and tethered a pony on land surrounding Odiham Cricket Club's new pavilion. Both Robinson and the club claimed ownership of the disputed land and, as an interim measure, the club obtained an injunction restraining Robinson from further trespass so that the cricketers could play cricket unimpeded.

On 8 November the case was heard at Basingstoke County Court before Judge Arthur Lee, who captained Winchester in 1932 and in the following three years played once for Hampshire and three times for Oxford without being awarded his blue. Robinson conducted his own case, as the judge said, 'ably and with good humour' and gave the court a history of the sale of land bordering on the Basingstoke Canal and claimed that some bits had been 'pinched' and some were 'trespassed on'. He also claimed that the disputed piece of land had been conveyed to him with some other land, which he had bought in

1964 from Edgar Vass. When the judge pointed out that Vass said he did not sell Robinson the disputed land because he did not own it, Robinson said the reason for that was because Vass did not know that he had owned it. For the cricketers it was argued that their president, Captain Robert Petre, had granted the club a lease at a peppercorn rent of the land on which the pavilion had subsequently been built and that the club therefore had a good title to the land. The club sought an order confirming its title, damages against Robinson for trespass and an injunction restraining him from further trespass.

Judge Lee said that a plan on an old conveyance on which Robinson had sought to rely was a bad plan and he found in favour of the cricket club. He awarded £10 damages and costs against Robinson and said that the club's occupation was solid in law and anything which interfered with the playing of village cricket 'must be damnified'. He also said that the club should continue 'for evermore' to occupy the land held under the lease from Captain Petre. Unfortunately this did not turn out to be the case, as a by-pass was subsequently built round Odiham, the course of which ran straight through the ground. The land was compulsorily acquired and a new ground was made available by the local council, which also provided some funds towards the cost of building a new pavilion.

Six years after Odiham Cricket Club took Squadron-Leader Robinson to court, damage inflicted on the pavilion of Little Waltham Cricket Club in Essex led to a case in the Chelmsford Crown Court. On Saturday 15 June 1974 6-year-old Shane Green was playing in the sandpit in the children's playground at Little Waltham, which was only 30 yards from the village cricket ground, when he was struck on the head by a ball which had been hit for six. Shane was knocked unconscious, his skull was fractured and his parents, Malcolm and Christine Green, were concerned that his brain might have been damaged. Shane was taken to hospital and Green left him there with his mother and went home worrying about him and brooding on the circumstances of the accident.

Many local parents had been concerned about the proximity of the cricket ground to the playground and several children had been hit before Shane, but none as seriously as he. Calls for the playground to be moved having proved unsuccessful, Green, a

31-year-old lorry driver and himself a former cricketer, decided to take matters into his own hands and, in the early hours of Sunday 16 June, he went to the cricket ground with a can of paraffin and set light to the pavilion, causing over £1,000 worth of damage. While the pavilion was still burning, Green admitted that he had started the fire and on 16 September, at Chelmsford Crown Court, he pleaded guilty to a charge of arson. Judge Peter Greenwood said that he realised Green had been through a traumatic experience with his small son but that revenge was never worthwhile and he sentenced Green to nine months' imprisonment, suspended for a year.

Given that Green's son had been injured and that the pavilion had been badly damaged, the incident had a reasonably happy outcome for all concerned. Shane made a full recovery, the playground was moved to a location about 300 yards from the cricket ground and no litigation ensued in the civil courts, as Green decided not to make a claim for his son's injury and the club took the view that the Green family had suffered enough and, therefore, did not seek compensation from Green.

George Davis is innocent – OK?

The next case also involved damage deliberately inflicted but, although the target was a cricket pitch, neither the perpetrators nor their purpose were connected with the game. The case was heard in 1976, the wicket was damaged in 1975 but the story really started in 1974 when a policeman was shot and injured during an armed robbery on an Electricity Board office in Ilford. George Davis, a 34-year-old mini-cab driver, was subsequently sentenced at the Old Bailey to twenty years' imprisonment for his part in the robbery and the wounding of the policeman. Some of his family and friends, however, maintained that Davis was innocent as he had been wrongly identified as one of the robbers and they started a 'Free George Davis' campaign.

In June 1975, after the successful Prudential World Cup tournament, the Australians started a short tour of England with four Tests instead of the usual five. Australia won the first Test by an innings, the second was drawn and the third started at Headingley on 14 August. England batted first, scoring 288 to which Australia replied with 135, Philippe Edmonds taking 5 for 28 in his first Test, and in their second innings England made 291, leaving Australia to score 445 to win the match. At close of play on the Monday night Australia were 220 for three with Rick McCosker 95 not out and Doug Walters 25 not out and, with seven wickets remaining, they thus needed to score another 225 runs on the last day, Tuesday 19 August. At about ten to seven on that morning George Cawthray, the head groundsman at Headingley, drew back the covers and saw that during the night the wicket had been deliberately damaged. Holes three inches deep had been dug in the wicket just about where the ball would pitch and oil had been poured on to it. Slogans had also been daubed on the walls round the ground, one of which read: 'G. Davis is innocent.' As it was impossible either to repair the wicket or to find another of similar pace and quality to the original one, it was decided to abandon the match. In the event rain set in before lunch and thus the match would have been washed out in any case, but McCosker was probably deprived of his maiden Test century. For the record, McCosker did make a hundred in the last Test which was also drawn, Australia thus retaining the Ashes.

The four responsible for the damage made no secret of their identities and one of them, Colin Dean, said that they had bought a gallon of oil from a motorway service station and taken the knives and forks, which they had used to dig up the pitch, from the motorway restaurant. Dean also said that the wicket had been spoiled because their campaign had so far failed to get a proper inquiry into Davis' conviction. Perhaps, however, the most appropriate comment was Dr Robin Birts' in a four-word letter to *The Times* on 21 August: 'Bring back the willow.'

On 1 September Dean, Peter Chappell and Richard Ramsey were remanded in custody and Geraldine Hughes was released on bail. All four were accused of conspiring to damage the wicket and the boundary wall, Dean and Chappell were also charged with damaging the pitch, while Ramsey and Mrs Hughes were also accused of damaging the boundary wall. During September the three men made further court appearances and the continued refusal to grant them bail provoked uproar in the public gallery from the Free George Davis supporters and resulted in Mrs Hughes giving up her own freedom in protest. On 19 September Ramsey was allowed bail and on 3 November bail was also granted to Dean and Chappell on their recognisances of £1,000 and a surety of £5,000. Meanwhile, on 17 October the case against the four had been transferred from Leeds Crown Court to Birkenhead Crown Court after defence submissions that Headingley and Leeds were 'synonymous with cricket'. As regards Davis, who was reported to have been horrified that the pitch had been damaged, on 11 December he was refused leave to appeal against his conviction, but his sentence was reduced from twenty years to seventeen years.

On 6 January 1976 all four accused pleaded guilty to the charges of damage, but the Judge, Frank Nance, ordered the charges of conspiracy to be deleted from the indictment. Dean was sentenced to nine months' imprisonment and Ramsey and Mrs Hughes to six months' imprisonment, in each case suspended for two years. Chappell was also sentenced to nine months' imprisonment, but this had the effect of activating two earlier suspended sentences imposed on him for criminal damage during the campaign and he was thus sent to prison with an eighteen months' sentence. As far as the four campaigners were concerned this was almost the end of the story, Chappell was released after serving thirteen months of his sentence and, in June 1977, he received a cricket bat signed by the Australian team, including his two namesakes Ian and Greg Chappell, to raise money for a London community project.

The campaign was successful in that a police review of the identification evidence at Davis' trial was ordered and, on 11 May 1976, the Home Secretary, Roy Jenkins,[2] told the House of Commons that he had recommended the exercise of the royal prerogative of mercy on the ground that the shift in the balance of evidence in the case was such that it would be wrong for Davis to remain in prison. The Home Secretary added that he had no evidence that Davis was innocent and which would justify a free pardon but, if the case was referred to the Court of Appeal, it was not clear that all the relevant material could be considered by the court. Davis was therefore freed, to the delight of his family and friends.

Fourteen months later Davis and three other men were arrested and charged with stealing 1,163 cases of whisky and

[2] Later Baron Jenkins.

261 cartons of coats, worth almost £100,000, from the Port of London Authority in 1973. On 11 July 1977 he was released on bail and on 23 September he was again arrested, this time by armed police after six men wearing stocking masks had attempted to rob the Seven Sisters Road branch of the Bank of Cyprus in north London. This time he was not allowed bail! On 18 February 1978 Davis was acquitted at Chelmsford Crown Court of the charge relating to the whisky and the coats but immediately taken back into custody on the bank raid charge. On 24 July he and five other men pleaded guilty to taking part in the £50,000 armed robbery on the Bank of Cyprus and Davis was sentenced to fifteen years' imprisonment. On appeal in May 1980 this was reduced to eleven years, which meant that with good conduct Davis could be free by the end of 1984. He had not long been released when, on 26 March 1986, he was arrested by British Transport police at Victoria station and charged with stealing a quantity of mail bags. The following January at Southend Crown Court he was given an eighteen months' prison sentence, with nine months suspended, after admitting the offence.

It is difficult to draw conclusions from the Davis saga other than the obvious one that, however reprehensible were the methods of his supporters, it was clearly right that Roy Jenkins should have had the original conviction investigated and that Davis should have been freed if there was any significant doubt about the validity of his conviction. However, it was probably lucky for Davis that the raid on the Ilford Electricity Board preceded that on the Bank of Cyprus to which he pleaded guilty, as had the order of events been reversed his supporters could well have been less numerous and less enthusiastic.

Damage and deprivation

On 1 August 1983 the groundsman at another Test-match venue noticed that his wicket had been – or rather was being – damaged when Harry Brind saw a man urinating on the wicket at the Oval. The police were called and Robert Shedan, a 32-year-old engineer, was charged with causing criminal damage to the Oval wicket. On the following day he appeared at Horseferry Road Court where evidence was given that Shedan's ministrations would necessitate part of the pitch being relaid. He was fined £10 and also ordered to pay £10 compensation to the Surrey County Cricket Club, but no first-class game was interrupted, as Surrey were playing Glamorgan at Swansea at the time.

As Mr Justice Chitty said in the case of *Ratcliff* v. *Jowers*, the preparation of a cricket ground required 'a considerable period of time' and damage to a wicket can quickly and easily be inflicted but not as quickly or easily repaired. It is, therefore, little consolation to those responsible for the preparation of wickets if someone who damages one does so unintentionally. Neville Cardus, in his *Autobiography*, relates an amusing incident when he was assistant cricket professional at Shrewsbury School. One wet afternoon in about 1915 the professional Ted Wainwright, the Yorkshire all-rounder who played in five Tests, saw the headmaster ride across the wicket on his bicycle. As Cardus puts it: 'Wainwright leaped to his feet, flung open the dressing-room window, stuck out his head, put two fingers into his mouth, emitted a piercing whistle, then shouted, "What the 'ell dost t' think tha doin'? Get off t' grass, tha bloody-looking foo-il." And he waved the Headmaster of Shrewsbury to a by-path.' The headmaster in question was the Reverend Cyril Alington, who played for Marlborough at Lord's in 1891, and was the son of H. G. Alington who was in the 1859 Oxford side. A contrite Alington admitted that he should have known better but, as he told Cardus the next day, 'I do think he [Wainwright] might have admonished me in language a little less – er – less drastic.'

On the other hand damage caused to a wicket may be unintentional but not really excusable and can land the malefactor in court. In 1984 the wicket of my own club, East Grinstead, was damaged by two youths riding motor cycles on the club's ground at West Street. In two separate hearings at East Grinstead's juvenile court one boy was fined £50 and ordered to pay £33 compensation and the other was made the subject of a six months' supervision order and also ordered to pay £33 compensation.

For a cricket club to have its wicket damaged or even its pavilion set alight is bad enough, but for a club to be threatened with the loss of the ground on which it has played its home matches for over sixty years is infinitely worse. This is what happened in February 1984 to the Berkshire village club of Waltham St Lawrence, which played its home games on land adjoining a substantial house known as Great Martins.

Waltham St Lawrence Cricket Club was formed over a hundred years ago and originally played on a ground known as Oak Meadow, but in 1921 started to use the ground at Great Martins, the legal title to which at all times remained with the owner of the house. Except for a short period during the 1939–45 war, the club used the ground on a regular basis during the cricket season and, in 1970, a substantial brick pavilion was built by the club in a corner of the ground. Until 1978 relations between the club and three successive owners of Great Martins were very good and apparently remained so when in 1978 the house was bought by Julian Wills. The club gained the impression that Wills intended to live at Great Martins for the rest of his life and was happy that the club should continue to play on the Great Martins ground during that period, although there was subsequently a difference of opinion whether or not a promise to that effect had been given by Wills to the club. In any event, believing that its use of the ground was not at risk, the club agreed to make a statutory declaration for which Wills asked them.

A resolution passed at a meeting of the club held on 9 February 1978 authorised the making of the declaration, the important part of which reads as follows:

1. The club has no claim to ownership of or right to the pavilion constructed at Great Martins.
2. That no club member in his individual or personal capacity has any such rights.
3. That the right to play cricket at Great Martins is and has at all times been by invitation of and with the consent of the owner for the time being of Great Martins which the owner may revoke at any time.

In 1978 and the following five seasons the club continued to play at Great Martins.

In February 1984 Wills' solicitors told Andrew Railton, the club's chairman, that Great Martins had been sold to Jan Pehrsson, who was moving to England from Sweden, and that

Pehrsson was not prepared to allow the club to continue to use the Great Martins ground. Correspondence and negotiations failed to budge Pehrsson and on 12 July his solicitors asked the club to vacate the ground by 31 August. The club thereupon took legal advice and was advised to commence proceedings for a declaration of its right to retain possession of the ground and use of the pavilion and also to seek an injunction, the effect of which would be to preserve the status quo pending the hearing of the action.

The club founded its claim to use and play on the ground on three bases, the first of which echoed almost two hundred years later the pleas of the defendants in *Fitch* v. *Rawling, Fitch and Chatteris*. The club maintained that there was a custom for the playing of games, including cricket, on the ground, which had existed long before the club started using the ground in 1921. The second basis was that the club had originally occupied the ground as a tenant at will but, as a matter of law, that tenancy had only lasted a year and the club had, therefore, since acquired title to the ground by virtue of adverse possession.[3] The third basis was that when the pavilion had been built in 1970 the then owner of Great Martins, who had also been president of the club, had by giving assistance and encouragement to the club, by implication recognised the club's title to the ground and to the pavilion. The club further maintained that the meeting and statutory declaration of February 1978 did not invalidate the Club's claim on any of the three bases put forward because the club had no power to waive the customary right to use the ground and, as to the other two bases, the resolution and statutory declaration were not sufficient to dispose of or adversely affect the club's title to the ground or to the pavilion.

The main plank of Pehrsson's defence was that the arrangement under which the club used the ground had never been more than an informal oral one and that this was evidenced by the statutory declaration. Pehrsson also maintained that even to grant an injunction pending the hearing of the main action would seriously inconvenience him and put him to additional expense

[3] Under adverse possession an unchallenged occupier of land, which he does not own but which he occupies with the permission of the true owner, acquires title to that land after twelve years.

in connection with certain work which he wished to carry out at Great Martins.

The application for the injunction was heard in the Chancery Division before Sir Richard Scott on 11 December 1984, but the court refused to grant the injunction and, as the club could not afford to take the matter further, it had to vacate the ground on which it had played its home matches since 1921. In fairness to Pehrsson, he had been told about the statutory declaration by Wills' solicitors when he bought the property and was also advised that the club had only an informal arrangement to use the ground and that this could be terminated at will. On the other hand Pehrsson did tell his architect that one day he and his family were picnicking outside the house and 'the occasion was spoilt from their point of view by a cricket match being played in such close proximity'. Clearly, Pehrsson, as John Woodcock wrote of Tony Greig in another context, was not an Englishman by birth or upbringing!

The club therefore lost, without any compensation, both its ground and the pavilion which the members had built, but fortunately Morlands Brewery, which owned Oak Meadow where the club had played before 1921, agreed to let it to the club, which set about reconverting it into a cricket ground. The club also bought a second-hand pavilion and, although heavily in debt, in June 1988 once again started playing home matches at Waltham St Lawrence.

XI

THE BOYCOTT MEETINGS

Reviewing John Callaghan's book *Boycott: A Cricketing Legend*, the 1983 *Wisden* remarked that, 'the number of books by, "by", and about Geoffrey Boycott must now surely exceed those credited to any other English cricketer.' Since 1983 there have been at least two important additions to the Boycott library, namely Don Mosey's *Boycott* and Boycott's own *The Autobiography*. I do not intend to add a further volume but a short introduction is necessary to set in context the two cases in which the Yorkshire County Cricket Club was involved in connection with Boycott.

I doubt if the history of cricket contains a more complex and controversial character than Geoffrey Boycott or one who has generated such fierce loyalty in his supporters and such bitter antagonism in his opponents. As Boycott himself might well point out, his career figures speak for themselves. In first-class cricket he scored 48,426 runs, including 151 centuries, at an average of 56.83, the highest of any Englishman who has scored over 10,000 runs, while in Tests he made over 8,000 runs, with 22 hundreds, at an average of 48. His detractors would, however, claim that figures do not tell the whole story and that Boycott's record would have been statistically less impressive had he always put the interests of his side first.

Boycott first played for Yorkshire in 1962 and was captain from 1971 until 1978, but during the latter period Yorkshire did not win any of the four main competitions and seldom looked like doing so. In October 1977 Don Brennan, a Yorkshire committee member and a former Yorkshire and England wicket-keeper, expressed the view that Boycott was not a suitable person to lead the county and the publicity given to this sentiment led to a number of pro-Boycott Yorkshire members forming the Reform Group. However, Boycott remained in office during 1978. In September of that year the committee decided to replace him as captain with John Hampshire, but expressed the

hope that Boycott would 'continue to extend his invaluable services as a player' and offered him a two-year contract to enable
him to do so. The action of the committee did not meet with the
approval of the Reform Group, which decided to requisition a
special general meeting of the county club. This required a petition signed by two and a half per cent of the members and on
12 October 1978, when the requisite signatures had been
collected, the Reform Group presented the petition to the
club, asking for a meeting to be convened to consider two
resolutions. These were:

> 1.   That this special general meeting has no confidence in the
> members of the cricket sub-committee and recommends
> their resignation from the general committee of the Yorkshire
> County Cricket Club forthwith, and
> 2.   That Geoffrey Boycott be reappointed captain of the
> Yorkshire County Cricket Club and be invited to serve as
> such for the 1979 season.

The club tried to head off the Reform Group first by raising
various technical points on the petition and secondly by itself
calling a general meeting to consider a resolution expressing
confidence in the committee of the club. This did not satisfy the
Reform Group, which considered that members might well have
confidence in the main committee while disapproving of the
cricket sub-committee and its decision to replace Boycott as
captain. The Reform Group therefore applied to the court for
an injunction to restrain the club from holding a special
general meeting and asking for an order compelling the club
to hold a meeting at which the Reform Group's two resolutions would be considered.

The case was heard by Vice-Chancellor Andrew Blackett-
Ord at Liverpool on 13 November 1978. On behalf of the
Reform Group, Brian Walsh QC contended that the county club
was seeking to outflank the Reform Group by calling a meeting
'at which no vote would be taken on the specific issues' raised
by the Reform Group, while, for the club, Donald Nicholls
QC denied that this was so and said that under the club's
rules the committee was responsible for the management of
its affairs, which meant that the decision to sack Boycott could
not be rescinded and that therefore the resolution to reinstate

him was ineffectual. However, Blackett-Ord ruled in favour of the Reform Group and ordered the club to hold a special general meeting at which the Reform Group's resolutions would be considered. In the event, the club and the Reform Group agreed that it would save expense and be in the interests of all parties if the two lots of resolutions were all considered at the same meeting.

The meeting was held on Saturday 9 December at the Royal Hall, Harrogate, and proved to be a lively occasion with over 1,300 members attending, but the issues were decided by the proxy votes, the committee winning on all three counts. The resolution expressing confidence in the committee was carried by 4,422 votes to 3,067, that expressing no confidence in the cricket sub-committee was defeated by 3,346 votes to 4,216 and that calling for Boycott's reappointment as captain was defeated by the larger majority of 2,602 votes to 4,826. The size of the votes against the committee, however, indicated that there was a large measure of dissatisfaction with the way in which the club was run and during the next five years the pot continued to simmer until it boiled over again.

The year 1983, under Raymond Illingworth's captaincy, was a season of mixed fortunes for Yorkshire. By finishing top of the John Player League, the club won its first major trophy for fourteen years but this was more than counterbalanced by the disgrace of Yorkshire, for the first time in its history, finishing bottom of the County Championship. On 3 October the cricket sub-committee met and unanimously decided to appoint David Bairstow as captain and not to renew Boycott's contract. This decision was approved by the main committee by a majority of eighteen to seven and the club issued the following statement:

> The committee feel that the time has come to make major decisions. We can go no lower. The rancour and controversy must end. We must now look to the future and give our youngsters the chance to show what they can do.
>
> With this in mind, we have appointed the ever-enthusiastic David Bairstow to captain them. Ray Illingworth will cease to play championship cricket, except in an emergency and will not of necessity travel with the first team. Geoff Boycott's contract will not be renewed. We realise that this will mean

he will not be playing during his testimonial year which is unfortunate, but the situation makes it unavoidable. We wish him every success with his testimonial which was awarded for his services to the club over the last ten years and we will give him every assistance to make it a success.

The sacking of Boycott incensed the Reform Group – now reconstituted as the Members' Group – those of its members who were on the Yorkshire committee objecting that the full committee had only been allowed to vote on the whole package presented by the cricket sub-committee and not on its constituent parts. On 24 October the Members' Group presented a petition requisitioning a special general meeting of the club for which, under the rules, the committee had to send out notice within three weeks. A meeting was accordingly convened for Saturday 3 December to consider three resolutions. These were first that Boycott be reinstated, second, that the members had no confidence in the general committee, and third, that the members had no confidence in the cricket sub-committee. Notice was not, however, sent to 680 members who had not paid their 1983 subscriptions as, surprisingly, under the club's rules it should have been. This was drawn to the attention of the committee and on Sunday 27 November, less than a week before the meeting was due to be held, it was called off. The cancellation incensed the Members' Group, which went to the court asking for an injunction restraining the club from postponing the meeting. Again the case was heard by Blackett-Ord, this time at Leeds.

The Members' Group's counsel, Matthew Caswell, a Yorkshire member who gave his services free, said that unless any of the resolutions were won and lost by less than 680 votes the failure to send the additional notices would be irrelevant and that, in such an event, the meeting could be adjourned to accommodate those members who had not been sent the original notice. Caswell also pointed out that for the court to allow the meeting to be postponed would necessarily involve a further breach of the rules, as a postponed meeting could not be convened within 21 days of the receipt of the original petition. For the club Gerald Godfrey QC mentioned that if the meeting went ahead on 3 December it would be totally invalid and that there was thus no alternative but to convene a new meeting as soon as possible. Blackett-Ord agreed with the club's view and said he thought it 'essential in the unfortunate state that the cricket club has got itself into, that there should be no possibility of questioning the validity of the notice of the meeting summoned to consider the resolutions' and that a fresh and valid meeting should be held as soon as practicable.

With the intervention of Christmas and the New Year the meeting was not held until Saturday 21 January 1984 when, as Don Mosey says, 'there was much verbal blood-letting, some virulent personal attacks [and] a brilliant speech by Brian Walsh',[1] a Boycott supporter who had been leading counsel for the Reform Group at the 1978 hearing. The meeting itself brought a resounding defeat for the committee: 4,115 voted for Boycott's reinstatement and 3,109 against, while the motions of no confidence in the general committee and in the cricket sub-committee were both passed, although in the former case by only 31 votes. The committee had no alternative but to resign, which it did, and at the subsequent election the Members' Group swept the board, winning all but four seats and among the successful candidates was Geoffrey Boycott himself.

In his dual capacity as committee member and player, Boycott continued to play for Yorkshire for another three years without compromising the standards of performance which he set himself. In the three seasons 1984 to 1986 he scored an aggregate of over 4,000 first-class runs for Yorkshire at an average of 65 and topped the county's batting averages in all three years. At the end of the 1986 season, however, the cricket sub-committee recommended that Boycott's contract should not be renewed and this recommendation was approved by the general committee by twelve votes to nine. This time there was no rebellion and no special meeting nor, although as John Woodcock wrote, Boycott was 'still hard and fit and full of runs', did he continue his career outside Yorkshire to enable him to score the 1,574 runs needed to reach a total of 50,000. For the record, in 1987, their first 'Boycottless' year since 1961, Yorkshire won the Benson and Hedges Cup and recorded more victories in the County Championship than in any year since 1978, which happened to be Boycott's last as captain.

[1] Walsh later became chairman of Yorkshire CCC.

XII

ASSAULT AND BATTERY

At law an assault need not necessarily comprise actual physical violence – words with a realistic threat of violence can be enough – but battery must involve physical contact. I am not an etymological expert, but the Oxford Dictionary shows that the verb to batter – and hence the noun battery – derive from the Old French word 'batre' and the Middle English word 'bat', the main modern English meaning of the latter word being 'an implement for striking the ball in cricket, baseball, etc.' It is fitting, therefore, that in several of the cases described in this chapter a cricket bat was the implement used by the assailant.

One Jacobean and four Victorian assaults
Ironically, although a cricket bat was used in the oldest of these cases it was not referred to as such. The record of the case is contained in an entry dated 26 March 1613 in the Court Roll of the Manor of Wanborough, which is about five miles west of Guildford. The original roll is in Latin and is held at the Guildford Muniment Room, where the following translation was made:

> Affray. Item. They [the homage or jury] present Nicholas Hockley in the month of August last year at Wanborough within this view made an assault and affray on a certain Robert Hewett and by and with a certain stick called 'a crickett staffe' value one penny drew blood therefore he is in mercy [is fined] 3s. 4d.

The words 'a cricket staffe' are not a translation, but appear in the original, which gives no indication whether Robert Hewett was assaulted at a game of cricket or whether the cricket staffe merely happened to be a weapon conveniently to hand.

A bat was again used in the next case, which occurred

240 years later, and in which the assault did arise directly out of an incident during a cricket match. The case was heard on 14 January 1853 by the Nisi Prius in Middlesex before Baron Platt and a jury and was an action by James Lane to recover damages from Christopher Barnes for an injury sustained when Barnes hit Lane with a cricket bat. Lane was aged about nineteen and helped his father in the latter's business of decorator, painter and paperhanger, which was based in the Horseferry Road, while Barnes was the son of a surgeon and also a pupil – but it seems a mature one – at Westminster School.

On 19 June 1852 the cricket club of which Lane and his brother John were members had a match at Shepherds Bush against Doctor White's pupils of Westminster School, one of whom was Barnes. White's pupils batted first and then the other side went in, but their innings was interrupted by a heavy shower and the teams sheltered in a shed belonging to the Wellington Tavern. During the interruption Barnes and some others went into the Wellington where, as *The Times* puts it, 'they had something to drink and subsequently he and others appeared to be very much excited'.

In due course the rain stopped and play was resumed, with James and John Lane as the not out batsmen. Barnes bowled a ball to John, which hit him on the leg, and Barnes appealed for l.b.w. and John was given out by the umpire at the bowler's end, who happened to be Barnes' brother. John Lane said that he was not out as his leg was not in front of the wicket and a quarrel arose during which Barnes, the bowler, hit James Lane, who was the batsman at the bowler's end, on the nose. This induced James to dare Barnes to hit him again, which provoked Barnes to grab a bat from his brother, the umpire, with which he tried to hit James, who ran off. James threw his own bat away, as he was afraid he might lose his temper and 'do some serious mischief with it', but Barnes chased him, trying to hit him with the bat. Eventually Barnes struck James on the back and then brought him down with 'a severe blow on the ankle'. This resulted in the other players gathering round and, after some argument and discussion, James was persuaded to continue his innings with a runner and the game was resumed.

Although history does not relate, presumably Barnes' brother did not reverse his decision and John Lane had to return to the shed. The game went on until eight o'clock in the evening, but by then James' leg was so bad that he had to be helped home.

The following day, which was a Sunday, the condition of James' leg had deteriorated so much that Doctor Burton Payne, the family doctor, was called out by the Lane family. At first the injury seemed to yield to treatment, but after about three weeks 'a violent inflammation of the ligamentary structure set in' and James had to be treated with mercury to make him salivate. Every time James went back to work the inflammation got worse and it was not until the beginning of 1853, more than six months after the assault, that he was sufficiently recovered to resume his occupation. He had thus only been back at work for two weeks when his claim against Barnes was heard on 14 January. Evidence was given that Doctor Payne's bill amounted to more than £17, which is currently worth about £550, and evidence was also given that James could earn up to £3 a week just as a decorative paperhanger, which was only one of his skills.

After the court had heard the plaintiff's case, and before Barnes had given evidence or any of his witnesses had been called, the counsel representing the two sides conferred and agreed that the claim should be settled on terms that James would be paid £60 damages. Even with a current value of about £2,000, this represents less than six months' earnings for James, and allows nothing for pain and suffering. It, therefore, hardly seems a generous settlement for James, even taking into account that it was his own brother who had questioned the umpire's decision!

Coincidentally the next case was also heard in 1853 and concerned a game of cricket played in the summer of 1852, in fact on 9 June, ten days before the game in which James Lane was injured. The match took place at King's Lynn and was between the Lynn Cricket Club, captained by their president Richard Bagge, and the nearby village of Litcham. Lynn played their home fixtures on a ground owned by a local builder called Salmon Robin, who on 7 April 1852 entered into an agreement with the Lynn Cricket Club under which

Robin agreed to let to the club a piece of land for it to use as a cricket field. The club agreed to pay Robin £10 a year and to keep the ground in proper playing condition and the right to use it was determinable by either party at the end of any current season by written notice given on or before 29 September.

The match on 9 June was played on Robin's ground and the playing area was 'tabooed' to everyone except the players. Litcham were batting when one of the Lynn fielders was called away and John Holmes, a committee member of the Lynn club, was asked to substitute. Then, as described in one of the reports of the case:[1]

> He [Holmes] complied, but did not take off his coat. Bagge, who was captain of the Lynn eleven, told him to do so: offence was taken at the tone in which the command was given; and the plaintiff would neither take off his coat nor leave the tabooed spot. He was then, by the direction of the defendant, forcibly removed from the tabooed ground; and the assaults were committed in so removing him.

Holmes sued Bagge and Thomas Fulcher,[2] presumably another member of the Lynn XI, for assault and the case came up at the 1853 Norfolk Spring Assizes, before the Chief Justice, Lord Campbell, who later became Lord Chancellor and also wrote biographies of the Lord Chancellors, which 'were said to add a new terror to death, as much for their inaccuracies as their asperities'.[3] The jury found for Holmes and he was awarded £20 damages, which has a current value of about £650.

Bagge and Fulcher appealed on the ground that the original twenty-two cricketers comprising the two teams were possessed of the cricket ground and that the assault on Holmes was justified, as it was committed in removing him in the exercise of

[1] Ellis & Blackburn's Reports. 1853.
[2] One of the reports gives his name as Fletcher and the name of the owner of the ground as Rolin.
[3] From *May It Please Your Lordship* by E. S. Turner.

that right of possession. Lord Campbell, this time accompanied by three other judges, also presided at the appeal, which was heard on 25 April 1853 by the Queen's Bench Court at Westminster. The court dismissed the appeal, holding that the Lynn club, of which Holmes was a member, was in possession of the ground and not the two teams, eleven of whom 'were strangers, invited by the Lynn Cricket Club to come as their guests to play'. However, the judgment also made it clear that, had the defendants framed their plea differently, they might have been successful. In the words of the judgment, the defendants were 'lawfully playing at cricket, and it appeared that a space was tabooed, and that no person could properly come there, and that the plaintiff did come within the tabooed part, and was requested to withdraw. Therefore, although there might be a justification showing that he was lawfully removed, this is not the basis upon which the plea is framed.' Thus, had Bagge and Fulcher been better advised, they might have won the case and saved themselves £20.

The next case involved a first-class cricketer, although not one whose name is widely known. Henry Stubberfield, otherwise known as 'Old Stubber', was a fast medium round-arm bowler, who played for Sussex in fifty-seven matches between 1857 and 1874 and, after his playing days, became a well-known umpire. On 14, 15 and 16 August 1871 a Gentlemen v. Players match was played at Brighton as a 'Farewell Benefit Match' for John Lillywhite. More than three pages in the 1872 *Wisden* are devoted to the match, in which W. G. Grace scored 217 in the Gentlemen's second innings.

Stubberfield did not play, but was serving in the members' bar on the first day of the match, where Richard Daft, who was playing in the match, and Henry Frere, who played once for Sussex, were talking when one James Adlam tried to enter the bar. Stubberfield told Adlam that he could not come in as the bar was a private one, but Adlam persisted and tried to push past Stubberfield and, when Stubberfield would not allow him in, started to swear at him and it was not until someone threatened to call a policeman that Adlam departed. Adlam subsequently sued Stubberfield for assault and the case came up at Hove Petty Sessions on 28 August. Not surprisingly, after hearing the evidence, the magistrates dismissed the case with costs.

Five years after John Lillywhite's benefit match was played at Brighton his cousin, James Lillywhite junior, who also played for Sussex, promoted a cricket tour to Australia and New Zealand in partnership with Alfred Shaw, the famous Nottinghamshire bowler. They recruited ten other professionals and set sail for Australia on 21 September 1876, hoping to make a profit. The wicket-keeper in the party – and the only one – was Edward ('Teddy') Pooley, who played for Surrey and at the Oval in 1868 shared in the dismissal of twelve Sussex batsmen, a record which is still unbeaten 120 years later. Pooley was also a useful hard-hitting batsman, who in fact was aged 38 when the team departed for Australia, although he only admitted to being 33. Apparently, when Pooley started as a cricket professional his father thought that he would have a better chance of success if he knocked a few years off his age and it was only when he was over 60 that Pooley revealed 1838 as his true year of birth.

After playing some matches in Australia, Lillywhite's side went to New Zealand in January 1877 for two months before returning to Australia for the final part of their tour. While the tourists were in New Zealand the Australians agreed among themselves to co-operate in selecting a combined Australian XI to play against Lillywhite's men on their return to Australia. In fact two such matches were played, Australia winning the first and England the second, but it was only some time later that they became recognised as the first Test matches ever played. England was probably lucky not to lose them both because Lillywhite's side was by no means the country's strongest as, in particular, it was made up solely of professionals thus omitting, among others, W. G. Grace. In addition, the first Test was played when the English team had not had enough time to recover from a rough crossing from New Zealand and also without the services of their wicket-keeper, Pooley, who had been compelled to remain behind in New Zealand. The party was thus reduced to a bare eleven players and John Selby, a good batsman but no wicket-keeper, found himself keeping wicket for England in what subsequently transpired to be the first two Test matches.

The reason for Pooley's absence is recorded by Shaw in his reminiscences. As all the versions which I have seen of the events in question appear to be derived, with or without acknowledgement, from Shaw's book, I cannot do better than reproduce his account of what happened.[4]

We were playing at Christchurch against Eighteen of Canterbury, on February 26th, 27th and 28th, 1877. In a discussion as to the prospects of the match that occurred in an hotel bar at night, Pooley offered to take £1 to 1s. that he named the individual score of every member of the local team. It is a trick familiar to cricketers, and in the old days of matches against local eighteens and twenty-twos it was not infrequently worked off against the unwary.

How safe it was for the nominator of the individual scores can be judged from the bowling record which had been credited to me at Auckland shortly before. In 55 overs of which 30 were maidens, I took 18 wickets for 39 runs, while in the second innings Emmett obtained 7 wickets for 8 runs . . .

But to return to Pooley's bet. The bet being accepted, Pooley named 'a duck' as the score of each batsman on the local side. A fair proportion of 'ducks' was recorded, and Pooley claimed £1 each for them, while prepared to pay the 1s. each for the other scores. The man with whom the bet had been made said it was a catch bet on Pooley's part, and he declined to pay. The man's name was Ralph Donkin. His refusal to pay led to a scene of disorder, and brought Pooley's services with the team to an unpleasant end.

We had to go next to Otago, and at the close of the match there Pooley was arrested on a charge of 'having at Christchurch maliciously injured property above the value of £5', and also of assaulting Donkin. For the assault he had £5 and costs to pay. In the other charge he had as partner in trouble Alf Bramall, a supernumerary attached to our team. The two were committed for trial, bail being allowed of £100, with two sureties of £50 each.

[4] *Alfred Shaw, Cricketer. His Career and Reminiscences*, recorded by A. W. Pullin ('Old Ebor').

We never saw Pooley again during the tour. He and his companion were tried before the Supreme Court at Christchurch on April 6th 1877, and found not guilty. The local public thought he had been hardly used in having been taken away from the team. They subscribed £50 for division between Pooley and Bramall, and in addition they presented Pooley with a gold ring. The old Surrey wicket-keeper had to make the journey back to England alone.

In justice to him it should be stated that he was not the only, and possibly not the chief, participant in the row that followed the bet.

Pooley continued playing for Surrey for another seven years but he never played for England. He is, therefore, the first of quite a long line of players who have been prevented by accident or misfortune from representing their country. He died in the workhouse in 1907, the same year as Shaw, and at the end of a long obituary *Wisden* refers to 'the faults of private character that marred Pooley's career and were the cause of the poverty in which he spent the later years of his life'. I suspect that these faults were not confined to an addiction to betting but, as *Wisden* also says, 'to the last he had a geniality and sense of humour that to a certain extent condoned his weaknesses'.

Branded for life
Roy Gilchrist, the West Indian fast bowler, was born in 1934 and was the twenty-second child of a Jamaican sugar estate and factory worker. If the other twenty-one were anything like their younger brother, the Gilchrist household must have been a lively place, as Roy was always in trouble. Gilchrist himself worked with his father on the estate and later helped one of his brothers, John, in his hairdressing salon, but 'snipping and cutting' were not to Gilchrist's taste and he abandoned hairdressing for a job where he could get more free time for cricket. Starting as a slow off-break bowler, Gilchrist changed to bowling fast and, with several spectacular performances in minor matches, quickly graduated to the Jamaica side.

At the end of his first season for Jamaica Gilchrist was chosen for the trial matches and did well enough to be selected for the West Indies' 1957 tour of England. Although not very successful on that tour, Gilchrist was a genuinely fast and hostile bowler and played in all the Tests, except the last when he was ill. The following season in the West Indies he played in all five Tests against Pakistan, taking 21 wickets in the series, which was more than anyone else on either side. In 1958–9 he was a member of the West Indies' party in India and Pakistan and played in four of the five Tests against India, finishing top of the Test bowling averages with twenty-six wickets at just over 16 runs each, including nine for 73 in the third Test. He did not, however, complete the tour as he was sent home by the West Indies' captain, Gerry Alexander, before the team went on to Pakistan for losing his temper and bowling 'beamers' at batsmen's heads.

After February 1959 Gilchrist never played in another Test match, but of the thirteen in which he did play three are very famous. His first Test was the one against England when Sonny Ramadhin was finally mastered. In their first innings England were dismissed for 186, Ramadhin taking seven for 49, but in the second innings Peter May with 285 not out and Colin Cowdrey with 154 put on 411 for England's fourth wicket, not only saving the match but almost winning it. In Gilchrist's first Test in the West Indies, Hanif Mohammad scored 337 for Pakistan, while in the third Test of that series Garfield Sobers made the record Test score of 365 not out, he and Conrad Hunte putting on 446 for the second wicket. Few men who played in such a comparatively small number of Tests can have played in three such historic ones. After being sent home from India, Gilchrist continued playing for Jamaica until 1962 and then had one season with Hyderabad, after which he played no more first-class cricket.

In 1963 Gilchrist's autobiography, *Hit Me For Six* was published and in it he admitted that he had been at fault in India and wrote that he was sorry for what had happened. He also said in the Introduction that he was 'a good boy now' and had decided to leave his 'wild moments' behind, but this was to prove a false hope. After leaving first-class cricket he had a successful, if controversial, career with a number of different clubs in the Yorkshire and Lancashire leagues. He started with Bacup in 1963, then had a season with Lowerhouse, followed by two seasons with Crompton and in 1967 he was playing for Heaton, which was in the Bolton League.

At about eleven o'clock on the night of Friday 2 June 1967 Gilchrist arrived back at his Manchester home and found his wife, Novlyn, doing some ironing. Gilchrist asked her to go to a party but she refused because of his behaviour at previous parties. An argument ensued which developed into a struggle, during which Gilchrist grabbed the iron with his right hand and, with his left arm round his wife's throat, pushed her against the wall. As counsel put it in the subsequent trials, the iron then 'came in contact with his wife's face', as a result of which Mrs Gilchrist received a four-inch burn on her left cheek, which left a permanent scar, although when he saw the injury caused by the iron, Gilchrist put some butter on the wound. Gilchrist appeared at Manchester City Magistrates' Court on 28 June when he pleaded not guilty to causing his wife grievous bodily harm and was granted bail on his own recognisance of £25.

When he was tried at Manchester Crown Court on 17 July he changed his plea to guilty and Mrs Gilchrist, who had been reluctant to give evidence against her husband, said that she did not know whether he had inflicted the injury on her deliberately, but she had now forgiven him and they were reconciled. Judge Edward Steel told Gilchrist, 'I hate to think that English sport has sunk so far that brutes will be tolerated because they are good at games', and put him on probation for three years. The judge added that Gilchrist had no one to thank for his lenient treatment except his wife and he trusted that Gilchrist would 'always remember that and treat her accordingly'.

Just over a year later Gilchrist found himself in court again. This time he had brandished a knife during an argument with a spectator at Manchester Corporation Transport Department's ground in Gorton. Gilchrist was found guilty of an assault occasioning actual bodily harm and fined £30 by the Manchester Stipendiary Magistrate. Unfortunately for him this further conviction constituted a breach of the probation order imposed in July 1967 and, on 8 November, he found himself again in the Crown Court before Judge Steel. This time Steel told him that he had shown that he was not worthy of leniency and sentenced him to eighteen months' imprisonment for breaking the probation order.

Gilchrist did not serve the full sentence and in December 1969 signed as professional for the Bradford League club of

East Bierley. His days in court, however, were not yet over. On 26 July 1975 he went to the police pound to retrieve his car, which had been stolen two days earlier. He was promptly arrested and charged with driving a car with excess alcohol in his blood on 23 April 1972. He came up before the Manchester Stipendiary Magistrate, John Bamber, on 28 July 1975, two days after his arrest but three and a quarter years after the offence. Gilchrist pleaded guilty but the magistrate said he found the delay in serving the warrant 'very disturbing' and while, in law, the delay might not be a reason for Gilchrist not being disqualified from driving 'in all justice and in all moral sense' it was. He therefore fined Gilchrist, who pleaded guilty, £5 and ordered that his licence should be endorsed.

Not quite cricket

The case of *Lane* v. *Barnes* shows that disagreement with the umpire's decision is not a twentieth-century phenomenon but fortunately, even in modern times, such disagreements seldom lead to physical assaults. One which did occurred in 1975 although, unlike the 1853 case, it was the umpire and not the non-striking batsman who was injured. On Saturday 17 May 1975 Elwaldo Jones, a 35-year-old resident of Handsworth, Birmingham, was batting in a game at Ward End Park when he was run out or, as Jones believed, wrongly adjudged by the 68-year-old umpire, George Carter, to have been run out. Jones made his disagreement with Carter's decision clear and an argument developed between the two men during which Jones struck Carter with his bat, bruising him badly and breaking his arm.

On 28 May Jones appeared at Birmingham Magistrates' Court when he pleaded guilty to unlawfully and maliciously inflicting grievous bodily harm on Carter. Jones told the court: 'I lost my temper. I am very sorry things should have happened like that. I have been playing in the park for thirteen years and I have never been in any argument.' The chairman of the bench, Sidney Lancaster, told Jones: 'You know perfectly well what the traditions of the game are', and fined him £50 (currently about £165), but there is no record of whether or not Carter obtained any compensation for his injuries. Unlike *Lane* v. *Barnes*, which was a civil claim for damages, Jones was the subject of a criminal prosecution and perhaps Jones paid up without being taken to court or Carter may have decided that he was not worth powder and shot.

In the next case it was not the umpire who was assaulted, nor even one of the opposition, but a member of the same team as the assailant. On 21 June 1980 Brook Motors were playing a 2nd XI game on their own ground against Gomersal, a village between Leeds and Huddersfield. Brook Motors, who were captained by Geoffrey Boyes, a 46-year-old lorry driver who also acted as groundsman, had not been having a successful season and in their previous three matches had been dismissed for 39, 44 and 55. Shortly before the match started Paul Woolerton, a 20-year-old export clerk who usually went in number three for Brook Motors, was in the pavilion talking to the wife of one of the home team and remarked that if Brook Motors were going to bat first she might as well start brewing up the tea. Woolerton's remarks were overheard by Boyes, who took exception to them and told Woolerton that if he was going to adopt that attitude he might as well stay at home and demoted him to number six in the batting order.

Later in the changing room hostilities were resumed and Boyes started prodding Woolerton on the side of the neck; Woolerton told Boyes to stop and pushed him away but Boyes then punched Woolerton in the face. According to one of the other players, he then swore at Woolerton and punched him six or seven times, although Boyes later maintained that he had only punched Woolerton once. In any event Boyes hit Woolerton hard enough to knock him down, remove three of his teeth and cut his lip. Not surprisingly, when he batted Woolerton was out first ball, but Brook Motors made the respectable total of 176 and only just lost the match.

Boyes was charged with assault and appeared at Huddersfield Magistrates' Court on 1 September. In evidence the police said that when seen by them Boyes had said that things had been building up for some time between himself and Woolerton and, in his own evidence, Boyes said that when he had told Woolerton he was demoted in the batting order he had prodded Woolerton, who had complained and sworn at him. Boyes also admitted that he had lost his temper and said: 'I was in the wrong, but I hit him only once.' The chairman of the bench, George Sheldrick, told

Boyes he had committed a vicious assault and fined him £100 and ordered him to pay £20 costs and £125 compensation to Woolerton. The incident also resulted in Boyes losing his place in the team and his job as groundsman and thus Brook Motors' cricket suffered as well as Boyes and his victim for, as Woolerton said after the case: 'It was a pity it happened because Boyes was a good medium pace bowler and a first class groundsman.'

Cricket and football

Many an impromptu game of cricket played by children on a recreation ground has been spoiled by a nearby game of football and one which suffered in this way took place on the Lyons Farm recreation ground at Worthing on Monday 19 May 1975. Gordon Mills was playing cricket with his 9-year-old son and four other children when some youths started playing football nearby. One of them kicked the ball into the middle of the cricketers and collided with the stumps sending them flying and so Mills asked the footballers not to kick the ball so hard. However, the trouble continued and an argument arose, during which Mills swung the bat that he had been using and caught one of the footballers, 20-year-old Robert Bridger, on his arm and then on the back of the head, causing a lump to appear.

On 29 May Mills appeared in Worthing Magistrates' Court and pleaded guilty to a charge of assault and occasioning actual bodily harm to Bridger. Mills said that he had been 'surrounded by bullies' and that one of them had punched him on the left ear and claimed that his act was carried out in self-defence and for the safety of young children. He added that he hoped his appearance in court would draw attention to the trouble that youths were causing at the recreation ground and said that if his action had saved young children from serious injury it had been worthwhile. The magistrate gave him a two-year conditional discharge.

Although a cricket bat was again the implement used in the next case, which also involved a game of football, no one was playing or attempting to play cricket nearby at the time. On Tuesday 4 November 1986 an amateur league match was played on a ground in Holloway and two of the players on one side, which won 4–0, were Noel Fitzgerald and Roger

McDermott, while one of the players on the losing side was Earl Braithwaite, the brother of Mark Braithwaite who was sentenced to life imprisonment for the murder of PC Keith Blakelock in the 1985 Tottenham riot. Braithwaite felt that he had been unfairly marked out of the game and later attacked Fitzgerald and McDermott with a cricket bat, telling one of them: 'You won't play football again for a while.' This was certainly a true statement, as he broke Fitzgerald's ankle and McDermott's arm.

Braithwaite, who was aged 25 and lived in Islington, was charged with causing grievous bodily harm to Fitzgerald and McDermott and his case came up at Snaresbrook Crown Court on 5 January 1988. What had happened fourteen months earlier is best described in the words of Fitzgerald, a 25-year-old builder:

> The tall coloured fellow I was marking approached me afterwards and called me a Paddy. He then pulled out something from a bag and hit me with it. I thought it was a cricket bat or a baseball bat with a black handle. He swung it at me and caught me across the middle of the back.
>
> I ran away but slipped on some cobbled stones and he came flying past me because he was running so fast. He hit me again on the left elbow, and swung at me again, catching me on the other one. He swung at me again, holding the bat in one hand, catching me on the calf muscle, and then on the ankle, saying 'You won't play football again for a while.' At this stage he walked off and I hobbled into the dressing room unable to put any weight on my right foot.

McDermott also gave evidence and told the court that Braithwaite had attacked him with the bat, breaking his arm. The case went into a second day when Braithwaite was found guilty and sentenced to one year's imprisonment.

Assaulting the police
As will be apparent from the chapter entitled 'Misbehaviour at the Match' cases arising from unruly behaviour by spectators at cricket matches are not a recent phenomenon, but all such cases that I have come across which involved assaults on the police have occurred in the last fifteen years.

The first World Cup tournament, officially called the Prudential Cup, which was held in England in June 1975 was an outstanding success. On Saturday 7 June England played India at Lord's in one of the Group A matches. England batted first and scored 334 for 4 in 60 overs, Dennis Amiss scoring 137, but India managed only 132 for 3 in their 60 overs, Sunil Gavaskar batting through the innings for 36 not out. As *Wisden* says, India 'gave such a disappointing exhibition that even their own large contingent of supporters showed their disapproval'. One of these was a 27-year-old lorry driver, Sharan Gill, who punched two policemen and on the Monday found himself in Marelybone Magistrates' Court, where he admitted to being 'a bit drunk and upset' and was jailed for six months. For the record, the only match which India won in the competition was that against East Africa, but they did, unexpectedly, win the third World Cup competition in 1983.

Most assaults and disturbances at cricket matches have taken place at one-day games, in particular the Sunday league matches and for a time Somerset, especially, gained a bad reputation in this respect. In 1979 Somerset won the John Player League and their penultimate home match was played at Taunton on 26 August, when they lost to Kent by 64 runs. At the time it seemed that the defeat had probably cost Somerset the title, as Kent only had to win their last two matches to win it, but they fell at the last fence, losing to Middlesex on 9 September before a crowd of 12,000 at Canterbury.

At Taunton on 26 August trouble started early in the game and the police went to a car park adjacent to the ground to investigate possible damage to the roof of a toilet block inside the ground. On the roof the police found several men, described by the Somerset Supporters' Club secretary as 'cider-swigging idiots', who greeted the police with abuse when asked to come down. Among them was 20-year-old John Coleman, who climbed down into the car park but became very abusive and threatening when told by the police to behave himself. One of the police, Sergeant Geoffrey Smith, arrested Coleman but he became violent and struggled, head-butting Smith and giving him a severe nose-bleed. Coleman was arrested and charged with assaulting the police and the next day appeared in court and was remanded in custody after the police had objected to bail.

On Tuesday 28 August Coleman appeared at Taunton Deane Magistrates' Court when he pleaded guilty to assaulting Sergeant Smith, causing him bodily harm and using threatening words and behaviour likely to cause a breach of the peace. Coleman's counsel, David White, pleaded on his client's behalf that the assault was not premeditated and that Coleman was 'not a man that is so far gone that prison is the only way to deal with him'. The magistrates, however, did not agree – not surprisingly as Coleman had previous convictions for assault, causing bodily harm, threatening behaviour, obstructing the police, theft, damage and giving assistance to a man who was unlawfully at large. Coleman was sentenced to six months' imprisonment and bound over in the sum of £50 to keep the peace for two years. Following that match, Somerset CCC banned all liquor from being brought into the ground by spectators and this was instrumental in improving the standard of behaviour.

On Sunday 3 May 1987, when Worcestershire beat Lancashire by six wickets in a rain-affected Refuge Assurance League match at Worcester, there were also incidents outside the ground when the police were obstructed and assaulted. On the following day six men, all in their twenties, appeared in court charged with a variety of offences and were granted bail. On 15 May at Worcester Magistrates' Court two of them, who their solicitor said were 'football supporters and have never been to a cricket match', admitted obstructing the police and were fined £50 each. The cases against the other four, all of whom pleaded not guilty to a variety of charges, were adjourned.

On 25 August Shaun Fenson, Alexander Stanfield, David Oakes and John Bird appeared again before the Worcester City Magistrates. The court was told that on 3 May a police superintendent had been punched on the side of the head, while other officers had been head-butted and punched during a fight which had flared up and spilled out of the ground. All four were found guilty of assaulting the police and all, except Fenson, of threatening or disorderly behaviour. Fenson was fined £200, Stanfield £250, Oakes £275 and Bird, who was found guilty of assaulting two policemen, £475. Imposing the fines, the chairman of the bench, Bernard Neil, expressed the hope that they would 'serve as a salutory lesson to people that law and order must be maintained, so that everyone can enjoy cricket or anything else', a sentiment that would surely have been echoed by PC Kevin Glanville, who had been assaulted by three of the four young men who were fined.

Definitely not cricket

As Sir Derek Hodgson said when giving judgment in the Court of Appeal in the next case, 'the events out of which this offence arose were somewhat confused'. In the early hours of Saturday 17 February 1979 a young man called Paul Turner was involved in a fight in a Manchester restaurant. Turner was then offered another fight with someone called Sutcliffe, which he accepted, but a third youth, seeing that Sutcliffe had various friends with him, ran to Turner's home and told his parents that Paul was involved in a fight. The Turner parents got out of bed and Paul's father armed himself with a baseball bat and went to Paul's assistance, while his mother, after telephoning the police, followed her husband armed with a cricket bat.

When Turner arrived at the spot near the restaurant where his son and Sutcliffe were going to have the fight, he found them arguing but not fighting and so Turner told his son to go home and he also started back for home himself. While he was running away Turner slipped on some ice and fell whereupon he was attacked by Sutcliffe, who was armed with a blunt knife, and also by some of Sutcliffe's friends. Meanwhile Mrs Turner had arrived on the scene and Paul relieved her of the cricket bat, which somehow then got into the hands of a friend of Paul's called Sykes. By this time Paul's father, who had dropped the baseball bat, was being hit with it by one Cassidy, a friend of Sutcliffe's who had picked it up. Sykes also then started hitting the unfortunate Turner, in his case with the cricket bat, mistakenly believing that he was hitting Sutcliffe, rather than his friend's father. Fortunately, although battered by bats of both the cricket and baseball variety, Turner's injuries proved not to be serious.

Sutcliffe, Cassidy and Sykes were all charged with offences under sections 18 and 20 of the Offences Against the Person Act 1861 and in addition Cassidy and Sykes were charged with, and pleaded guilty to, occasioning actual bodily harm. On 27

February 1980 at Manchester Crown Court Sutcliffe, who had been armed with a knife, was sentenced to eighteen months' imprisonment for affray while Cassidy and Sykes each received six months' imprisonment for assault occasioning actual bodily harm. Sykes appealed against the sentence imposed on him on the ground that it should have been less than Cassidy's because Cassidy had no fewer than ten previous convictions, including assaulting the police, threatening behaviour and possessing offensive weapons, whereas Sykes only had one previous conviction which was for a very minor offence committed some five years earlier. Giving judgment, Mr Justice Hodgson said the court felt that there was a real disparity between the sentences imposed on Cassidy and Sykes and that if, having regard to their different records, they received the same sentences the good character of Sykes as a mitigating circumstance would seem not to exist. In the circumstances, therefore, the court substituted for Sykes' sentence of six months' imprisonment such sentence as would secure his immediate release. In fact by the time the appeal was heard on 20 May 1980 and Sykes became a free man, he had already been in prison for almost three months.

When the incomparable Don Bradman and the sixteen other cricketers making up the 1948 Australian side signed a number of presentation bats, they could not have expected one of them would be used thirty-seven years later as a weapon in a dispute between two neighbours in Dorset. The incident in question was the culmination of a history of disputes concerning access and rights of way between John Rew, a 44-year-old accountant and investment adviser who lived at Thorn Hill House, Stalbridge, and Paul Evans, a 67-year-old former Wing-Commander who was awarded the DFC for his exploits during the siege of Malta and lived in a converted stable block in the grounds of the Thorn Hill House estate.

On 16 November 1984, Evans and his wife, Evelyn, returned home by car from a local Conservative meeting at Shaftesbury, but as Mrs Evans got out of her husband's MG her fur coat caught on the horn, sounding it. Rew heard the horn and said he saw Evans' headlights flashing at his window and went out with his prized cricket bat to remonstrate with Evans, whom he thought was trying to wind him up. Evans, having seen his wife indoors, saw Rew approaching with the bat and got back into the car to reverse it into his garage, locking the car doors but leaving the driver's window open. Rew then told Evans to 'buzz off' while, as he later claimed, standing in front of Evans' car making cricket strokes. According to Evans, Rew was swinging the bat, which caused him to drive on to adjoining land belonging to Rew in order to avoid it. In any event, Evans' response to being told to 'buzz off' was to tell Rew that the reason he was not accepted in the district was not a question of money but of manners and lack of breeding whereupon, unable to think of a suitable reply, Rew flicked Evans' cigar out of his mouth.

Rew's version of what happened next is that he shouted to his wife, Pauline, to call the police because Evans was on his property. As Evans made another remark he moved forward to hear what he was saying but Evans drove the car forward over Rew's foot. In court later Rew said that he then 'thrust the handle of the bat into the window because I wanted to say "stop"'. Evans denied he had driven over Rew's foot and said that Rew had aimed a punch at him and smashed the window of his car with the bat, showering him with glass.

In due course the police arrived in the shape of Sergeant John Hatton, who arrested both men for conduct likely to cause a breach of the peace. Rew was also charged with destroying a car window without lawful excuse, which he denied. Evans and Rew appeared at Sturminster Newton Magistrates' Court on 10 January 1985, when Rew was found guilty of criminal damage and conditionally discharged for two years, while both men were bound over to keep the peace. History does not relate whether the bat which, unlike the window of the MG, was irreplaceable suffered in the dispute.

The Ealing Vicarage case

This case is interesting on several different levels, of which the first and most basic is that it featured a vicar, a virgin, a robbery and a rape and all these elements were fully exploited by the tabloid press. Also of interest are the reactions of the victims, the criticism of the sentences passed on the offenders, the appeal by one of the three criminals against his sentence and the report of the Press Council on the case. As far as this book is concerned, the case qualifies for inclusion as it involved a particularly savage instance of battery with a cricket bat, in fact a well-used 'Don Bradman' bat, if a televison news item on the case depicted the bat in question.

The events took place on Thursday, 6 March 1986, when three men set out to rob a house in Ealing. The three, all of whom were unemployed, were Robert Horscroft, who was 34 and had thirteen convictions including some for burglary and inflicting actual bodily harm, Martin McCall, who was 21 and had two convictions for similar offences and one for possessing cannabis, and Christopher Byrne, who was also 21 and also had three convictions, in his case for handling, theft and possession of cannabis. The previous evening the three had robbed an off-licence and on the morning of 6 March they had all been drinking, apart from which both McCall and Byrne had a perennial drink and drugs problem.

On 6 March the three, having failed to gain admission to a house in Queen Anne's Gardens, went to Ealing Vicarage which is nearby. In the vicarage were the vicar of St Mary's, 53-year-old Prebendary Michael Saward, David Kerr a 20-year-old friend of the family and a girl, who was aged 21. McCall rang the bell and when the door was opened by Saward he spun round with a knife in his hand and forced his way into the house, followed by Horscroft and Byrne. Once inside the three men forced Saward into his study, cut the telephone wires and demanded jewellery and money. Kerr and the girl were also forced into the study at knifepoint. The girl was subsequently taken upstairs and raped by McCall and also indecently assaulted and forced to commit a sexual act by Byrne. Horscroft, however, had nothing to do with the sexual attacks on the girl, telling McCall and Byrne: 'We didn't come here for this, we came here for money.'

Saward and Kerr pleaded in vain for the girl to be left alone, but their pleas were ignored by Horscroft and Byrne who bludgeoned them over the head with the vicar's cricket bat. Both men were rendered unconscious, or virtually so, and Saward spent seven days in hospital recovering from his injuries while Kerr, whose skull was fractured, was not released for ten days. While Horscroft and Byrne were battering the vicar and Kerr, McCall drank some vodka from a bottle on which his fingerprints were later found. The gang then left the vicarage with a video-recorder, some jewellery, a small amount of cash, some credit cards and the cricket bat. The next day they all went to a barber in Isleworth for a 'short back and sides', where they aroused the suspicions of the assistant, Tracey Hennessy. The descriptions that she was able to give, with the information given by the victims and the fingerprints on the vodka bottle, all helped the police to trace the culprits who were arrested on 15 March, four days after the cricket bat had been found in the garden of a house in west London.

On 2 February 1987 all three appeared at the Old Bailey before Mr Justice Leonard. Also in court was Jacqueline Defelice, Horscroft's 36-year-old lover, who admitted trying to pervert the course of justice by concealing clothes used in the raid by Horscroft and disposing of two knives and some stolen goods. She was sentenced on 2 February to eighteen months' imprisonment, suspended for two years, and her's was the only sentence which did not subsequently arouse bitter controversy. Also sentenced on 2 February were McCall and Byrne. McCall received five years' imprisonment for aggravated burglary and another five to run consecutively on the rape charge, making a total of ten years. Byrne was sentenced to five years for aggravated burglary, three years for rape, two years for the assault on the vicar and three for the assault on Kerr. However, in Byrne's case the latter three sentences were to run concurrently and his total sentence was thus one of eight years' imprisonment. Sir John Leonard left the sentencing of Horscroft over until the following day.

Horscroft had been charged on two indictments, the first of which related to the Ealing Vicarage case and the second to entirely separate matters. On the first indictment there were four counts, aggravated burglary, rape, inflicting grievous bodily harm on the vicar and inflicting grievous bodily harm on Kerr. On the second indictment there were seven counts of burglary, and on this indictment Horscroft asked for twenty-four offences, mostly of burglary and similar crimes, to be taken into consideration. On the counts under the first indictment Horscroft pleaded not guilty to the rape and the assault on Kerr which the judge ordered to remain on the file. On the count of aggravated burglary Mr Justice Leonard sentenced Horscroft to seven years' imprisonment and on the charge of assaulting Saward he was given three years' imprisonment to run consecutively. On the second indictment Horscroft received a variety of terms of imprisonment varying between two and four years, all to run concurrently with each other but consecutively with the sentences on the first indictment. Thus Horscroft was sentenced on both indictments to a total of fourteen years' imprisonment, of which ten related to the Ealing case.

Before Horscroft was sentenced, however, a storm of criticism had broken on the shortness of the sentences given to McCall and Byrne for the rape and it intensified when a comparison was made with the sentences given to Horscroft, who had not taken part in the rape. The sentences were also criticised by the victims, who made the point that the terms imposed for rape and aggravated burglary gave the impression that the two were 'roughly comparable crimes'. Nevertheless, Saward also made it clear that he did not feel any hatred or desire for personal revenge and throughout the aftermath of the affair his attitude and comments were a credit to himself and his faith and the girl won praise for her courage and resilience. Once McCall and Byrne had been sentenced their terms of imprisonment could not be increased, but Horscroft clearly felt that his own sentence was unjust in the context of those imposed on the other two and on 8 June his appeal against sentence was heard in the Criminal Division of the Court of Appeal.

After hearing counsel for Horscroft, the court said it accepted that Horscroft had helped the police over the crimes on the second indictment and that the vicar had not been as seriously injured by Horscroft as Kerr had by Byrne. Nevertheless, the court dismissed Horscroft's appeal and its reasons for doing so are interesting and, in my view, difficult to fault.

The court considered that, as far as the second indictment was concerned, there was a long catalogue of offences and that a sentence of four years' imprisonment for these 'was by no means out of the way' and that such a sentence certainly gave credit for the information which Horscroft had given to the police, without which the sentence might well have been twice as long. In so far as the events at the vicarage were concerned, the Court of Appeal regarded seven years' imprisonment in respect of the burglary, the holding up of the occupants at knife-point and the way in which the burglary was committed to be by no means too long in the light of the part which Horscroft had played. Likewise the court regarded the three-year sentence in respect of Horscroft's attack on the vicar with the cricket bat to be 'by no means out of the ordinary'.

That left the court to consider the complaint of the disparity with the sentences imposed on Byrne, who received, in effect, three years' imprisonment for two cricket bat assaults, while Horscroft received the same term for one assault of a less serious nature. The Court of Appeal considered that the judge at first instance had been too lenient with Byrne, rather than too severe with Horscroft and therefore saw no reason to interfere with Horscroft's sentence on that ground either. In a way it seems that the court was applying the lesson to be drawn from the parable of the Labourers in the Vineyard, in that leniency or generosity shown to one person is no reason for another not receiving his just deserts.[5]

In addition the Court of Appeal commented on the criticism by the media of the sentences imposed on McCall and Byrne for rape. In the judgment the Lord Chief Justice, Lord Lane, pointed out that a judge does not simply add together all the sentences which he thinks correct for a particular defendant, as this would result in an inordinately long term of imprisonment, but that he either passes longer sentences to run concurrently with each other or shorter sentences to run consecutively. In the case under review the court said that it would have led to less rancour and criticism if Mr Justice Leonard had imposed longer sentences on McCall and Byrne for the rape and further long sentences for the burglary and assaults, all to run concurrently. Thus ten years and eight years respectively for the rape, five years each for the burglary and three years each for inflicting grievous bodily harm, all running concurrently would have resulted in the same total sentences for McCall and Byrne and would probably have prevented some of the public outcry that the sentences imposed for rape were too short, as well as providing an answer to some of the points made in the Court of Appeal on behalf of Horscroft. Overall the Court of Appeal concluded that a 'fair-minded bystander' (presumably the modern equivalent of the man on the Clapham omnibus)

[5] *St Matthew*, Chapter 20, Verses 1 to 16.

would not think Horscroft had been hard done by and that to reduce his sentence would be to reduce it below its proper level.

Meanwhile on 5 March 1987, between the date of the original trial and the hearing of Horscroft's appeal, the Press Council had issued a report on the case. *The Sun* and the *News of the World* were both censured and several other papers were criticised for their treatment of aspects of the story in February 1986 when the crimes were committed. In its report the Council drew attention to what it described as the 'jigsaw puzzle identification' of the victims of rapes, which reports in different papers made possible. Indeed the Council pointed out that one newspaper, which was criticised but not censured, had published the two pieces of the jigsaw necessary to reveal the victim's identity on different pages of the same issue.

Indisputably all three victims of the crimes committed at St Mary's Vicarage on 6 March 1986 suffered horribly, but to end on a happier note, in November 1987 Mowbray's published an important new book written by Saward entitled *Evangelicals on the Move* while, coincidentally, in the same month the girl's engagement to be married was announced.

Botham and Qadir

To continue with another biblical reference, it is doubtful if the author of the Book of Job had Ian Terence Botham in mind when he wrote: 'Man is born unto trouble, as the sparks fly upward,' but there can have been few people who better exemplify the truth of that maxim. Even the publicity material for his own wife's book, *Living with a Legend*, described Botham as a 'larger than life personality' and his career as 'a decade of tempestuous activity both on and off the field', with 'every year bringing a fresh set of dramas'. Two of these dramas fall within the scope of this chapter – or to be strictly accurate – one, as the second was enacted after Kathy Botham's book was published.

One of the greatest all-rounders the game has produced, Botham attained the double of 1,000 runs and 100 wickets in 21 Tests, fewer than anyone else. In 1980, at the age of 24, he captained England in a five-match series against the West Indies and also in the Centenary Test against Australia, but Botham's own performance in these matches was disappointing, as in six games he scored only 169 runs at an average of under twenty and his fourteen wickets cost over 35 runs each.

The Bothams lived at Epworth, which is in South Humberside, and in 1979 Scunthorpe United, a side in the fourth division of the Football League, had signed Botham as a non-contract player and for the following five seasons he appeared fairly regularly for one or other of the Scunthorpe sides, including the first team. Botham was regarded as a good team and club man at Scunthorpe and he played football with the same zest as cricket, although with less skill and inspiration. In the 1980–81 season Scunthorpe drew 0–0 with Altrincham in the FA Cup, but lost the replay 0–1 as a result of a penalty awarded against Scunthorpe's goalkeeper Joe Neenan. There was more than usual disappointment in Scunthorpe at this defeat as victory would have meant playing Liverpool in the next round.

Although knocked out of the Cup, the Scunthorpe footballers decided to have a pre-Christmas party on Monday 22 December and, as a player, Botham was invited to attend and, in spite of his wife's misgivings, decided that he should go. There were about eight in the party, which went first to a Berni Inn in Scunthorpe and then by minibus to Tiffany's dance hall, where they arrived at about half past ten. Botham did not dance but had a few drinks and chatted and the party broke up at about two o'clock on the morning of 23 December when Botham and the others left and went outside to find the minibus. A series of events then took place, which resulted in Botham and Neenan appearing in the local magistrates' court on 14 January 1981 charged with assault. Neenan pleaded guilty and was fined £100, while Botham denied the charge and elected to go for trial before a jury. The case against Botham was not heard until September and before then his cricket career had passed through one of its most dramatic periods.

From January to April 1981 Botham captained the England side in the West Indies which lost the rubber by two Tests to nil. As a player, Botham had a poor tour, although he did take most wickets for England both in Tests and on the tour as a whole. The tour itself, which *Wisden* describes as 'ill-fated and unsuccessful', was over-shadowed by the sudden and tragic death from a heart attack of the assistant manager

Ken Barrington on 14 March 1981 and by the Jackman affair. The latter led to the Test in Guyana being cancelled because the Guyanese government would not allow Robin Jackman into the country on account of his South African connections. The following summer in England Botham captained England in the first two Tests against Australia but in the second game his Test career probably reached its nadir when he scored nought twice, in the second innings having to return to the England dressing room at Lord's through a pavilion of silent and stony-faced members after being bowled first ball. Mike Brearley took over the captaincy for the remaining four Tests, in three of which Botham won the Man of the Match award with some of the most astonishing performances in the history of Test cricket. The feats are well known but, in essence, Botham took 7 wickets and scored 50 and 149 not out at Leeds, he and Bob Willis turning virtually certain defeat into an England victory, he took 5 wickets for 11 runs in Australia's second innings at Edgbaston, scored an unforgettable 118 at Old Trafford and took 10 wickets in the final game at the Oval. Botham was indisputably the Man of the Series, but after the season was over he still had the assault charge to face.

The case was heard at Grimsby Crown Court and opened on Monday 21 September before a jury of six men and six women and was presided over by Richard Hutchinson, who had been a circuit judge since 1974. Graham Richards appeared for the prosecution while Alan Rawley QC led the defence for Botham. As might be expected, both the incident and the subsequent case attracted a lot of publicity but at the end of the day the vital details of what happened in the early hours of 23 December remained in dispute, although the main course of events is clear.

After Botham left Tiffany's, he was standing outside talking to Neenan when Steven Isbister, a 19-year-old naval rating who had also been at Tiffany's, came up and offered Botham his autograph. Botham thought Isbister was seeking his autograph and when he realised that, as a joke, Isbister was offering his own autograph, Botham said he did not want it, to which Isbister replied that he did not want Botham's either. In his evidence Botham said that Isbister then called him a name and there were then 'a few words and shoves with Joe and Steven Isbister telling each other to get lost'. To continue with events as recalled by Botham, a fight then developed on the other side of the road between Isbister and Neenan and Botham went across to see what was going on. Botham dragged Neenan away and they were walking over to the minibus when he heard Isbister 'mouthing off' up the road. Isbister 'had a pretty full vocabulary of swear words' and Botham said he decided to find out what was the matter with Isbister and so set off after him, followed by Neenan. When he caught up with Isbister he said, 'Right, what the hell's this all about?' In his evidence Botham said that Isbister's reply was 'not very coherent', but that when Neenan joined them Isbister said, 'You can fuck off, you ginger headed bastard.' Botham then told Neenan that Isbister had had too much to drink and he turned to go, but the next thing he knew was that Neenan and Isbister were fighting again. Botham said that Isbister, who was bleeding from the lip, refused his offer of help and walked away. Botham added that 'at no time' did he kick Isbister.

Isbister, who was six feet two inches tall and weighed thirteen and a half stone, gave a rather different version of events. According to him, he tried to hide in an alley when he realised that Botham and Neenan were chasing him, but Botham caught him and said, 'Let's see how big you are now,' and punched him in the face. Isbister also said that when Neenan arrived on the scene he joined in and both he and Botham punched and kicked him in the face and all over his body. While Neenan had admitted, and been fined for, assaulting Isbister, he was adamant that Botham had nothing to do with the assault. On the other hand, Isbister's version was, as Botham conceded, supported by three witnesses but one of these admitted to having convictions for burglary and malicious wounding. Isbister also had a criminal record, having pleaded guilty to assaulting a fish and chip shop proprietor in 1980 and of causing criminal damage to a telephone box.

In his closing speech for the prosecution Richards said that there was no doubt that Isbister was an ill-behaved young man, who acted with scant regard for social custom or common manners. However, at the end of the day, the jury must be concerned with what actually happened in the alley and he maintained 'that Botham ran down the road to teach Isbister a lesson'. For the defence Rawley described the allegations 'as a load of codswallop from a parcel of rogues'. After the jury had been out for three hours the judge intimated that he would accept a majority verdict of ten to two, but after a further hour and three quarters the jury returned to say that there was no prospect even of such a verdict within the reasonably near future. This left the prosecution with the choice of seeking a re-trial or deciding to offer no further evidence. Richards stated that he had 'very grave doubts of the ability to find a fresh jury in England that would not be influenced in some part by media coverage' and that he was satisfied a fair trial would not result. The judge said he entirely approved of the prosecution's decision, but did not agree that the matter should 'lie on the file' and said that Botham must be entitled to a verdict of not guilty and that is what he was given. *The Daily Telegraph* ended its account of the case with the comments of Botham's parents. Mrs Marie Botham said: 'There's nothing to celebrate. We knew all along there was nothing to worry about.' As for Isbister, Botham's father had no hard feelings, after all, Leslie Botham said: 'He's just a nonentity.'

Botham's second appearance in court for assault could hardly have taken place further away from his first, as the venue was Perth, Western Australia. After his acquittal at Grimsby in 1981, Botham's life, both on and off the field, continued its exciting and controversial course, each year certainly bringing at least one 'fresh set of dramas'. Apart from various controversies in which he was involved and some sensational, but unsubstantiated, allegations made against him, Botham was fined for a variety of offences both by the courts and by various cricket authorities. The fines included one of £200[6] imposed in March 1988 by the Victorian Umpires' Association for offensive language during a Sheffield Shield game. In July 1987 Botham had signed to play for Queensland for three years, but his troubles in Australia did not end with this fine and his contract to play for Queensland was not to run its full course.

On Tuesday 15 March 1988 the Queensland team flew to Perth on Ansett Flight 55 to play Western Australia in the final of the Sheffield Shield competition, a game which in

---

[6] The approximate sterling equivalents of Australian and West Indian currency are sometimes shown.

fact Queensland lost. During the four-hour flight Botham's voice had been loud and his language colourful and shortly before the plane reached Perth he got into an argument with the Queensland and Australian captain Allan Border. Another passenger, Alan Winter, who was sitting immediately in front of Botham, turned around and said, 'Come on, fella, keep it down. It's becoming a bit common in here.' Botham's response was to abuse Winter and tell him it was none of his business. He then grabbed Winter by the scalp and hair and shook his head forcefully from side to side. Botham then told another passenger to keep his eyes to the front or he would be next and also abused a woman passenger, to whom he later apologised.

Botham was charged with offensive behaviour and assault against Winter and on 22 March appeared in the Perth Court of Petty Sessions, where he pleaded guilty to both charges. The magistrate, Peter Michelides, told Botham that fame did not give him a licence to misbehave and indeed, because he was in the public eye, he had a duty to show more restraint. On the two offences Botham was fined a total of £320 and ordered to pay £35 costs. A charge against Botham of assaulting another passenger was withdrawn, but a charge of offensive behaviour brought against one of Botham's team-mates, Greg Ritchie the former Test batsman, was adjourned for seven months as Ritchie pleaded not guilty.

The matter having been dealt with by the courts, it then fell to be considered by the Australian Cricket Board, together with an incident in which Botham and Dennis Lillee, the former Australian fast bowler, were alleged to have caused about £400 worth of damage to a dressing room at Launceston, Tasmania, on 28 February. The Board fined Botham £1,250 for the assault on the plane and fined him and Lillee £750 each for the dressing-room incident, but for Botham this was still not the end of the road. His conduct was then investigated by the Queensland Cricket Association Executive, which considered that he had not complied with the provisions of his contract with the Association and therefore decided to terminate it. Botham's career as a Queensland player thus came to an abrupt and inglorious end. By the time this last decision was made, however, Botham was thousands of miles away in the south of France preparing to retrace Hannibal's footsteps in a 500-mile walk in aid of the Leukaemia Research Fund and was reported as saying that 'he couldn't give a stuff about what's happening 12,000 miles away'.

While Botham was trudging towards Turin, the West Indies and Pakistan were starting an exciting three-match Test series in the West Indies. The Pakistanis were led by Imran Khan, who had yielded to immense pressure to lead the side having previously announced his retirement from Test cricket. Pakistan easily won the first Test, when the West Indies were without Vivian Richards and Malcolm Marshall. The second game was a match of fluctuating fortunes and eventually it was Pakistan who held out for a draw, the leg-spin and googly bowler, Abdul Qadir, surviving the last five balls of the match. The final Test at Bridgetown, Barbados, was another exciting game and, after being three runs behind on the first innings, West Indies were set 266 to win. When they lost their seventh wicket still needing 86 runs, Pakistan must have been favourites and they still appeared to be in the driving seat when, with 59 needed, the eighth wicket fell and Winston Benjamin came in to join the not-out batsman, Jeffrey Dujon.

As the West Indies score gradually mounted, some of the Pakistan side found it difficult to keep their heads as several appeals were rejected, including two in the same over from Qadir, a world-class bowler with a mercurial temperament. At the end of that over Qadir snatched his cap from the umpire and stalked off to long leg, where he was fielding. On the boundary he was jeered by the spectators, in particular by Albert Auguste, a 21-year-old car washer, who suggested to Qadir that he should try and get a wicket fairly. This was too much for the already irate Qadir, who vaulted the boundary board and started punching Auguste, until the twelfth man, Haafiz Shahid, came and led Qadir away.

Auguste was examined by Doctor Rudi Webster, who sent him for an X-ray examination in case he had a fractured rib or hand. Webster himself had been a first-class cricketer, appearing as a fast medium bowler in the 1960s for Scotland, Warwickshire and Otago and in 1961 he had the distinction of taking 11 wickets for 100 runs on his first-class debut, including a wicket with his first ball. To return to 1988, Qadir's assault on Auguste had the effect of holding up the Test for about five minutes and when play was resumed Dujon and Benjamin saw the West Indies home to a two-wicket victory, Benjamin twice hitting Qadir for six and clinching the issue with a straight drive for four.

After the game Qadir was ordered to appear in the local magistrates' court, but before doing so he attended a meeting with Auguste, Intikhab Alam the Pakistani manager and two members of the West Indies Cricket Board of Control, where Qadir apologised to Auguste, who is also believed to have been paid about £600 by way of compensation. Consequently, when Qadir appeared in court and pleaded not guilty to a charge of unlawful beating, Auguste declined to give evidence and the case was dismissed. A day or two later in London, Qadir expressed his regret for hitting Auguste, something he admitted that 'should not have happened, no matter how severe the provocation from the crowd'. This was the last of a series of unsavoury incidents from which the image of cricket suffered throughout the world in the 1987–88 season but, as this chapter has shown, assaults by cricketers, both on and off the field, have been taking place almost as long as the game has been played.

XIII

MISBEHAVIOUR AT THE MATCH

Early troubles

Cases arising from bad behaviour at cricket matches are, like cricket-related cases of assault, not a recent phenomenon, although they have become more common in the last twenty years. Indeed the distinction between the two categories of cases is somewhat arbitrary as certain cases in each chapter could properly be included in the other. One of these is a case which was heard almost two hundred years ago and involved both riot and battery, but of which very few details are known. Such details as there are appear, not in an account of the case itself, of which none seems to have survived, but in connection with a petition relating to the fines imposed. Volume XVI of *Sussex Notes and Queries* records a note in the *Calendar of Treasury Books* for 6 June 1693, which refers to a petition to the Queen of Thomas Reynolds, Henry Gunter and Elenor (sic) Lansford seeking remission of the fines imposed on them for riot and battery committed against Ralph Thurston in Sussex, 'they being only spectators at a game of crickett'. There is no indication of the nature or location of the riot, but it is interesting to note that the petition was addressed to Queen Mary alone and not to King William as well.

Forty years on, even on a weekday, the mere playing of cricket was regarded as misbehaviour, as in April 1733 some 'loose idle and disorderly persons' at Moorfields were presented by the Grand Jury for Middlesex Sessions for 'behaving themselves in a very loose idle and disorderly manner by playing at crickett', such conduct, in the view of the Grand Jury, tending 'very much to the depravation and corruption of youth and good manners'. Some fifty years later, although apparently no case was involved, *The Times* reported trouble in White Conduit Fields, Islington. The item in question, which appeared on 22 June 1785, reads:

It is recommended that the Lordling Cricketters who amuse themselves in White Conduit Fields, to procure an Act of Parliament for inclosing their play ground, which will not only prevent their being incommoded, but protect themselves from a repetition of the severe rebuke which they justly merit and received on Saturday evening from some spirited citizens whom they injured and attempted vi et armii to drive from the footpath, pretending it was within their bounds.

The cricketers who patronised White Conduit Fields were, as the extract indicates, aristocrats and in some cases titled. However, they did not take *The Times*' advice and obtain the passing of an Act of Parliament but, at the suggestion of the Earl of Winchilsea, solved their problem by moving in 1787 from the public ground at Islington to a private one, of which Thomas Lord had taken a lease from the Portman family, in what is now Dorset Square. Thus the White Conduit Cricket Club was the precursor of the Marylebone Cricket Club, which is generally regarded as having been founded in 1787.

The conduct of cricketers continued to attract criticism and more than a hundred years after the Middlesex Grand Jury had made known its views on the corrupting effect of cricket on the young, a similar opinion was expressed by a resident of my home town, East Grinstead. Thomas Cramp was the founder of the Temperance Society in East Grinstead, having in 1837 given up not only alcoholic drinks but also tea and coffee, so that water was his only beverage. For many years he kept a diary and on Monday 22 August 1842 he wrote:

A cricket match with East Grinstead and Lingfield in the Chequer Mead. A great number of persons present. At about 3 o'clock a heavy thunderstorm stopped the play. They are now (10 p.m.) singing and rioting at the Crown. Such are the usual endings of cricket matches. They have led many a young man astray and brought him to ruin.

Disturbance at Sydney

As mentioned in connection with the Pooley assault case, it

was only some time after they were played that the first two Test matches came to be recognised as such. The same can be said of the third Test, which was played at Melbourne on 2, 3 and 4 January 1879. The 1880 *Wisden* entitles its account of the game, 'Lord Harris's Eleven v. The Australian Eleven', although the account of the game itself refers to 'England'. In fact there should have been two representative matches on this tour, but the return match was cancelled after what *Wisden* calls 'the disturbance' at Sydney during a game against New South Wales.

The team which Lord Harris took to Australia in 1878–9 consisted of eleven amateurs and two professionals, George Ulyett and Tom Emmett, who were included to strengthen the bowling. Also a member of the side was A. N. ('Monkey') Hornby, the diminutive but tough Lancashire batsman, later immortalised in Francis Thompson's poem, who played for England three times at cricket and nine times at rugby, captaining his country at both games.

Lord Harris's side played thirteen matches, of which eight were against odds, and six games were won, three lost including the Test and four drawn. In late January the tourists played a game on level terms against New South Wales and were beaten by five wickets and, after decisively beating eighteen of Bathurst, a return match against New South Wales was played at the Association Ground at Sydney starting on Friday 7 February 1879. The umpires in this match were Edmund Barton, who was later knighted and from 1901 to 1903 was the first prime minister of the Australian Commonwealth, and George Coulthard, a 22-year-old Victorian, who was accompanying Harris's team as an umpire and had stood in the Test at Melbourne.

Lord Harris won the toss and his side batted first and were all out for 267, after at one stage being 217 for two. *The Australasian* newspaper's description of the fall of the third English wicket is worth quoting: 'Ulyett hit a ball from Spofforth towards the pavilion enclosure; Evans running at full speed made a kangaroo-like bound at the flying leather, and secured it with one hand.'[1] New South Wales were dismissed

---

[1] F. R. Spofforth ('the Demon') who had taken 13 wickets for 110 runs in the Test and Edwin Evans a right-arm spin bowler who played six times for Australia.

for 177, W. L. Murdoch carrying his bat for 82 not out and Emmett taking 8 for 47. At about four o'clock on the Saturday afternoon New South Wales followed on and Murdoch and A. C. Bannerman had put on 19 when, to quote *Wisden*, 'an appeal to Coulthard, the umpire, resulted in Murdoch being run out, then arose The Disturbance'.

The disturbance or the Sydney riot, as it is more usually called, is described at length in contemporary Australian newspapers, in the 1880 *Wisden* and in various histories of Australian cricket. *The Sydney Morning Herald* summarises its fuller account in its sporting columns with a shorter version in the 'News of the Day' section. The relevant part of this reads:

> . . . demonstrations of disapproval, originating in the pavilion, culminated in hundreds of roughs and larrikins rushing the ground. Lord Harris was assaulted, and other members of the English team were hustled about in a most cowardly manner. Eventually the visiting team, assisted by the police and a number of gentlemen from the grand stand and pavilion, managed to get back to the pavilion. The man who struck the captain of the English team was at once seized by Mr. Hornby, and despite the frantic efforts of the mob to rescue him, was brought into the pavilion and afterwards released on giving his name and address. Attempts were afterwards made to continue the match, but as the English eleven declined to allow a substitute for Coulthard, the mob obstinately refused to leave the ground and it was arranged that the contest should be resumed today, . . .

In its fuller account the *Herald* said:

> It is a significant fact the hooting and groaning proceeded first of all from about a dozen persons in the pavilion, some of whom, at all events, were known to be pecuniarily interested in the result of the match. One well-known betting man himself acted as fugleman, and the crowd outside, encouraged by this bad example, worked themselves into a state of violent excitement, and presently broke through all the bounds of decency and fair play.

Kerry Packer and Tony Greig

Adrian Murell and All Sport.

The captains, Tony Greig and Ian Chappell, inspect the damaged wicket at Headingley on 19th August 1975.

Press Association

George and Rosemary Davis leaving Waterloo Station on 11th May 1976 after Davis had been released from prison.

The Times

Boycott supporters, Sid
Fielden and Reg Kirk
(arms aloft), celebrate
victory after the Yorkshire
C.C.C. meeting held at
Harrogate on 21st
January 1984.

Yorkshire Post

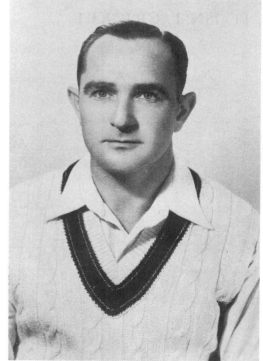

Sidney Barnes, cricketer,
turnstile hurdler and
litigant.

Thorsons Publishing Group

'Strewth Marge! You sat next to Ian Botham on the plane and you didn't get his autograph?'

Mac's comment in the Daily Mail on Ian Botham's journey to Perth in March 1988.

Daily Mail

Michael Angelow celebrates England passing 400 in their second innings of the Lord's Test against Australia in 1975.

Sport & General

Nets erected by Water Orton Cricket Club to protect
Eric Orme's bungalow.

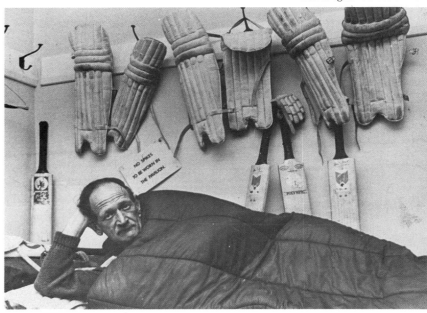

Michael Rowley beds down in Stourbridge Cricket Club's pavilion.

Protective netting erected by Lintz Cricket Club to protect houses built on land adjoining the ground. The Millers' house is the left-hand one.

Allan Glenwright

John and Brenda Miller in their garden.

Allan Glenwright

Arthur Coningham who was involved in a sensational divorce case in Australia in 1900–01.
Jack Pollard and Angus & Robertson

Francis Henry Bateman Champain playing a straight bat in about 1899.

To an extent this is supported by the Reverend Vernon Royle, the brilliant Lancashire cover-point who was one of Harris's team. Writing of the riot in his diary of the tour,[2] Royle says: 'It was a most disgraceful affair & took its origin from the sons of the "better" class in the pavilion.'

No further play having been possible after the riot on the Saturday, the game was resumed on the Monday on a difficult wicket which had been affected by rain on the Sunday. The remaining New South Wales wickets added only another 30 runs and the England XI thus won by an innings and 41 runs, Emmett finishing with a match analysis of thirteen for 68. Even more remarkably Ulyett, who took four for 13 in New South Wales' second innings, took his wickets with four consecutive balls, although the 1880 *Wisden* wrongly attributes one of his wickets to Emmett. Also, this match is the only one throughout the tour for which *Wisden* names the umpire and it is perhaps unfortunate, in view of what happened, that it does not restrict itself to giving their names as it adds 'for N.S.W.' in the case of Barton and 'for England' in the case of Coulthard.

Some two weeks after the riot two of the larrikins, William Rigney and John Richards, appeared at Water Police Court charged with having participated in the disorder. Rigney and Richards, one of whom was the man who had hit Lord Harris and been grabbed and taken to the pavilion by Hornby, pleaded guilty and expressed their regret for what had happened. They were both fined £2 and ordered to pay £1 6s. costs and were told that it was only because of their 'rather tardy contrition' and good characters that they were not being sent to prison for seven days. It was also stated in court that inmates of the pavilion who had initiated the disturbance, including a well-known Victorian bookmaker, had had their membership subscriptions of £1 11s. 6d. returned to them and that they would never again be admitted to the ground. Finally, the magistrate referred to the hospitable treatment which Australian cricketers received in England and expressed his regret that Lord Harris and his team should have encountered such a disagreeable experience in Sydney.

[2] *Diary of the Reverend Vernon Royle, Australia 1878–1879.* A photocopy is held in the library at Lord's, but the diary does not appear in Padwick's *A Bibliography of Cricket.*

There was a strange postscript to Coulthard's umpiring career. Having stood in the Test at Melbourne in 1879, he played for Australia at Sydney in the second Test in the 1881–2 series, thus becoming the first and perhaps the only person to umpire in a Test match before playing in one. Played as a bowler, Coulthard batted at number eleven and scored six not out in his only innings, but his captain did not ask him to bowl. Who was Australia's captain? William Lloyd Murdoch, whom two years earlier Coulthard had adjudged run out on the same ground. A year after his sole Test appearance, and still under 30, Coulthard died of consumption.

Since 1879 there have been many disturbances, or worse, at cricket matches, especially Test matches and one-day internationals. In his book *The Wildest Tests*, which was published in 1972, Ray Robinson describes some of the games that have been worst affected. Most of the Tests in question took place in the West Indies, India or Pakistan and although spectators were guilty, among other things of bottle throwing, arson and invading the playing area to damage the wicket, I do not know in which instances, if any, the offenders were prosecuted. If there were any such prosecutions, the charges would probably have been in respect of public order offences and dealt with in magistrates' courts or their local equivalent.

The flasher and the streakers

In his book, Robinson includes two Tests which took place in Australia, the Adelaide Test in 1933, when W. A. ('Bert') Oldfield was hit by a ball from Harold Larwood, and the Test against England played at Sydney in February 1971. The latter game was in fact the seventh Test of the series, as an extra game had been added when the third Test at Melbourne was completely washed out.

In 1970–71 England were captained by Raymond Illingworth and his side came to the final Test one up but, as Australia held the Ashes, England had to avoid losing to regain the Ashes. It was to prove an eventful match. England were dismissed for 184 in their first innings and during Australia's reply Terry Jenner was hit on the head by a ball from John Snow, who was thereupon warned by umpire Lou Rowan about the persistent bowling of bumpers. This led to protests by Snow and

Illingworth, who disagreed with Rowan's interpretation of the laws of the game. Their reaction upset an already tense and partisan crowd, some of whom started throwing cans and bottles on to the ground. This resulted in Illingworth leading his side off the field as he said that he had a duty to safeguard his players. However, they returned after the ground had been cleared and Illingworth had been warned that he risked the match being awarded to Australia if England did not come back on to the field.

Australia had a first innings lead of 80 runs and in England's second innings John Edrich and Brian Luckhurst made a good start, putting on 94 for the first wicket. Not long before he was out for 57, Edrich complained to umpire Tom Brooks, the former New South Wales bowler, that a mirror was being flashed in his eyes. Brooks stopped play and ran to the sight screen to tell the police of Edrich's complaint. They located a young man who was reflecting the sunlight on what appeared to be a lunch tin, and arrested him, but I do not know whether or not he was subsequently charged.

Proceedings were, however, taken against some of the can and bottle throwers. At the Central Court in Sydney eleven men were fined amounts varying from A.$20 to A.$100 and two others were remanded. One of the cans was reported as having hit a policeman on the head, while one of those fined maintained that he had thrown his can, not before the Englishmen left the field, but in protest at them doing so.

Australia regained the Ashes in 1974–5 and the following summer in England they won the first Test of a four-match series by an innings. The second, which was eventually drawn, was played at Lord's in very hot weather. On the fourth day, towards the end of England's second innings in which John Edrich scored 175, the proceedings were suddenly enlivened by the appearance of a stark naked young man, who ran across the ground vaulting both sets of stumps en route. In fact that description is not quite accurate, as he kept his shoes and socks on for the run.

The man in question was Michael Angelow, a 24-year-old ship's cook from St Albans, who had done the streak for a £20 bet. On the following day, Tuesday 5 August, at Marylebone Magistrates' Court the magistrate, Colonel William Haswell said:

'The court will have that £20' and deprived Angelow of it by fining him £20. After the case Angelow, who admitted he had drunk a lot of lager and 'wouldn't have passed a breath test', set off back to Lord's for what remained of the last day's play. An official at Lord's was quoted as saying: 'I can not see how we could keep him out, even if we wanted to. I doubt whether we would recognise him with his clothes on.'

While there was a certain style and originality about Angelow's streak the same can not be said of most of his imitators, either in England or overseas. In December 1975 an invader at Perth staged an encore during the Test against the West Indies and in 1984 Lord's was again the venue of another such exhibition when on 2 July, the fourth day of the Test against the West Indies, two members of the staff of The Cricketers Hotel at Bagshot ran onto the field naked and were each fined £50 for insulting behaviour. More worthwhile, both from the spectators' point of view and from her's, was the appearance on the second day of the 1986 Lord's Test against India of Ashley Summers, a 22-year-old model, wearing only a pair of satin knickers and waving her skirt, which bore the legend 'Bring back Botham', the Somerset cricketer at the time having been suspended by the TCCB from first-class cricket for nine weeks. Miss Summers won some of the loudest cheers of the day and appeared on the following day, appropriately undressed, on page three of *The Sun* newspaper, where she was reported as saying: 'Even the policeman who took me away said it was a shame to cover up such a lovely body.' In any event she was not charged: sex discrimination, perhaps!

The disappearing bails

While streaking is one of the more ostentatious ways of disrupting a cricket match, removing the bails is one of the most discreet. Twice in the 1980s a Test match was interrupted in this way. The first occasion was during the Old Trafford Test against Australia in 1981, which England won by 103 runs thus retaining the Ashes by going three-one up in the series.

In this match England batted first and were out for 231, but Australia collapsed in their first innings and England had a first innings lead of 101. England's second innings, in which they scored 404, was dominated by Botham's 118, to which reference is made elsewhere, and Australia were thus set 506 to win, a score only exceeded once in the fourth innings of a Test and that in South Africa in 1938–9, when England scored 654 for five and although the Test was meant to be 'timeless' it had to be left drawn so that the English team could catch the boat home. In fact, although Australia lost the Old Trafford Test, they did well to score 402, both Graham Yallop and Allan Border scoring centuries. It was while these two were batting on the fourth day of the match, Sunday 16 August, that the interruption occurred.

As England's captain Mike Brearley describes in his book *Phoenix from the Ashes*, 'two sinister-looking men in shirt-sleeves walked deliberately up to the stumps. We all watched in amazement as they quietly picked off the bails, turned, and walked back unhurriedly the way they came.' One of the men then neatly side-stepped a policeman on his way back to the stand. The two men were 25-year-old David Considine and 21-year-old Joseph Daly, who had gone to the match with a friend who had bet them £5 that they would not dare to go on to the pitch and grab a bail. They won their bet, but were fined £40 each with £5 costs after admitting to being drunk and disorderly, a charge they would have found it difficult to deny as Daly said that between the three of them they had consumed a bottle of whisky, two bottles of wine and two bottles of cider.

The background to the removal of the bails in the other 1980s Test was somewhat different. The incident occurred in July 1986 during the Edgbaston Test against India, a series which has already qualified for a mention in the immediately preceding section of this chapter. At Edgbaston the reason for taking the bails was not surreptitiously to win a bet but demonstrably to protest about the proposed deportation from Britain of a 25-year-old Jamaican called Metso Moncrieff.

Pervais Khan, who was aged twenty-four, and Joanna Duchesne, who was seventeen, ran on to the ground, staged a demonstration in mid-pitch and stopped play. Khan unfurled a banner saying: 'Metso Must Stay – No Deportation', while Miss Duchesne removed one of the sets of bails and stuffed them down her trousers, whence they were subsequently re-coverd by a policewoman. On 8 September Khan and Miss Duchesne appeared before the Birmingham magistrates at the

Victoria Law Courts, while outside Workers Against Racism staged a demonstration in support of the pair. In court the police failed to produce any witnesses in support of charges of using threatening words and behaviour and the prosecution therefore offered no evidence and the cases against Khan and Miss Duchesne were dismissed. Whether Metso Moncrieff was allowed to stay in Britain, I do not know.

Pitch invasions

Usually when the pitch is invaded by demonstrators, hooligans or larrikins – as they were called at Sydney in 1879 – the players suffer nothing more than irritation and, if battling, a break in concentration. Unfortunately, at Perth on 13 November 1982, Terry Alderman, the Australian fast bowler, sustained an injury which put him out of cricket for the rest of the season. The incident occurred towards the end of the second day of the drawn first Test when England, who had been put in by Australia, reached a total of 400. This was the pretext for about thirty young England 'supporters' to invade the pitch.

One of these was Gary Donnison, a 19-year-old machinist from the Perth suburb of Gosnells, who before emigrating some twelve years earlier had lived in York. One of the invading youths made an unfriendly approach to Alderman, who pushed him away, but shortly afterwards Alderman was thumped on the back of the head by one of the other youths, who turned out to be Donnison. As there were no police nearby, Alderman, assisted by his fellow fast bowler Dennis Lillee, chased Donnison to try and apprehend him. Alderman caught up with Donnison and brought him down with a rugby tackle but dislocated his shoulder in doing so. As Alderman said afterwards, it was sickening to be injured like that and ruled out of the Tests and he would have second thoughts about chasing an intruder again, 'but it was an instinctive thing to do'.

Detective Sergeant Graeme Lienert then arrested Donnison and asked him why he had hit Alderman. Sergeant Lienert alleged that Donnison replied: 'I hit him. I was excited. I didn't mean to hurt him. I just ran out for a stir. I gave him a cheeky hit across the head.' Donnison was charged with disorderly conduct and assault and appeared at Perth Magistrates' Court on 23 February when he pleaded not guilty. Alderman, Lillee and Sergeant Lienert all gave evidence for the prosecution, while Donnison maintained that he had not hit Alderman but merely tried to flick off his hat, although he did admit to having drunk a lot of beer. The magistrate, Con Zempilas, reserved his decision until the following Monday, 28 February, when he said that he did not believe Donnison's evidence whereas Alderman and Lillee impressed him as 'most reliable and credible witnesses'. He found Donnison guilty and fined him A.$500 (about £320) on the charge of disorderly conduct and gave him a year's probation with an order to complete two hundred hours of community service on the assault charge. This involved Donnison in performing such tasks as chopping wood and sweeping pensioners' gardens and would, as the magistrate put it, enable him to atone for his anti-social conduct.

The next case was another where, like the George Davis and the Metso Moncrieff cases, a Test was disrupted by people demonstrating about something which had nothing to do with cricket. The first day of Sri Lanka's first ever Test in this country, which appropriately was played at Lord's, was 23 August 1984, and nine Tamils saw this as an opportunity to demonstrate for a separate Tamil state. They accordingly disrupted the game for a short time by invading the pitch. On the following day at Marylebone Magistrates' Court they admitted behaviour likely to cause a breach of the peace and were bound over in the sum of £100 each to keep the peace for a year. The demonstration certainly did not unsettle the Sri Lankans, who scored 491 for 7 declared in their first innings and generally had the better of a drawn game in which their performance and approach to the game won them many friends.

Unfortunately, as mentioned earlier, bad behaviour by spectators has recently become more common and the last decade contains several further examples of it. As such incidents became more common they were reported less fully and anyhow a catalogue of exhibitionists disrupting games or otherwise misbehaving and subsequently being punished in the magistrates' courts would not make interesting reading. Among the matches which suffered in this way were the 1985 Old Trafford Test against Australia, the 1986 Benson and Hedges Cup Final between Middlesex and Kent at Lord's and a 1987 one-day international between England and Pakistan where Perth again saw a pitch invasion by hooligans, the majority of whom were described by the police as being 'definitely English'.

Inevitably such behaviour led eventually to someone being badly hurt and this happened during the third one-day international match against Pakistan at Edgbaston on 25 May 1987. England won the match by one wicket and took the Texaco Trophy by two matches to one and, as *Wisden* said, it was particularly sad that 'marvellous cricket was marred by ugly scenes . . . provoked by racial pride, racial prejudice and alcohol'. During the match police were called in to separate rival supporters who were fighting on the terraces and sixteen arrests were made. One spectator, Mohammed Riaz, suffered a severed jugular vein and wind-pipe injury when he was hit by a jagged missile thrown into the crowd. His life was probably saved by WPC Teresa Sharples, who held the wound together with her hands until an ambulance arrived.

Although WPC Sharples probably did not know it, in saving Riaz's life in this way she was emulating a similar feat by W. G. Grace exactly one hundred years earlier. In 1887, when fielding for Gloucestershire against Lancashire, Arthur Croome impaled himself on a spiked railing trying to save a boundary. Then, as A. A. Thomson relates in his life of Grace:

> W. G. held the jagged edges of the wound together. It was a matter of life and death that the injured parts should be kept perfectly still and the Doctor's hand never shook for one instant. He literally held the victim's life in his hand for nearly half an hour and such a feat would only have been possible to a man of his iron nerve and fantastic stamina.

Since the injury to Riaz in May 1987 matters seem to have improved in the light of firmer action by the police and the cricket authorities, but it is sad that threats, restrictions and restraints are necessary to ensure the good behaviour of a small minority of spectators at important matches.

XIV

BOTHAM AGAIN

The three years 1984, 1985 and 1986 were ones in which, judged even by his own high standards, Ian Botham provided a lot of copy for the popular press. During this period he was concerned in at least four court cases, although he was a party in only two of them. In February 1984 Botham made an uncomplimentary joke about Pakistan, saying it was an ideal place to send your mother-in-law on holiday, for which he was subsequently fined by the Test and County Cricket Board, but it was in March that the storm really broke.

On Sunday 11 March Botham returned to England and was greeted by an article in *The Mail on Sunday* headed: 'Botham named in drugs sensation'. The article alleged that while on tour in New Zealand the previous winter Botham had smoked, possessed and supplied prohibited drugs. The following day Botham saw his solicitor Alan Herd of Watts, Vallance and Vallance and on Wednesday 14 March it was announced that a writ had been issued against *The Mail on Sunday* and its editor Stewart Steven for what Herd described as 'a most serious libel'. *The Mail on Sunday* said that it would defend the action and, undeterred, on 8 April printed another article alleging that Botham had offered marijuana to two girls who had gone to his hotel room in New Zealand. On the following day writs for libel were issued against *The Mail on Sunday* and its editor in respect of the second article.

This second week in April was a particularly busy one for Botham and Herd as, two days after issuing the second batch of writs on Botham's behalf, Herd was defending his client in Whitminster Magistrates' Court for driving at 100 m.p.h. on the M5 near Cheltenham. Botham, who was driving his Saab endorsed with advertisements, pleaded guilty and was fined £100 and banned from driving for four weeks, in spite of a plea that the loss of his licence would cause difficulties in his testimonial year. On Friday of the same week Botham was fined £1,000 by the TCCB for his remarks about Pakistan.

The 1984 cricket season, in which he captained Somerset, was the year of the West Indies' 'blackwash' of England and a rather poor one for Botham personally, but during the season he did complete 4,000 runs and 300 wickets in Test cricket. For the Botham family, however, 1984 had a sting in the tail. On New Year's Eve Botham's wife, Kathy, was in the kitchen preparing for a small family party when four policemen arrived at the door. They stated that a small packet of drugs had been found in the pocket of some trousers of Botham's, which his wife had taken to the cleaners, and asked to search the house for which, in any event, they had a warrant. During the search the police found a bank bag containing cannabis in a drawer in the Bothams' bedroom and, when asked by the police about it, Botham said that someone had given it to him two or three years previously and he had forgotten all about it. On analysis the substance was found to contain 2.19 grammes of cannabis, valued at £4. Botham was charged with possessing cannabis and appeared at Scunthorpe Magistrates' Court on 14 February 1985. He pleaded guilty and was fined £100, with £25 costs. Mrs Botham had originally been arrested with her husband but, as Herd pointed out in court, although she was not subsequently charged, she suffered a great deal on account of all the attention from the media and the distress and disruption to her family's life which that entailed.

The year 1985 was a season of spectacular personal success for Botham, especially for Somerset for whom he scored 5 hundreds and finished with a batting average of over 100. However, Somerset finished bottom of the Championship table, winning only one match and that when Botham was not playing. In early October Botham resigned as captain and Peter Roebuck was appointed in his place. Later in the same month Botham started on his 870-mile walk from John O'Groats to Lands End which, while itself not without incident, raised £880,000 for the Leukaemia Research Fund. In the winter of 1985–6 Botham was an unsuccessful member of David Gower's unsuccessful side touring the West Indies, where England suffered another 'blackwash'. On 6 April 1986, between the fourth and fifth Tests, the *News of the World* published a sensational article describing a 'Botham cocaine and sex scandal' which, among other things, alleged that Botham and Lindy Field, an ex-Miss Barbados, had 'snorted' cocaine together and had made love several times, on one occasion so vigorously that they had broken the bed on which they were performing. The article also referred to the 'drug incidents' in New Zealand, which had been the subject of *The Mail on Sunday*'s article two years earlier. Botham's solicitor forthwith issued a writ for libel against News Group Newspapers, the publishers of the *News of the World*. On 10 April the *News of the World* intimated that it intended to publish a further article on 13 April containing more allegations about the use of drugs on the 1984 tour of New Zealand. This resulted in the Attorney General applying for and being granted an injunction by Mr Justice Leggatt 'restraining News Group Newspapers Limited, as publishers of the *News of the World*, from publishing any narrative allegations covering substantially the same ground as the allegations contained in *The Mail on Sunday* articles of 11th March and 8th April 1984.'

It may be wondered why the Attorney General should intervene in a dispute between two newspapers and a private citizen, where the latter was suing the papers for libel and the papers were proposing to defend the actions on the ground of justification. The answer is that there is a common law rule, known as 'the strict liability rule', which says that, regardless of intent, conduct which might interfere with legal proceedings constitutes a criminal contempt of court. This rule conflicted with the rule in the 1891 case of *Bonnard* v. *Perryman*, which said that the court had a duty not to fetter the right of free speech in a case of libel where there was a plea of justification and the issue was also affected by the Contempt of Court Act 1981, which restricts the circumstances in which the strict liability rule applied.

Taking account of both the above rules and of the 1981 Act, Mr Justice Leggatt considered that, as Botham was a public figure, an average juryman in the case between Botham and *The Mail on Sunday* would be likely to remember what he had read in the *News of the World* and that if he did, there was a substantial risk of him being severely prejudiced by what he had read, although the trial was not due to come on before March 1987 at the earliest. News Group Newspapers at once appealed against Sir Andrew Leggatt's decision and, on 16 and 17 April, the appeals were heard by the Master of the Rolls, Sir John Donaldson, sitting with Sir Roger Parker and Sir George Waller. At the conclusion of a two-day hearing, the Master of the Rolls announced that the appeal would be allowed for reasons to be given later. On 30 April, while Botham was playing against Derbyshire at Chesterfield, the Court of Appeal gave its reasons.

The main judgment was given by Sir John Donaldson who started with the words: 'In this appeal we have been called upon to consider the interaction of two fundamental freedoms – the right to free speech and the right to an unprejudiced trial by jury.' He went on to review the rule in *Bonnard* v. *Perryman*, the strict liability rule and the relevant parts of the Contempt of Court Act. With regard to the Act he said that the most relevant provision was contained in part of section 2, which provided that the 'strict liability rule applies only to a publication which creates a substantial risk that the course of justice in the proceedings in question will be seriously impeded or prejudiced'. The Act, Sir John pointed out, provided a double test, namely that there must be a 'substantial' risk of the proceedings being 'seriously' prejudiced and, in his view, this provision and not the rule in *Bonnard* v. *Perryman* was the crux of the matter. He considered the proximity of the trial was a factor of great importance and that 'many wickets will have fallen' by the time it took place the following year. It was primarily on this ground that he and the other two judges concluded that it was not possible to say that the proposed article in the *News of the World* would present a substantial risk of the actions against *The Mail on Sunday* being seriously prejudiced, although such a time would come when the trial got nearer.

The *News of the World* took full advantage of the Court of Appeal's decision and on 20 April published an article, described as the 'Story they tried to ban' and which was spread over three pages. The article contained further allegations about Botham and ended by saying:

To-day's publication of our findings is made possible by a historic court victory. The Appeal Court overturned a ban on publication imposed following a plea by the Attorney-General. He wanted to gag the paper because a libel action by Botham against another newspaper is still pending.

Although the outcome of News Group Newspapers' appeal revolved round Botham's pending libel action against *The Mail on Sunday*, neither that paper nor Botham were parties to it and when the 1986 cricket season started, therefore, Botham's action against *The Mail on Sunday* was still pending. At about that time Botham and his wife were advised by Herd to settle the case as – win or lose – Botham would incur large legal fees and he and his family would come under the full glare of the media. The Bothams accepted Herd's advice and he negotiated a settlement with *The Mail on Sunday*, which involved both Botham and his wife writing articles for that paper. These appeared on 18 May 1986, two years and two months after the 'Botham named in drugs sensation' article had appeared.

The Mail on Sunday's headline on that day was 'Botham – I *did* take pot' and a long article under Botham's own by-line included the following passages:

> I did something then that I have regretted ever since because I have had to live with the consequences of that decision. I denied that I had ever smoked pot at any time in my life and started legal proceedings against *The Mail on Sunday* for what it had said about the New Zealand tour. I know that what I am now saying will shock many people, particularly those who have stood by me for so long. The fact is that I have, at various times in the past smoked pot. I had been with a group of people who had been doing it and I went along with it. On other occasions I have smoked simply in order to relax – to get off the sometimes fearful treadmill of being an international celebrity, trying to forget for a moment the pressures that were on me all the time.

and later on:

> *The Mail on Sunday* is not a paper which prints scandal for the sake of scandal. This does not, of course, mean that all Fleet Street reporting is of the same order. . . . I do

believe . . . that I should be protected from those journalists
who simply make up stories in order to get their salacious
headlines, hoping to sell more newspapers. I have, however,
decided that I am not going to bother suing everybody in
sight. Life is too short.

The article ended:

My ambition is to continue to represent my county and my
country. The new Ian Botham is determined to take on the
world and win!

The paper also contained a short and sensible article by
Mrs Botham, who said that she could not pretend that she
was 'thrilled to bits' about her husband's confession but was
proud of him for having been man enough to make it. She
also dismissed as 'laughable' the things that had recently been
written about Botham in other newspapers.

The Bothams hoped that disposing of the pending libel
actions would enable Botham to get on with the 1986 cricket
season with, as Mrs Botham put it, 'the slate wiped clean'. The
cricket authorities, however, did not view the revelations in the
same light and on 29 May Botham appeared before the Disci-
pline Committee of the TCCB. The official statement issued
after the meeting of that committee said:

I. T. Botham faced charges of bringing the game into disrepute
since becoming an England cricketer by: a) using cannabis; b)
admitting to using cannabis; c) denying in the past that he had
used cannabis; d) making public pronouncements without the
clearance of his county. Finding Botham guilty on charges b),
c) and d) the committee suspended him from all first class
cricket until and including 31st July.

On 4 August Botham celebrated his return to the first-class
game by hitting the Worcestershire bowlers for 104 not out in
64 minutes from 66 balls. Then, selected for the final Test
against New Zealand, he took a wicket with his first ball and
scored 59 not out, his first 50 coming from 32 balls, a record
for Test cricket in terms of balls received, where the number has

been recorded. Shortly before this amazing innings Botham had been one of thirty-five cricketers asked by the TCCB whether they would be available, if selected, for the forthcoming tour of Australia.

In making its approach, the TCCB had asked the possible tourists to sign letters undertaking that they would comply with restrictions imposed by the TCCB on players writing newspaper articles and otherwise being involved with the media. The terms of this undertaking would have prevented Botham from writing for *The Sun*, which he was contractually bound to do. On 20 August *The Sun* announced that it would sue the TCCB for inducing Botham to break a legitimate contract with it and that it would 'have great pleasure in suing the pants off the TCCB'. On 1 September Mr Justice Turner refused to order the issue of an injunction preventing the TCCB from imposing the restriction. *The Sun* said that it would consider making an appeal against Sir Michael Turner's decision but the following day announced that it would not be doing so. The TCCB's pants remained intact.

Botham was selected for the Australian tour and on Saturday 8 November, when he was playing against Western Australia at Perth, Somerset County Cricket Club held a special general meeting at Shepton Mallet to consider a resolution calling for the resignation of the committee, following the decision not to re-engage Vivian Richards and Joel Garner. The motion of no confidence was defeated by a majority of over two to one and, as was known at the time, when Richards and Garner were not re-engaged, Botham also left Somerset and, after a lot of speculation, joined Worcestershire. Thus three eventful years ended with Botham's litigation settled, his ban ended and with a new county to play for. On 1 January 1987 he celebrated the New Year by hitting 68 off 39 balls in a one-day international against Australia in which he was nominated as Man of the Match.

XV

A LIBELLED ELEVEN

In its editorial on 10 May 1963 *The Cricketer* commented: 'Research suggests that in the whole history of the game this [i.e. a cricketer bringing a successful action for libel] is a unique circumstance; it is surely not the first case where redress for defamation might have been sought.' *The Cricketer* ended its comment by saying that the whole character of cricket had been 'put in jeopardy by the tone of much modern writing and in taking the action he did Mr. May has done the game a most signal service'. That, since 1963, the tone of some reports has continued to leave something to be desired is evidenced by the half-dozen or more successful libel actions that have been brought since P. B. H. May 'opened the batting' in 1963.

Peter May
Peter May has often been described as perhaps the finest English batsman since the Second World War; certainly the name of a better one escapes me. Retiring from first-class cricket while still under 35, he scored over 27,000 runs at an average of over 50, including 85 hundreds, and played for England 66 times, 41 of them as captain. It was, however, the way in which he made his runs rather than their number which marked him out as a player of the highest class and Surrey's and England's success during the years that he played for them were in no small measure due to May's own contributions. In 1959–60 May captained England in the West Indies, but he became ill during the tour and his doctor ordered him home before it was over. He missed the 1960 season due to illness, returning to the England side against Australia in 1961, but after that season retired from Test cricket. He succeeded Stuart Surridge as captain of Surrey in 1957 and in 1962 the Surrey committee looked forward to him not having to miss county matches because he was playing for England.

E. M. Wellings, who was born some twenty years before May,

was an Oxford cricket blue who played for Surrey in 1931 as an off-break bowler and lower-order batsman. In his four appearances for the county he scored 33 runs and took only 2 wickets, but although he did not make his mark in county cricket he later became a well-known cricket writer. For many years he was cricket correspondent of the *Evening News* and also covered public school cricket for *Wisden*. He also wrote several books on cricket, of which the best is *Vintage Cricketers*. On 14 May 1962, less than a month after the start of the season, an article appeared in the *Evening News* by Wellings under the headline 'May and Surrey rumpus – Decision to miss more matches shocks county'. In the article Wellings stated that a difference of opinion had arisen between May and Surrey about the obligations of a county captain and that the county was 'deeply hurt by May's apparent off hand attitude to the captaincy'. Wellings went on to state that May had originally said that he would be available to play in most of Surrey's matches, but he had now let the committee know that 'he will not play in any away games and will turn out in only half the home matches'. The article went on to say that:

> far from becoming the asset anticipated this year May has turned himself into a liability. An absentee captain who disrupts the side by making occasional visits does not give the players a chance to settle down as a team. It is clear that May should either change his mind and play regularly or resign the captaincy.

May, who in fact appeared in seventeen of the county's twenty-eight championship matches, took exception to the article and decided to sue Wellings and Associated Newspapers, the publishers of the *Evening News*, for libel. On 1 April 1963 settlement of the action was announced. It was stated in court that the defendants recognised that there was no truth in the statements upon which the article had been based and that they had come to court to acknowledge that and had agreed to make a substantial payment to May by way of damages and to indemnify him against his legal costs. It was also stated that May intended to make a donation to the Surrey County Supporters Club of part of the sum which he received. For his part, it was stated that May accepted that Wellings had relied for his information on a source which he thought to be trustworthy but which had proved not to be so. Sincere apologies were expressed on behalf of Associated Newspapers and Wellings for the publication of hurtful and inaccurate statements concerning so distinguished a cricketer. Thus, like many libel cases, although the matter came to the court, no case was heard, the court merely acting as a forum for announcing the terms of settlement agreed between the parties and obtaining an order that the record of the case should be withdrawn.

Ossie Wheatley

O. S. ('Ossie') Wheatley won cricket blues at Cambridge as a fast bowler in 1957 and 1958, in the latter year taking 80 wickets, a record for a University season. While up at Cambridge Wheatley became a member of Hawks, the well-known social and sporting club, whose Oxford equivalent is Vincents. From 1957 to 1960 Wheatley played for Warwickshire, but in 1961 he moved to Glamorgan to take over the captaincy from the redoubtable Wilfred Wooller.

Tuesday 16 July 1963 was the last day of the University match and also the night on which the Hawks' annual dinner was held at Quaglino's Restaurant in London. On that day Glamorgan were playing Kent at Dover and, following a declaration by Glamorgan, Kent won the match with a quarter of an hour to spare. Wheatley was due to attend the Hawks' dinner but realised that he would arrive late unless he changed into his dinner jacket at Dover and went straight to Quaglino's. He therefore did this and arranged for the rest of his clothes to be sent with the Glamorgan team's luggage direct to Colchester, where Glamorgan were due to play Essex the next day. Wheatley left the dinner at about midnight, went to bed soon afterwards and left for Colchester early the next morning dressed in his dinner jacket. Well before the start of play and with only a few people on the ground, Wheatley tossed for innings with the Essex captain, Trevor Bailey, still wearing his dinner jacket and then went and changed into his cricket clothes.

The following day the account of the match in the *Daily Express* included the statement that the 'Glamorgan skipper Ossie Wheatley tossed up in evening dress at Colchester when arriving from an all-night London party'. The *Daily Sketch* went into the matter in more detail. In its gossip column under the heading 'He even won the toss', it said that the Hawks' dinner 'must have been quite a night' and implied that, although Quaglino's had survived intact, it had been too quiet an evening for Wheatley, who had gone on somewhere else after the dinner and then gone to Colchester still wearing his dinner jacket.

Wheatley objected to the articles which suggested that, instead of going to bed, he had attended an all-night party as he considered this suggestion was damaging to his reputation as a professional cricket captain. He therefore started an action for libel against the *Daily Sketch* and against Beaverbrook Newspapers, as proprietors of the *Daily Express*. As in May's case, the defendants did not dispute the libel in court where, on 31 July 1964, the terms of settlement were announced. Brian Neill for Wheatley explained the circumstances which resulted in his client tossing up dressed in his dinner jacket and said that Wheatley would have had no objection to this being reported, had the two papers confined themselves to the facts and not also made inaccurate and damaging statements and imputations. It was also stated in court that the defendants regretted that the articles were worded so as to convey the damaging imputations, which they accepted were untrue, and in the circumstances Wheatley was paid an appropriate sum by way of damages and to cover his legal costs.

The selectors

From 8 to 13 June 1967 England played India at Headingley. England batted first and at the end of a full first day's play were 281 for three, of which Geoffrey Boycott had scored 106 not out. On the second day England batted for another three and a half hours before declaring at 550 for four, Boycott then being 246 not out. In their first innings India scored 164 and following on made 510, but nevertheless England won by six wickets on the last day. Boycott's lack of enterprise did not meet with the approval of the English selectors, Douglas Insole, Alec Bedser, Don Kenyon, Peter May and, as England captain, Brian Close, and they dropped Boycott for the second Test. In his autobiography, written nearly twenty years later

Boycott describes this as 'the deepest wound in my professional life'. At the time his omission provoked a lot of controversy which was manifested, in particular, in an article by
Michael Parkinson in *The Sunday Times* of 25 June.

The article referred to the selectors dropping Boycott as
an act of 'priceless folly and stupidity' and said that Boycott's 'sin was that he scored 246 not out' while he was out
of form. Parkinson went on to say that Boycott had made
enemies 'particularly among that small but influential section
of administrators and cricket writers, whose first criteria in
assessing a cricketer is whether or not they would like him
to marry their daughter'. He ended by saying that what had
happened to Boycott was 'an unnecessary, hurtful and shaming
insult' and that 'the England selectors are a bunch of palsied
twits'.

While the selectors fully accepted that their choice of an
England side was a legitimate matter for criticism, they considered that Parkinson's article went too far, as it suggested
that in omitting Boycott they had been actuated by 'unworthy
and discreditable motives'. When the selectors' views were made
known to it, *The Sunday Times* published a disclaimer to the
effect that it was not the paper's contention that the selectors
were actuated by such motives, but it did not accept that
Parkinson's article conveyed that impression. This was not a
view which commended itself to the selectors and their legal
advisers and they decided to proceed with an action for libel
against Parkinson and Times Newspapers, as publishers of *The
Sunday Times*.

By the time the parties reached court on 25 July 1968,
The Sunday Times had changed its mind and come to recognise
that, after all, the article was capable of the construction put on
it by the selectors, although the defendants still maintained their
criticism of the dropping of Boycott. Through their counsel,
Brian Neill, QC, who four years earlier had represented Wheatley,
Parkinson and *The Sunday Times* apologised to the selectors for
the distress which the passages in question had caused them.
The selectors, whose object in bringing the action had been to
clear their names, did not seek any damages but were content
for the case to be settled on the basis of the defendants' apologies and the payment of their costs.

Ray Illingworth and Alan Knott

The 1970–71 series in which England, with Ray Illingworth as captain and Alan Knott as wicket-keeper, retained the Ashes was a difficult and controversial one for the England team. The final Test in particular saw a number of unpleasant incidents, some of which led to prosecutions and are described in the chapter entitled 'Misbehaviour at the Match'. The controversy was revived less than two months after the side's return to England by an article written by Denis Compton in the *Sunday Express* of 9 May 1971.

Throughout his playing career Compton, one of England's greatest cricketers, always played both cricket and football, at which he also excelled, in a most generous and sportsmanlike spirit and was clearly distressed that such a spirit did not seem to have prevailed in the England side during the 1970–71 series. Unfortunately, in making this point for the readers of the *Sunday Express*, Compton overstepped the mark. Under the headline 'Is cheating now a part of cricket?' Compton criticised certain aspects of some of the England players' behaviour and was especially critical of their showing open dissent with umpires' decisions. The article referred to Illingworth's 'obvious encouragement to his players to intimidate if necessary in order to win' and also said that Knott had told Compton that he had appealed for a catch at the wicket off Peter Lever when he knew that the batsman, Keith Stackpole, had not hit the ball, the purpose of the appeal having been 'to put further pressure on the umpire'.

Illingworth and Knott objected to being branded as cheats and decided to sue Compton and Beaverbrook Newspapers for libel. Like the three cases already described, this one was settled, although the negotiations between lawyers seem to have taken a long time, as it was almost three and a half years before it came to court. On 2 November 1974 Mr Justice Cusack was told that Compton only had the interests of cricket at heart and that while he 'certainly intended that his article should raise in a provocative form a matter which he considers to be important for the well-being of cricket, he did not intend to allege that either Mr Illingworth or Mr Knott had cheated and he very much regrets that such an interpretation could have been put upon what he wrote.' An undisclosed amount of damages was paid to Illingworth and Knott, who said that they would be making donations to charity, and their costs were also paid by the defendants.

Max Walker

Reviewing the 1977 Australian tour of England, *Wisden* wrote that although the team could not be described as colourless, it had taken on 'a very light shade of grey'. On the face of it this may seem surprising as Greg Chappell's side contained several other very talented players, but the team was racked by the Packer affair, which broke in May while the tourists were playing in Sussex at Hove. Thirteen of the seventeen tourists were revealed to have signed for Packer, including Max Walker, the fast medium bowler who played for Victoria. Apart from four of the players, the team's manager Len Maddocks, a former Australian wicket-keeper, had not signed for Packer.

Maddocks, who was also a member of the Australian Board of Control, made clear his total opposition to the Packer concept and this led to an unhappy tour, the party gravitating into two opposing camps. Midway through the tour the *Daily Express* made out that things had got so bad that Walker had threatened Maddocks with assault. This allegation was not true and on 17 March 1980 Walker accepted an apology and undisclosed damages in settlement of his libel action against Express Newspapers.

Clive Lloyd

Another cricketer who signed for Packer was Clive Lloyd, the West Indies' captain. He was one of the most important recruits for World Series Cricket, as not only was he a magnificent player in his own right, but he was also a highly respected and influential captain of the West Indies and it was likely that his lead in signing or not signing for Packer would be followed by other members of the West Indies team. This proved to be the case as, although Lloyd left the other players to make up their own minds, Michael Holding, Vivian Richards and Andy Roberts all signed up before 9 May 1977 and others followed afterwards, including Lawrence Rowe.

Rowe was an attacking batsman, who had scored 214 and 100 not out against New Zealand on his Test debut and 302 against England at Bridgetown in 1974. He played in World Series Cricket and subsequently went on the 1979–80 West Indies tour to Australia, by which time the dispute between WSC and the 'cricket establishment' had been resolved. Rowe was dogged by injury on the 1980 West Indies tour of England and did not play in any of the Tests, nor was he chosen for any of the home Tests against England in 1980–81, although he made 116 against the tourists for Jamaica. In 1983 Rowe captained a rebel West Indies' side on a tour of South Africa and, not surprisingly, this outraged the West Indies' cricket authorities, who banned all members of Rowe's team from Tests for life, while some of the territories including Jamaica also banned their players for life from local cricket. Among those who criticised Rowe for going to South Africa was the West Indies' captain, Lloyd.

Rowe hit back at Lloyd's criticism and, on 19 February 1983, *The Sun* published a short article in which Rowe was quoted as saying:

He has no right to attack us. We are professional men and have the right to make our own decisions. It's hardly the way for Lloyd to talk. He wasn't worried about taking money from Kerry Packer. He not only signed West Indian players but also took ten per cent of their wages. You can't have double standards. We consider ourselves to be just like other businessmen who trade in South Africa.

A similar article appeared in the *Daily Express* under the headline 'Rebel Rowe hits out at Lloyd'. Rowe's allegation was untrue and clearly very damaging to Lloyd as a captain with a responsibility to exercise a good influence on the other players and to lead them by example.

Lloyd instituted proceedings for libel against the two newspapers, but not it seems against Rowe as well. Both actions were settled quickly and on 15 June in the High Court in Manchester it was announced that Lloyd had been paid substantial damages by Express Newspapers and on 12 July, at the same venue, it was announced that *The Sun* had paid up as well. In both cases, through their counsel, the newspapers apologised to Lloyd and also agreed to pay his costs.

When the Rowe case was settled, Lloyd was also engaged in another libel case arising out of his involvement with World Series Cricket, but this action was not settled quickly, or indeed at all. This case had its origins in Australia on 19 January 1982 and it did not finish until 11 November 1985 when the Judicial Committee of the Privy Council gave its judgment in London.

From November 1981 to January 1982 the Benson and Hedges World Series Cup competition took place in Australia. There were three teams competing, Australia, West Indies and Pakistan. The form of the competition was that the countries played each other five times and then the two teams with the best record played a final consisting of the best of five matches. When on 19 January Australia and the West Indies came to play the fifteenth and last match of the preliminary round, the West Indies were already through to the final, but whether their opponents would be Australia or Pakistan depended on the result of this match. If Australia won they would go through to the final on a faster scoring rate and a final in which Australia appeared would obviously be more popular with the public and thus more profitable for Packer and the Australian Cricket Board, with whom he was now reconciled. Lloyd was unable to play for the West Indies as he had flu and in the event Australia won a rain-spoiled game on the faster scoring rate. West Indies scored 189 in their 50 overs and Australia were 168 for seven after 43.1 overs, with Border 30 not out, when rain stopped play.

In the light of the libel case which was to arise out of its article on 21 January, the *Melbourne Age*'s headlines on 20 January over its account of the match are interesting. They were: 'Rain enables Australia to qualify for finals on fractionally better run rate' and 'Win a gift from the heavens'. These headlines seem to imply that the *Age* expected the West Indies would have won the match had rain not intervened. However, in his *A History of West Indies Cricket*, Michael Manley, takes a different view, commenting that it was reasonable to suppose that Australia would have won 'since they only needed another 22 runs from six overs and five balls with Allan Border not out on 30 and seemingly in charge'.

On 21 January in its features section the *Age* contained

an article by David Thorpe headed 'Come on, dollar, come on'. The article started by referring to the World Baseball Series of 1919, which had been 'fixed' and continued by making the point, at some length, that in Australia it was an 'article of faith' in important sporting contests that both sides were trying to win and that neither was 'tainted with the "taking the dive" concept of the prize-fighting booth'. The article went on to consider the World Cup Series and to point out that a West Indies–Australia final would be much more popular and more profitable than a West Indies–Pakistan final. Thorpe then continued, 'One wonders about the collective state of mind of the West Indians' and referred to the possibility that in the game on 19 January both sides had the common goal of ensuring that they were the two sides to qualify for the final. The article ended:

> Two opposing teams with a common goal cannot be said to be competing in good faith to win each game as it comes, but rather indulging in a mutely arranged and prolonged charade in which money has replaced that vital cog and is running the incentive machine. Somebody is playing with the faith of the people – with the single mindedness of a burglar blowing a safe.

Although no player on either side was named in the article, the *Age* must have realised that it had overstepped the mark because on 27 January it published a statement saying that it had been suggested that the article may have been read as meaning that the outcome of the match had been 'dishonestly pre-arranged' and that if the article had been so read by anyone, 'the *Age* sincerely regrets that and apologises to Mr Packer and the members of the two teams.' The damage, however, had already been done and Lloyd took legal advice on behalf of himself and his team and the Australians also sought legal advice on the basis that one side could not 'fix' the result without the connivance of the other. Both teams decided to sue David Syme & Co., the proprietors of the *Age*, for libel and it was also decided that, although he had been unable to play in the match, Lloyd, as captain of the side primarily involved, would bring the action as a test case for the other players.

One of the first steps in the action was to obtain a decision on the preliminary issue as to whether the words of the article were capable of being understood as bearing the defamatory imputations alleged by Lloyd. These, in essence, were that, in concert with others, he had defrauded the public for financial gain by 'fixing' the result of the match and would be prepared to do the same again. Mr Justice Maxwell decided that the article was capable of bearing the defamatory meaning alleged and Syme did not appeal against this decision.

The next stage was the hearing of the case itself and this took place before Mr Justice Begg in the New South Wales Supreme Court in April 1984. During the hearing it emerged that the West Indies players had taken part in the World Cup Series on the basis of a flat fee and that the West Indies Cricket Board had also received a fixed amount for the series and that, therefore, no financial advantage or disadvantage accrued to the players or to the Board, whether the final match was against Pakistan or Australia. The jury found for Lloyd and awarded him A.$100,000 damages. Syme appealed and early in 1985 the New South Wales Court of Appeal allowed the appeal by a majority of two to one and Lloyd thereupon appealed to the Judicial Committee of the Privy Council. The case was one of the last Australian cases to be referred to the Committee, as shortly afterwards Australia abolished the right of final appeal to London and the case also raised a number of interesting legal points. It was heard in London on 2 and 3 October 1985 and both sides were represented by members of the New South Wales bar, Syme also instructing a member of the English bar.

The outcome of the case did not depend on the general law of libel but on the 1974 Defamation Act of New South Wales, which applied only in that state. The Act gives a cause of action in respect of the publication of defamatory imputations. It was common ground in this case that the only imputations relied on by Lloyd were comment and that the 1974 Act replaced the common law defence of fair comment on a matter of public interest with a statutory defence of comment. The Act provided that it was 'a defence as to comment that the comment is the comment of a servant or agent of the defendant' and provided also that such a defence could only be defeated if it could be shown that the servant or agent 'did not have the opinion represented by the comment'.

On 11 November 1985 Lord Keith of Kinkel gave the judgment of the Judicial Committee and he found that the article contained ample material which was capable of supporting the defamatory imputations alleged. Lord Keith then referred to the answer given by Syme to one of the interrogatories[1] in which Syme said that they did not intend the article to convey any of the imputations pleaded by Lloyd. This, Lord Keith said, amounted to an admission that Thorpe, the author of the article who was Syme's servant or agent, did not hold the opinion represented by the defamatory imputations and that therefore the defence of comment was defeated, as Thorpe did not have the opinion represented by the comment. Lord Keith also said that Syme's employee, who had answered the interrogatories, had been under a duty to make proper inquiries before answering them but, once an answer had been given that the article did not intend to convey the libellous imputations alleged, that answer had to be taken by the court as being made on behalf of the relevant servant or agent, namely Thorpe. In the view of the Judicial Committee, the New South Wales Court of Appeal had been wrong to hold that the words of the article were incapable of being understood as bearing the defamatory imputations and thus the jury at the original trial were entitled to have reached the verdict which they did. In view of this, therefore, and as under the 1973 Act the defence of comment was defeated, the Committee allowed the appeal with costs and restored the jury's verdict.

It seems that the defendants might well have succeeded had Syme admitted that by publishing the article the *Age* could have been making a defamatory imputation, but that the view expressed was the comment of Thorpe, their servant or agent who wrote the article, and that he held the opinion represented by the comment. This, however, would have been inconsistent not only with Syme's answer to the interrogatory but also with the statement published in the *Age* on 27 January 1982. As it was the award of A.$100,000 damages to Lloyd was reinstated and the other West Indian and Australian players accepted an out-of-court settlement of A.$25,000 each.

---

[1] Formal preliminary questions addressed to the defendant.

Graham Gooch

Graham Gooch, the Essex opening batsman, first played for Essex in 1973 and won his first Test cap in 1975 and in 1981–2 he toured India and Sri Lanka with the England side. He played in all six Tests against India and also in the inaugural Test against Sri Lanka, which finished on 21 February 1982. Less than a week later Gooch was on his way to South Africa as one of the members of a 'rebel' tour sponsored by South African Breweries. The tour lasted a month and, at the request of his fellow players, Gooch captained the SAB English team.

On 19 March the Test and County Cricket Board held a special meeting after which it was announced that the fifteen players who had gone on the tour would be banned from selection for England for three years. This ban was subsequently approved by the International Cricket Conference. When the tourists returned to England some of them took legal advice with a view to challenging the ban but they were advised that, although the TCCB had imposed a restraint on the fifteen players earning their living which would normally be unlawful, the TCCB might well have a defence on other grounds to such an action. As Geoffrey Boycott put it: 'The TCCB had polished up its legal act considerably since Packer.'

Consequently Gooch did not play in any of the six Tests against India and Pakistan in 1982, nor was he eligible for selection for the England side which toured Australia and New Zealand in 1982–3. It was while England were losing the Ashes in Australia that *The Sun* published a 'Sun Exclusive' under the headline: 'I couldn't care less about England!' The article, a large part of which consisted of what purported to be statements made by Gooch, made out that he was losing no sleep over England's humiliation in Australia. For example Gooch was alleged to have said 'bitterly': 'I'm far too busy enjoying my cricket in Cape Town to worry about what England are doing in Australia.'

At the time the article was published Gooch was in South Africa playing for Western Province and he was sent a copy of the article by his father, who asked him why he had said such things. The answer was that Gooch had not said them and he decided to sue News Group Newspapers, as proprietors of *The Sun*, and Ian Todd, the reporter under whose name the article appeared. The case opened on 9 July 1984 and, after a two-day hearing, the jury took 50 minutes to return a unanimous verdict in favour of Gooch and awarded him £25,000 damages. Following the case, Gooch said he felt that his reputation had been vindicated and, if selected, he would be happy to play again for England. After serving his three years' suspension, Gooch returned to Test cricket in 1985 and became a regular member of the England team. Indeed he captained England in the last Test against the West Indies in 1988 and was chosen to captain the side selected to tour India that winter, but the South African connection of Gooch and some of the other players caused the tour to be cancelled.

The Eleven

Finally, an explanation of the title of this chapter. There are, in fact, eleven different individuals who appeared as plaintiffs in the eight cases. In possible batting order they are: Gooch, Kenyon, May, Lloyd, Insole, Close, Knott, Illingworth, Walker, Bedser and Wheatley. All except Wheatley are Test cricketers and they comprise a formidable and well-balanced side. Which of the eight Test and county captains should lead the team I leave to the reader.

XVI

THE TURNSTILE HURDLER

In his book *10 for 66 and All That*, Arthur Mailey, the Australian leg-break bowler, writer and cartoonist, included a chapter entitled 'Rebels of Cricket'. In it he wrote: 'The most spectacular rebel Australia has had in years is Sidney Barnes, who first came into prominence as a turnstile hurdler.' Barnes himself would not have denied that his jumping the turnstile in Melbourne during the Test against England in the 1946–7 series attracted a good deal of attention, but he would also justly claim that he was already prominent as a cricketer. In the previous Test he had scored 234, putting on a world record 405 for the fifth wicket with Don Bradman who also scored 234.

There are various versions of the turnstile hurdling incident and Barnes gives his own in his book *It Isn't Cricket*, which was published in 1953. Barnes recounts that he had arranged to give his two complimentary tickets to a New Zealand friend and his wife and that he met them outside the ground, but when he reached the turnstile Barnes found that he had forgotten his own entrance ticket, which had his name written across it. He failed to persuade the gate-keeper either to admit him without a ticket or to send someone to find Bradman or the Australian manager who could vouch for him. Realising he was not getting anywhere and, as he was already late, Barnes said to the gate-keeper, 'You know I'm Barnes and I'm running late already. You're not sending for anybody so I'm coming in' and with that he stepped over the turnstile. I do not know if Barnes' description of the incident is accurate or whether, as has been alleged, he either sold his own ticket or gave it to a friend as well as the two complimentary ones. What is certain is that the context in which Barnes sets the incident is wrong. He says that he was one of the not-out batsmen at the time and that he went on to make 42 and that Australia got 365 but England 'hit back' and were over 150 for one when Bill Edrich was l.b.w. to Ernie Toshack. In fact Barnes made 45 and Edrich was l.b.w. to Ray Lindwall but, more importantly, Barnes was out soon after lunch on the first day and he cannot, therefore, have been one of the not-out batsmen when he arrived at the ground. Probably the incident took place on the fourth day when Barnes was not-out overnight and went on to score 32.

Barnes first played for New South Wales in 1937 and, at the age of 21, was chosen for the 1938 tour of England. Unfortunately he broke a wrist playing deck games on the journey to England and was only able to play in the second half of the tour. He made his Test debut at the Oval when England made their record score of 903 for 7 and Australia, with Jack Fingleton and Bradman injured, were defeated by an innings and 579 runs. Barnes, however, performed creditably, scoring 41 and 33 in addition to taking one wicket. After the war, he played in a further twelve Tests for Australia and was particularly successful on the 1948 tour of England when, having backed himself to do so, he scored a hundred at Lord's and, in what proved to be his last Test, put on 117 for Australia's first wicket with Arthur Morris at the Oval. Barnes' career batting average was well over 50 in first-class cricket as a whole and in Tests it was 63.05, a figure exceeded among those who have played at least fifteen Test innings only by Bradman and the New Zealander, Stewart Dempster. He was also a fine close fielder and an occasional change bowler. In 1949 Barnes declared himself unavailable to tour South Africa in 1948–50, saying that he could not afford to go as the players, who were unpaid, were offered only £450 to cover their expenses. He also missed the 1950–51 season, when Freddie Brown's side was in Australia, as he was offered a lucrative contract to write on the tour, but he resumed playing in the 1951–2 season, when the West Indies were the tourists, and he was determined to get back into the Australian side.

Following their very successful tour of England in 1950 the West Indies, with much the same side, were expected to do well in Australia, but their performance fell so far below expectation that they won only one Test, losing the other four, and were victorious in only one of the six games against state teams. However, although Australia won the first two Tests, Ken Archer did not prove a success as Morris's opening partner and Barnes meanwhile had been performing quite well for New South Wales. In particular, he and Morris put on 210 for New South Wales' first wicket against Victoria in a Sheffield Shield match immediately following the second Test.

A few days after this match Barnes was in Sydney when he noticed a newspaper placard which bore the legend 'Barnes in – Barnes out'. On buying the paper, Barnes discovered that the Australian selectors, Sir Donald Bradman, Edward ('Chappie') Dwyer and Jack Ryder, had chosen him as one of the thirteen players from whom the team for the third Test would be chosen, but that the Australian Cricket Board had referred the list back to the selectors as it objected to one of the thirteen. The player in question was not named by the Board or by the selectors, but it was pretty obvious that the press had identified him correctly and a bitterly resentful Sidney Barnes set out to discover why his selection had been vetoed. Barnes, however, was met by a wall of silence and the Board would not even confirm or deny that he was the player of whose selection it had disapproved. All he did know, because of the Board's constitution, was that his rejection had been for 'reasons other than cricket ability'.

In late February, having made no progress in almost three months, Barnes consulted J. W. Shand QC, one of Australia's leading barristers, and on his advice Barnes made a statement to the press which included the following paragraph:

> After it was published that I had been rejected by the Board for reasons other than cricket ability, my wife and I have suffered constantly from the suggestions implied in such rejection and the rumours consequent upon it. I fear that unless the position is immediately cleared up it may affect myself and also the future of my children. By this statement I am inviting and hoping to secure from the Board a statement of any reason which they had for rejecting me upon such a ground.

Also on Shand's advice, Barnes wrote to each of the nine members of the Board asking him whether he was in favour of the Board's rejection and, if so, what his reasons were. In reply Barnes received nine identical letters which read:

Dear Sir,
I have your letter of 11 inst., and have noted the contents. I am unwilling to enter into any correspondence with you on the subject matter set forth in your letter.

Barnes still seemed to be getting nowhere when on 24 April 1952 a letter appeared in the *Sydney Daily Mirror*, written in response to a letter which it had published condemning the Board's action. This second letter was written by Jacob Raith, who was a master baker and a former president of Petersham Cricket Club. It read:

Dear Sir,
I have noticed that in his letter, which was published in your paper, Mr Stacy Atkin comments that he has seen no support for the attitude of the Board of Control in the many statements that have been made concerning Mr Sid Barnes. Because the lips of the members of the Board are sealed it should not be assumed that they are without support. The Board is an impartial body of cricket administrators made up of men who have given outstanding service to the game.
   It must be abundantly clear to all that they would not have excluded Mr Barnes from the Australian XI capriciously and only for some matter of a sufficiently serious nature. In declining to meet his request to publish reasons the Board may well be acting kindly towards him. In common with the vast bulk of the cricketing public, I say that the Board has my whole-hearted support and I suggest to Mr Barnes and his supporters that the matter be allowed to fizzle out.

Yours faithfully
J. L. Raith

The publication of this letter handed Barnes the stick he needed with which to beat the Board. He decided to sue Raith seeking damages for libel, but more particularly in order to clear his name. Raith pleaded that the words in the letter did not bear a defamatory meaning and that they were true and in the public interest. The case opened in the Sydney District Court before Mr Justice Lloyd and a jury on 21 August 1952. Shand appeared as leading counsel for Barnes and J. W. Smyth QC led for Raith.

William Jeanes, the secretary of the Board, was called to produce the minutes of meetings of the Board held since 1 September 1948 and all other documents relating to Barnes. Jeanes said that he objected to doing this as the documents were the property of the Board, but he was over-ruled by the judge who said that the documents were not privileged and must be produced. The minutes did not reveal the reason for Barnes' rejection, but did show that a resolution had been passed which read:

> The approval of selections of Australian teams shall be dealt with upon a confidential basis; no minutes shall be recorded in respect thereof and no publication shall be made of the names of any persons who may be disapproved or the reasons therefor.

After Barnes had given evidence, the chairman of the Board, Aubrey Oxlade, was called. Oxlade said that although Barnes was 'a bit childish', he did not look upon his misdemeanours as serious and thought that he should not have been rejected by the Board. In fact it transpired that of the thirteen members of the Board one had been away in England and, of the rest, nine had voted for Barnes' exclusion and three against it. The two who opposed his exclusion, in addition to Oxlade, were Frank Cush and Sir Donald Bradman, the only selector who was also a member of the Board.

The next witness was Keith Johnson, a member of the Board who had been manager of Bradman's 1948 Australian side in England. Johnson was in the box for some time and did not finish giving evidence until the second day of the trial. He admitted that he had been one of the nine who had voted against Barnes and said that, in his opinion, the cumulative effect of three incidents was enough to disqualify Barnes from the team, although none of them would have been sufficiently serious on its own. The three incidents were the turnstile hurdling incident, which has already been described, the royal photograph incident and the Toshack incident.

The latter two incidents turned out hardly to be capital

offences either. The royal photograph incident happened at Lord's on 19 July 1948 when the Australian and Middlesex teams were presented to King George VI and Queen Elizabeth during the tea interval. Barnes, who was not playing, took some photographs with the permission of the Earl of Gowrie VC, the president of MCC. It was, however, pointed out to Barnes afterwards by Ronnie Aird, the assistant secretary of MCC, that he should not have taken the pictures because MCC, as the owner of Lord's, had sold all the filming rights. Apparently Johnson had seen Aird speak to Barnes, but did not also know that he had received Lord Gowrie's permission to take the photographs. The Toshack incident had arisen in June 1948 in the match against Northamptonshire, in which Toshack was twelfth man and Barnes was not playing. Johnson said that Barnes had taken Toshack away from his duties at the match to play tennis on a nearby court, although he admitted that he did not know whether Barnes was the abductor or the victim. There was also a difference of opinion as to whether the court was about 50 or about 300 yards distant from where the game was being played, but there was no dispute that Toshack, like Barnes, was over 21 years old, indeed both were over 30 at the time.

Johnson was given a particularly uncomfortable time by Barnes' counsel in the witness-box, because on returning from the 1948 tour Johnson, as manager, had made a written report in which he said that the behaviour of the team, both on and off the field, had been exemplary. This was clearly inconsistent with his opinion that the two incidents involving Barnes, taken with the turnstile incident, warranted excluding him from the team over three years later. The following exchanges between Shand and Johnson are given in Barnes' book:

Shand: How could you have really thought that he had behaved in a manner befitting worthy representatives of Australia and [that] on and off the field his conduct was exemplary if you thought his conduct was so serious as to warrant his omission from the team?

Johnson: After a lot of thought . . .

Shand: I am not asking for a lot of thought.

Johnson: I gave a report on the team as a whole and
            that is my opinion.
Shand: You admit that that applies to every one of them?
Johnson: Yes.
Shand: And yet one of them was guilty of conduct
            so serious in your opinion as to warrant his
            ommission?
Johnson: With subsequent events. In making a report of
            the team I made it in a general way after a lot
            of thought.
Shand: You said that applied to every member of the
            team. That is not what you thought, is it?
Johnson: With one exception it was.
Shand: I am not talking about exceptions. I am talking
            about every member of the team. It was wrong?
Johnson: Yes.
Shand: As applied to Barnes it was wrong?
Johnson: Yes.
Shand: Your report was false?
Johnson: It was misleading on that point.
Shand: Not up to that point – just false, is it not?
Johnson: Yes.
Shand: Do you still call yourself a responsible person?
Johnson: Yes.

By the time that Johnson left the witness-box it was pretty clear
the way things were going, even before evidence had been given
by Dwyer, a selector, and Cush, a member of the Board, both
of whom had supported Barnes. After their evidence, Smyth,
addressing the jury on behalf of Raith, said that in order for
his client's plea to be successful he had to prove that Barnes had
been excluded for a sufficiently serious reason. He continued:
'Let me make it quite clear at the outset that I am bound to
confess that seldom in the history of libel actions has such a
plea failed so completely and utterly.' Smyth said that he was
bound to accept that the jury would award damages but asked
that they should not reflect 'the contempt that you and every
decent citizen must feel' for the nine members of the Board,
who excluded Barnes from the Australian XI on 'such silly,
trivial grounds'. Smyth concluded his address by saying he

had 'instructions unreservedly from [his] client to withdraw publicly any suggestion against Barnes that may be contained in Mr Raith's letter. In the circumstances it is the only proper thing to do.'

There was then a short adjournment after which Smyth announced that the case had been settled on condition that he made a statement in open court. This statement was that, after hearing the reasons for which the Board had excluded Barnes, Raith admitted they did not justify Barnes' exclusion and that Raith's defence could not be upheld. Smyth also stated that, had his client known the facts, he would not have written the letter in question and Raith agreed to pay Barnes' costs. On behalf of Barnes, Shand acknowledged that in writing the letter Raith had not been motivated by any malice. Thus Barnes won a complete victory against an unfortunate defendant who, when he got to court, found that the Board had supplied him with dud ammunition with which to defend himself. The case also, incidentally, predates by over a decade *May* v. *Associated Newspapers*, although Barnes' case is in a very different category from those described in the chapter entitled 'A Libelled Eleven'.

Barnes' reputation had been vindicated, but he was never again to play for Australia. By the time the case came to court, the 1951–2 season was, of course, over but Barnes still hoped to regain a place in the Australian team during the 1952–3 series against South Africa and to win a place in the 1953 side to tour England. In November 1952 he scored a commanding 152 for New South Wales but, when this was not followed by selection for the Test team, Barnes demoted himself for the next state match to twelfth man and when drinks were served accompanied the steward on to the field, brushed the players' flannels, combed their hair and handed round a box of cigars. He was not chosen for the 1953 tour either and played no more first-class cricket after 1952–3, returning to the press box. Some of the comments in books and articles which appeared under his name made him few friends and it is possible, as Barnes hints in his book, that his pen may also have had something to do with the Board's decision to exclude him from the Tests against the West Indies in 1951–2. Barnes quotes from an article in the *Melbourne Sporting Globe*, which appeared before the team was chosen and in which H. de Lacey wrote:

If Barnes doesn't make the third or fourth Test teams don't blame lack of ability on the selectors. If the selectors are unanimous in wanting Barnes I doubt whether their wishes would be granted . . .

I don't presume to know the mind of the selectors but I do know that Barnes's peccadilloes with the Board and his one season of newspaper prominence, in which he often ridiculed cricket management, have brought him into sharp conflict with the most powerful section of cricket control.

After he left the game Barnes became a successful businessman, but prosperity neither lessened his eccentricities nor made him easier to deal with. Finally, on 16 December 1973, at the age of 57, he took his own life, the police finding him at his home in Collarory, New South Wales with a bottle of sleeping tablets by his side. Difficult he certainly was, but undoubtedly he was also a fine cricketer who, with more luck and a more equable temperament, could have been one of Australia's greatest batsmen. His fiercest critics, however, were not those who knew him best for, as Ray Robinson wrote of him in his book *From the Boundary*:

In all the criticism of Barnes for flagrant showmanship and cross-grained behaviour, the most severe comments come from those who knew him from afar, the least from the cricketers who have played with and against him.

XVII

RETIRED HURT

As mentioned in the 'Sudden Death' chapter, people have often been injured while playing cricket and sometimes the person injured has, although wounded, continued to take part in the game. First-class cricket provides several instances of heroic performances by batsmen who have been badly hurt, including Denis Compton's 145 not out against Australia at Old Trafford in 1948 and Bert Sutcliffe's 80 not out for New Zealand against South Africa at Johannesburg in 1953 when, head bandaged, Sutcliffe hit Hugh Tayfield for three sixes in one over. However, injuries to players in any class of cricket have seldom resulted in litigation because accidental injury is a normal risk of playing the game. In fact, I know of only three such cases.

An eye lost
On Saturday 12 July 1902 Eton were playing at Lord's, the Gentlemen were playing at the Oval and the Cleveland CC were playing at Hackney Marshes, a recreation ground owned by the London County Council on which there were as many as a hundred cricket pitches. In order to enable players and spectators to find a particular pitch and to demarcate it from its neighbours, the LCC provided indicators. These consisted of metal flags with numbers painted on them, attached to the top of iron uprights about 4 feet 6 inches high.

For the game on 12 July 1902 Cleveland had been allocated pitch number twelve and when the team arrived they saw that one of the groundsmen had stuck an indicator into the middle of the wicket to identify it. Before the game started the indicator was removed and the Cleveland wicket-keeper put it about twenty yards 'to the rear and slightly to the right of the batsman's wicket', in other words at very fine and fairly short leg. Cleveland fielded first and one of their players was a 17-year-old assistant librarian surnamed Giles. While he was

trying to stop the ball, which one of the opponents' batsmen
had hit towards the indicator, Giles ran into it and one of the
points 'ran into his eye and destroyed the sight thereof'. Being
under 21, Giles could not sue the LCC himself but, through his
father, brought an action claiming damages due to the LCC's
negligence. The case was heard by Mr Justice Kennedy, sitting
with a jury, on 24 November 1903 and the leading counsel for
the LCC was Henry Dickens, a son of Charles Dickens, who
had taken silk in 1892 and was to be knighted in 1922.

On behalf of Giles it was alleged that the LCC had 'wrong-
fully erected and maintained certain dangerous or improper
posts on the cricket ground' and that the posts were 'required
to remain in an upright position on the cricket ground during
the playing of games'. The plaintiff also alleged that before the
game started the players were told by the groundsmen to move
the indicator from the wicket and replace it 'in an upright position elsewhere on the pitch'. In view of this the LCC, through
its employees the groundsmen, were negligent either in not
protecting the sharp edges of the indicator or in requiring it
to remain on the ground where Cleveland were playing and,
it was maintained on behalf of Giles, this negligence was the
cause of his accident.

Counsel for the LCC 'denied that the indicators were
dangerous or improper' and denied too that the groundsmen
had insisted on the indicator being in the playing area and in an
upright position during the game. Had the indicator constituted
a hazard, the defence maintained, Giles knew it and could have
moved it but he voluntarily took the risk of playing with it where
it was. Therefore, the LCC contended, the accident was either
one incidental to playing the game of cricket or had been caused
by Giles' own carelessness.

Giving judgment, Sir William Kennedy agreed with Dickens
that Giles and the other Cleveland players had voluntarily
incurred the risk of injury as the indicators were not a concealed
or lurking danger. He also said that there was no evidence that
the groundsmen had required that the indicators should be in
an upright position during play and that therefore there was no
basis on which a jury could find that the LCC had been negligent. The jury were not, therefore, asked to reach a verdict and
judgment was entered for the defendant.

A skull fractured

In 1885 one of the members of the Shrewsbury School XI was R. S. T. C. Humphreys who, as Travers Humphreys, later became famous as a barrister and judge. In 1895 the birth took place in Brighton of Maurice William Tate, who later became famous as a superb fast-medium bowler and hard-hitting batsman for Sussex and England. On 11 December 1939 Tate gave evidence in a case tried by Humphreys at Lewes and it was partly the latter deciding 'with fear and trembling and with as much courage as I can assume' to disagree with an opinion expressed by Tate, that led Humphreys to reach the verdict which he did.

The case in question was *Barfoot* v. *East Sussex County Council* and concerned a claim brought by Terence Barfoot, on behalf of his 11-year-old son John, against the Council, as the local authority responsible for the school in Seaford where Barfoot was a pupil. When playing cricket at school Barfoot had been struck on the head by a ball which had fractured his skull. The game had been umpired by one of the masters, George Stevenson, and Barfoot was, according to Stevenson, fielding at square leg where Stevenson had told him to stand about twelve yards from the bat. In court Stevenson admitted that Barfoot had moved in three or four yards and that he had not noticed this until Barfoot had been injured, but Stevenson denied that Barfoot had been placed at silly mid on rather than at square leg. Tate was called as a witness by the defence and expressed the opinion that it was no more dangerous to field forward of the wicket than square with it and it was this opinion with which Mr Justice Humphreys dared to differ.

Sir Travers decided that Barfoot had been fielding in a position which Stevenson knew to be dangerous and that he would not have allowed Barfoot to have fielded there if he had noticed where he was standing. Humphreys found that 'owing to his other duties as umpire, Mr Stevenson failed to exercise the care which the law requires from a master in charge of a pupil'. In the circumstances he found for Barfoot and awarded him £750 damages (currently worth about £16,000), with £20 special damages to his father. Sir Travers refused a request for a fourteen-day stay of execution, saying that if the Council wished to appeal they could go to the Court of Appeal, but that he considered the matter which he had decided was one of fact and not of law.

Four teeth lost

The third case also concerns a game of cricket in which young boys and a school master were involved, although on this occasion it was the master who was injured. In 1954 Robert Macrory, who was 53 at the time, was on the staff of Watcombe House, a preparatory school at North Cheriton in Somerset. On Saturday 5 June Macrory was playing in the annual match between the boys and the staff although, as he said later, 'Cricket isn't my game.' While he was fielding, Macrory had four teeth knocked out and was concussed when he collided with the games master. He applied for industrial injuries benefit and, on being refused, appealed to the Industrial Injuries Appeals Tribunal and his case came up at Taunton on 26 August 1954.

The basic principle governing entitlement to industrial injuries benefit is that the injury must have been caused by an accident arising out of and in the course of the injured person's employment. Macrory gave evidence at the hearing that masters at Watcombe House were expected to umpire, referee and play cricket and other games as necessary. Had he refused, Macrory said, he was sure he would 'have been given notice at the first opportunity'. The tribunal found that, although he had no written agreement, Macrory was under a duty to play in the match and that the injury therefore arose 'out of and in the course of his employment' and entitled him to benefit. The tribunal, however, made it clear that its decision had been made on the particular facts of the case and should not be taken as applying to the teaching profession as a whole.

XVIII

SIX AND OUT

From its earliest days cricket has occasionally resulted in injury to spectators and others not participating in the game. Such injuries have usually been caused by the ball being hit out of the ground and this has also resulted in damage to property and in the risk of people being injured and property damaged.

An early example of such an injury happened on 7 June 1731 when Mr Legat, a cooper and dealer in brandy and rum, was passing what is now the Honourable Artillery Company's ground in London and was struck on the nose by a cricket ball, which had been hit over the wall. A contemporary account stated that 'when the bleeding was stopt outwardly he bled inwardly, and when stopt inwardly he bled outwardly'. As a result, on 6 July the unfortunate man died in nearby Basinghall Street from loss of blood.

An early instance in first-class cricket of an injury caused by a ball hit out of the ground occurred at Harrogate on 1 August 1901 when Jimmy Sinclair, the South African all-rounder, hit Wilfred Rhodes out of the ground and knocked down a cab-driver, who was having a free view of the game from the top of his cab. This incident was followed by a solicitor's letter, but it was ignored and nothing more was heard of the matter. The first such accident which I have come across and which was followed by legal proceedings occurred in Scotland seven years later.

A Scottish case

On 2 July 1908 Arthur Abraham, 'an elderly man', was playing cricket with three 11 or 12 year-old boys, Charles Thomas, Gilbert Cunningham and Charles Robinson. The game was being played at Cambuslang near Glasgow on the 'back-green' behind the row of terraced houses in one of which Abraham lived. In a nearby row of houses lived John Ward and his daughter Mary and these houses also had a green behind them for the use of the tenants. The two greens were separated by a 5½-foot-high stone wall and by a lane, which was about 11 feet wide. Between seven and eight o'clock in the evening of 2 July Miss Ward was sitting in 'her' back-green when she was struck on the head and badly injured by a cricket ball, which had been hit by one of the four playing cricket. Through her father, as tutor of his pupil child, Miss Ward brought an action against Abraham and the boys claiming damages for the injuries which she had sustained.

The case was first heard by the Sheriff-substitute on 20 August 1909 and the report of it contains many words peculiar to Scottish law. On behalf of Ward, the pursuer, it was alleged that the greens were meant primarily for use as drying greens and not as playgrounds and that the defenders, and especially Abraham, knew or ought to have known that 'there was a grave danger of the ball being hit outwith the boundaries' of the green, as had happened several times previously. It was not known which of the four was batting and who, therefore, had hit the ball which struck Miss Ward, but evidence was given that the distance between the stumps and where Miss Ward was sitting was 55 yards. The defenders pleaded that Ward's 'averments were irrelevant' and the Sheriff-substitute assoilzied (acquitted) them.

Ward appealed and on 15 November 1909 the Sheriff of Lanarkshire heard the appeal and also dismissed the action as irrelevant. His reasons, however, are interesting. As far as the pupil defenders were concerned, the Sheriff considered it was unreasonable to assume that they would have 'the foresight to anticipate danger to the neighbours' and that therefore the action against them should be dismissed, but Abraham gave the Sheriff more difficulty. He thought that if four adults had been playing they would all have been liable but in this case, as it was not known who had 'projected the ball which caused the injury', Abraham could not be held liable. To support this the Sheriff cited an earlier case in which it had been held that one of four people who had gone out shooting could not be held liable for an accident as it was not known which of the four had fired the shot in question.

Not surprisingly in the light of the reason given by the Sheriff for his decision, Ward decided to appeal again, this time to the Court of Session, where the case was heard on

27 January 1910. Similar arguments were again put forward on behalf of Ward, but these were again rejected by the court, which 'came practically to the same conclusion as the Sheriff'. However, the Court of Session did not agree with the analogy drawn with the shooting case, as rifle shooting was only legal with proper arrangements to make it safe and, in the absence of such arrangements, the person discharging the shot would be liable. This was very different from cricket, which was only dangerous in very special circumstances, and in the case before it the court considered that the conditions and manner of play were not such as to make those playing it negligent and thus liable for the injury caused to Miss Ward. In the circumstances it was immaterial whether Abraham or one of the boys had actually hit the ball which caused the injury and the court thus 'affirmed the interlocutor appealed against' and dismissed Ward's action.

Struck on the shoulders

On Sunday 28 August 1932 Frederick Foster, a 69-year-old resident of Chadwell Heath in Essex, stopped to speak to a friend while he was walking along Whalebone Lane on his way to church when he was struck on the shoulder by a cricket ball, which had been hit out of Becontree United Cricket Club's nearby ground. Foster was hurt badly enough to need medical attention and subsequently had to attend hospital several times for treatment. He decided to claim damages from the club and brought an action for negligence against H. M. Cashman and W. T. Beechman, as representatives of the members of the club. The case was heard by Judge John Crawford at Romford County Court on 18 September 1933.

Evidence was given that the pitch was 80 yards from the road and that there was a 6- or 7-foot-high chestnut fence between the ground and the road, through which a cricket ball could not pass. Evidence was also given by Foster's son that he had seen balls hit out of the ground on previous occasions. On behalf of the club Henry Leon[1] submitted that the members could not be held responsible for what had happened, that they had

---

[1] Henry Cecil Leon, better known under his pen name of Henry Cecil, wrote several books including *Brothers in Law*.

not been proved negligent and that the club therefore had no case to answer. The judge agreed that there was no evidence of negligence by the club and added that cricket was a legal game played all over the country on grounds near roads and that, if Foster was to succeed, it would make people who played on such grounds liable. Crawford also said that, while he had heard nothing about the man who had actually hit the ball, he could understand that an action might lie against him, although not against the club as a whole and he dismissed Foster's claim without prejudice to any action which he might take against the person who had hit the ball in question.

Even allowing that the accounts of the case are only short newspaper ones, I find two things surprising. First that the judge, and apparently counsel, considered it relevant who hit the ball and secondly, that, in the circumstances, the court did not ascertain who had hit it. It seems to me that if there was negligence, it would have been the negligence of the home club for allowing cricket to be played in circumstances which it should have foreseen as being likely to endanger members of the public and that, therefore, who actually hit the ball was irrelevant. The only sort of circumstances in which an individual, rather than a club, might be liable for such an injury would be where, for example, some members or visitors were engaged in an unofficial practice and, because they were too near the fence, were doing so negligently.

Three years after Foster's claim failed in Romford, Miss or Mrs Vince was more fortunate in Birmingham. Ms Vince's house adjoined a sports' ground maintained by Barrow's Stores Limited for the use of their employees and one day, while sitting in her garden, she was struck on the shoulder by a ball, which had been hit by a batsman playing in a Married v. Single match. Ms Vince was not seriously injured, but incurred some medical expenses and she claimed £50 (currently worth about £1,200) for negligence or alternatively for nuisance, the distinction between the two being that while negligence can result from a single act or omission, nuisance involves a continuing state of affairs, in this case, Ms Vince alleged, the dangerous siting of the cricket pitch.

The case came up at Birmingham County Court in November 1936 and evidence was given that the distance from the wicket to the boundary was 65 yards and that the sports' ground was separated from Ms Vince's property by a net. However, the mesh of the net, although narrow enough to stop a football, was wide enough to allow 'three cricket balls abreast to pass through each hole' – an alarming prospect! Barrow's Stores denied negligence and nuisance and the batsman who had hit the ball said in evidence that he was sure it had not landed where Ms Vince said that she had been sitting. The defence also contended that Ms Vince was an old lady in a neurotic condition and that her injuries were the product of an over-wrought imagination. Judge Alfred Ruegg found for Ms Vince and awarded her £25 damages and Barrow's Stores also had to pay her costs. It is not clear from the reference to the case in *The Law Journal* whether the judge held Barrow's Stores liable on the basis of negligence or nuisance, but the journal does state that the case 'must be taken as having been decided on special facts, and not as laying down any wide principle'.

Bolton v. Stone

On being asked to name a well-known case involving cricket most lawyers would probably reply *Bolton* v. *Stone*. It is a case which differs from its main contender, the Packer case, in three respects. First the facts are simple, secondly, the case went right up to the House of Lords and thirdly, the case is an important legal precedent. Indeed, the opening section on negligence in the current edition of *Halsbury's Laws of England* contains a reference to the case.

On Saturday 9 August 1947, while Cyril Washbrook was scoring 128 for Lancashire against the South Africans at Old Trafford, Cheetham Cricket Club 2nd XI were playing a home match against Denton St Lawrence 2nd XI in another part of Manchester. The northern end of Cheetham's ground was bounded by Beckenham Road and Miss Bessie Stone, who was in her early fifties, lived at number ten. On that Saturday she had just stepped out of her garden on to the pavement when she was struck on the head and injured by a ball which had been bowled by Cheetham spin bowler Geoffrey Topham and hit for six by a Denton St Lawrence batsman called Leadbetter. Miss Stone brought an action for damages against the committee and members of Cheetham CC, but did not sue

Leadbetter or, except as a member of Cheetham, Topham.

Cheetham Cricket Club had existed and played on the ground since about 1864 and in 1910, when Beckenham Road was constructed, the club gave up a small strip of land at the north end of the ground in exchange for a similar strip at the south end. The wicket, however, which ran north to south, had continued to be pitched in the same area opposite the pavilion and, after 1910, the northern boundary was thus about 15 yards shorter than the southern one. The ball which struck Miss Stone had been straight driven from the southern wicket and the distance from that wicket to the northern boundary was about 73 yards. Some 5 yards beyond the boundary was a 7-foot high fence, but the upward slope of the ground at the point where the ball was hit into the road meant that the top of the fence was about 17 feet above the level of the wicket. Thus the distance from the wicket to the fence, which the ball had cleared, was about 78 yards and it was a further 20 yards to the spot where Miss Stone was hit, giving a total distance of just under 100 yards.

The case came up at Manchester Assizes before Mr Justice Oliver on 15 December 1948 and Miss Stone based her claim on three grounds. First, that the club had been negligent in allowing cricket to be played in circumstances where someone on the adjoining road was liable to be injured. Secondly, that the presence of a cricket ground near roads on which balls were sometimes hit constituted a nuisance, and thirdly, under the rule in *Rylands* v. *Fletcher*. *Rylands* v. *Fletcher* was an 1868 case, which is authority for the rule that if a person brings on to his land something liable to do mischief that person is responsible for the consequences of its escape, whether or not he was negligent, but the rule applies only to the non-natural use of land. Sir Roland Oliver found in favour of the cricket club on all three counts, dismissing the claim under the rule in *Rylands* v. *Fletcher* with the memorable words: 'I hope it will never be said of cricket in this country that it is a non-natural use of land.' Although the case subsequently went to the Court of Appeal and to the House of Lords, this effectively disposed of Miss Stone's claim under that head and, although it was thrown in for good measure in the higher courts, it was not seriously pursued there.

Miss Stone appealed against Mr Justice Oliver's decision

and her case came up before Lords Justice Somervell, Singleton
and Jenkins in October 1949.[2] Here, although Miss Stone again
lost on the ground of nuisance, she succeeded by a majority of
two to one on the ground of negligence, Lord Justice Somervell
dissenting. On the question of nuisance the court held unanimously that, although over a period of about thirty years balls
had occasionally been hit into the road, this was not enough
to make the playing of cricket on the ground a nuisance. The
Court of Appeal distinguished Miss Stone's case from a 1922
case where a golf club, which had constructed a hole alongside
a road on to which balls were frequently hit, was held liable
on the basis of nuisance. As to negligence, the majority held
that, as the club knew balls had been and could again be hit
into Beckenham Road, the members had failed in their duty to
take reasonable care to prevent users of the road being injured
or nearby property damaged. Judgment was therefore entered
for Miss Stone, who was awarded damages amounting to £104
19s. 6d., which is currently worth almost £1,200.

The club decided to appeal to the House of Lords and,
as the outcome of the case was important to all cricket
clubs, the MCC and the National Cricket Club Association
helped with the costs of the appeal. This enabled the club
to bring out the big guns in the House of Lords, instructing
Sir Walter Monckton KC and W. A. ('Bill') Sime as its counsel. As
mentioned in the 'Taxes and Wills' chapter, Monckton played for
Harrow in 1910 and, as Viscount Monckton, was president of
MCC in 1956–7. Sime, who was made a circuit judge in 1972,
captained Nottinghamshire from 1947 to 1950 and was later
president of his county club and also of the XL Club. As in
the Court of Appeal, Henry Nelson KC was leading counsel
for Miss Stone, with Henry Burton and Francis Clark as his
juniors. This formidable array of legal talent appeared before
five law lords in March 1951, approaching four years after the
mighty six had been hit into Beckenham Road. The House of
Lords heard arguments from both sides over two days and then
took two months to consider the case, delivering judgment on 10
May. In their judgments the law lords all considered the question of negligence in detail, two of them quoting with approval

---

[2] Later Lord Somervell and Lord Jenkins.

words used by Lord Atkin in a famous 1932 case: 'You must take reasonable care to avoid acts or omissions which you can reasonably foresee would be likely to injure your neighbour.' While their lordships considered the case 'finely balanced' and 'not far from the borderline' they decided unanimously that the Cheetham Cricket Club had not been negligent. The House of Lords also found for the club on the nuisance issue, two of the judges saying that Miss Stone's counsel had conceded that the claim for nuisance could not succeed if the claim for negligence failed. The fact that, in Nelson's view, he had made no such concession can have been of little comfort to Miss Stone, as her claim had now failed on all counts in the highest court of the land. However, the residents of Beckenham Road now no longer run even a remote risk of being hit by a six as Cheetham Cricket Club ceased to exist in 1967 and the ground has since been built on.

Although the cases in this chapter are dealt with chronologically, it so happens that the first four are the only ones in which the actions were brought by people who had actually been struck by a ball hit out of the ground. The length of the hits varied between 55 yards in *Ward* v. *Abraham* to almost double that distance in *Bolton* v. *Stone*, in which *Ward* v. *Abraham* was, in fact, the only one of the three earlier cases considered. It does seem, on the rather brief report which is available, that Ms Vince may have been lucky to win her case, although Barrow's Stores must have been negligent in erecting a boundary net with a mesh through which cricket balls could so easily pass. However, contrary to what is sometimes supposed, *Bolton* v. *Stone* does not preclude a successful claim being brought for negligence against a club out of whose ground a cricket ball is hit causing injury or damage. Indeed, the House of Lords described *Bolton* v. *Stone* as a borderline case and it is clear, from later cases and from occasions where clubs have settled claims out of court, that each case depends on its own facts. In a situation where, for example, there was a small ground near a busy road or a children's playground, the club and possibly, if different, the owner of the ground could well be liable in negligence for injuries caused by a ball hit out of the ground.[3]

Sixes in the sixties

Three cases in the 1960s involved balls being persistently hit out of cricket grounds and the club in question being taken to court because of the consequent damage and annoyance and the risk of someone being injured. In the first case Eric Orme sued Water Orton Cricket Club because balls were continually being hit into his garden and against the side of his bungalow, which he had built alongside the ground where cricket had been played since about 1890. At Birmingham County Court on 24 June 1963, Orme applied for an interim injunction restraining the club from playing cricket on its grounds in such a manner as to constitute a nuisance or annoyance to him. Orme's bungalow at 41 Coleshill Road was said to be only 38 yards from the nearer wicket and 60 yards from the farther one and, if these distances are correct, it is not surprising that, when he got tired of handing them back, Orme quickly found himself with a collection of twenty cricket balls.

In 1962, in response to an approach from Orme, the club had erected 100 feet long and 20 feet high wire-netting fence along the boundary with 41 Coleshill Road, but Orme did not consider that this afforded him adequate protection and therefore, with 'the greatest regret' he brought proceedings against the club. Judge Robert Nicklin did not, however, have to decide whether or not to grant Orme's application for an injunction as the parties reached a compromise on the basis of the club undertaking to erect a wire fence 125 feet long and 30 feet high, with a further 100 feet of netting 25 feet high. Giving details to the court of the compromise, the club's counsel, Michael Davies,[4] said that the additional fencing 'should afford protection, unless Water Orton Village Cricket Club entertained the West Indian touring side, an event which I am assured does not at present appear in their fixture list'. The club said that the fence would be erected quickly and the judge was pleased to be able to adjourn the case generally, as he said that he had not been attracted by the prospect of putting members

---

[3] The circumstances in which Shane Green was hurt might well have been such a case (see 'Pitches and Pavilions' chapter).
[4] Later Sir Michael Davies.

of Water Orton CC at 'risk of going to prison if a member of a visiting team continued to hit boundaries after an injunction was granted'.

The facts of the next case were similar to those at Water Orton, but the nature of the court proceedings was very different. Egham Cricket Club was formed in 1930 and moved to its ground in Windsor Road in 1932. The ground was held under a lease in which the club agreed not to do or allow anything to be done on the ground, which was or might be a nuisance to the owner or occupier of any nearby property. From 1932 onwards, however, cricketers had hit balls into the garden of Iford, which overlooked the cricket ground, and the balls were recovered with the permission of the owner who, since 1954, had been Hector Tidd.

In 1960 the club had suggested for the first time that it had a right to hit balls into Iford and to collect them and this claim was resisted by Tidd. The 'ensuing correspondence varied from the conciliatory to the defiant' and eventually, in October 1965, Bernard Horton, the captain of Egham CC, took Tidd to court seeking a declaration upholding the club's alleged right to hit balls into Iford and then to recover them. It must be almost unique in such cases for the club to be the plaintiff and another unusual feature of the case was that Horton appeared in person on behalf of the club.

Horton based the club's claim on three grounds, namely that an implied easement[5] had been granted to the club in 1932, that the right claimed had been exercised for over twenty years and that there was a lost grant to the right claimed. In the High Court on 22 October 1965 Sir Maurice Lyell found in favour of Tidd on all three grounds and refused to grant the declaration which Horton had sought. The judge held first that the grant of an easement was inconsistent with the terms of the 1932 lease, secondly, that there was no evidence of any right having been claimed before 1960, balls before that date having been recovered with the permission of the owner of Iford, and thirdly, that, as no right had ever been granted, there could be no question of a lost grant of right.

[5] An easement is a right over another person's land.

Sir Maurice ruled that Tidd was entitled to peaceful enjoyment of his property and granted him an injunction restraining members of Egham CC from hitting balls into Iford and from trespassing on his property to recover them. Horton was, however, awarded £2 nominal damages in respect of his claim for an assault by Tidd during a dispute over a lost ball, but this sum did not go very far towards meeting the five-sixths of the costs of the case which were awarded against Horton.

Following the case both sides were reported to have received anonymous threats by post or telephone, the treasurer of the club receiving an anonymous postcard with a West Ealing post mark threatening action by 'toughs from the East End'. More constructively, however, Tidd offered to pay the full cost of an 18-foot high wire fence if the members of the club would erect it. The club's committee met and decided to write to Tidd accepting his offer, subject to sorting out certain details, including whether the fence would be erected on Tidd's land or on the cricket ground.

The last of the 1960s cases concerned Trent Bridge, a ground which has been associated with cricket since 1837 and has been the headquarters of Nottinghamshire Cricket since about 1856. The problem in this case arose from balls being hit, not from the playing area, but from the practice nets. On its north-eastern side the ground is bounded by Fox Road where William Freitag lived at number nine and was headmaster and owner of Angela House Preparatory School, which was at number eleven Fox Road. Nottinghamshire County Cricket Club had taken precautions against balls being hit into Fox Road but, in spite of these, many balls were hit into the road and some broke windows. Freitag was concerned for the safety of his pupils and so, in November 1969, he took proceedings against the county club asking Nottinghamshire County Court to grant an injunction restraining the county club from hitting balls into his properties and seeking nominal damages. For the club it was stated that Freitag had been compensated for a broken window and could not justifiably claim further damages and also that steps had been taken by the club to stop balls being hit out of the ground during net practice. However, Freitag was awarded £2 damages and the costs of the case, and Judge Abraham Flint granted him the injunction which he had sought. After the case

Freitag said he was delighted with the result, but the county club refused to comment.

Miller v. Jackson

The facts of this case are similar to those involving the Water Orton and Egham cricket clubs but, like *Bolton* v. *Stone*, *Miller* v. *Jackson* is a significant case legally, because the unsuccessful party appealed, resulting in important judgments being given by the appellate court. The facts of the case, which in a surprising turn of phrase the staid *Solicitors' Journal* described as 'redolent of the smell of the roast beef of old England', concerned a field in the Durham village of Lintz, which is near Gateshead, where cricket had been played since 1905. Lintz Cricket Club had a long lease of the land from the National Coal Board, which in 1965 sold the freehold reversion and some adjoining pasture land to the Stanley Urban District Council. In 1972 the Council sold the pasture land to Wimpey's, who built a road named Brackenridge and a row of semi-detached houses on it. In June 1972 number twenty Brackenridge was bought jointly by John Miller and his wife, Brenda, both of whom were in their early thirties. The cricket ground was small and the 'square', on which wickets were prepared, measured about 32 by 30 yards.

The distance to the Millers' garden from the northern end of the square was only 34 yards, while from the southern crease it was about 67 yards to the garden and about 87 yards to the house. The distances were thus significantly less than in *Bolton* v. *Stone*, where the distance from the wicket to the fence which the ball cleared was about 78 yards and to where Miss Stone was hit almost 100 yards. When the Millers bought their house there was a 6-feet high concrete fence along the northern boundary of the cricket ground and in 1972, 1973 and 1974 balls had been hit into the Millers' garden on a number of occasions and the house itself was hit several times. The Millers complained and at the beginning of the 1975 season the club, at a cost of £700, erected a chainlink fence, which was fourteen feet nine inches high, along the northern boundary. This resulted in a sharp reduction in the number of balls hit into the gardens in Brackenridge – in 1975 six balls clearing the fence while in the following year the number was eight or nine. The Millers claimed that in the two years seven of the balls had landed in their garden, one of them just missing a window of a room where their 12-year-old son was sitting.

The Millers were still unhappy about the situation and complained again to the club, which offered to put unbreakable glass and shutters in the windows and doors at the rear of the houses which backed on to the cricket ground. This offer was rejected and the Millers decided to sue the club through its chairman, Robert Jackson, and its secretary as representatives of the members as a whole. The Millers claimed that the club had been negligent in playing cricket in circumstances which might result in balls being hit into their garden and also that the continued use of the field as a ground on which cricket was played, in such close proximity to their house and garden, constituted a nuisance to their enjoyment of the property. They sought an injunction to restrain the club from playing cricket on the ground without taking adequate steps to prevent the ball being hit into their garden and also claimed damages, including compensation for the cost of replacing a broken window and repairing the roof.

The case came up before Sir Trevor Reeve at Newcastle-upon-Tyne Crown Court in October 1976, when a number of the Millers' neighbours gave evidence that they too had suffered from balls being hit into their gardens and one, Colin Craig who lived next door to the Millers, said that a ball had just missed him when he was picking raspberries. In a reserved judgment delivered on 3 December, Mr Justice Reeve awarded the Millers £174 14p. damages, of which £24 14p. represented compensation for repairing the window and the roof. More importantly, he also granted the injunction in the terms requested by the Millers.

The consequences of this decision were likely to prove fatal to Lintz Cricket Club, as it was not feasible to erect a higher fence, because of the exposed position of the ground, and the practical effect of the injunction was, therefore, that Lintz would have to look for another ground. The consequences, however, were also serious for cricket clubs throughout the country because, although not inconsistent with *Bolton* v. *Stone*, the judgment would have repercussions, especially for clubs where recent building development created a problem which had not previously existed. When Lintz decided to appeal, therefore, the

National Cricket Association and the Test and County Cricket Board agreed to underwrite the legal costs.

The appeal was heard in the Court of Appeal on 31 March and 1 April 1977 by Lord Denning, Sir Geoffrey Lane and Lord Justice Cumming-Bruce.[6] In the Court of Appeal the leading counsel for the club was Michael Kempster QC, who six months later was to head the cricket establishment's team in the Packer case. On 6 April judgments were delivered and, although the Court of Appeal found in favour of the Millers on the legal issue, the practical effect of the judgments was a victory for the cricket club. There were really three issues involved and on each one of these one of the judges dissented from the opinion of the other two. On the question of negligence the Court of Appeal held that the club was liable and it reached the same conclusion on the issue of nuisance. On both issues Lord Denning disagreed with the majority, considering that the members were entitled to run the club in the way in which they had been accustomed to do before the houses were built and that 'it was not a nuisance, nor was it negligent of them so to run it'. Lords Justice Lane and Cumming-Bruce, however, both considered themselves bound by an 1879 case, where a doctor had built a consulting room near a noisy confectionary shop and the fact that, before the doctor arrived on the scene, the confectioner's pestle and mortar had not caused a problem for over sixty years was held to be no defence to a claim for nuisance.

It was on the question of the appropriate remedy, however, where Sir Geoffrey Lane was in the minority, that the club effectively won. On this issue the court held that, in deciding whether or not an injunction was appropriate, it had to weigh the interests of the public against those of the individual and that in this case the former should prevail, particularly as the Millers must have realised when they bought their house that there was a risk of balls being hit into their garden. As the Court of Appeal decided to discharge the injunction, it increased the £150 special damages to £400 in order to cover future, as well as past,

---

[6] Later Lord Lane and Lord Chief Justice. Lord Justice Cumming-Bruce has a quadruple-barrelled name: Sir James Roualeyn Hovell-Thurlow-Cumming-Bruce.

inconvenience. An additional point raised by Lord Denning in his judgment, and which was relevant both to the question of nuisance and to whether or not an injunction was the appropriate remedy, was the question of planning permission. He said: 'I am surprised that the developers of the housing estate were allowed to build the houses so close to the cricket ground ... The planning authorities ought not to have allowed it. The houses ought to have been so sited as not to interfere with the cricket.' To what extent this is a factor which, either before or after *Miller* v. *Jackson*, planning authorities take into account in considering applications it is impossible to assess.

Needless to relate, the Millers were unhappy that the Court of Appeal decided to discharge the injunction. Mrs Miller was reported as saying that she felt 'numbed by the decision' and that she and her husband might consider moving but felt that, because of the publicity, they might lose money if they tried to sell their house. The club, however, was delighted and Jackson hailed it 'as a victory not only for the club but for sport in general'. As for Lord Denning, who had found for the club on all counts, his clerk told *The Daily Telegraph* that his lordship was 'not a sporting man' and that his passions extended to 'rice pudding and the law'.

Like *Bolton* v. *Stone*, *Miller* v. *Jackson* found its way into legal textbooks and is authority for the proposition that it is a ground for refusing an injunction in a case of nuisance if the nuisance is in the public interest. However, three years later the case was not accepted as a binding precedent in circumstances which led to a limited injunction being granted where noise from power-boat racing on a lake annoyed someone who had built a house nearby. *Miller* v. *Jackson* is a decision which has not escaped criticism and, although this was all important to Lintz Cricket Club, it was only on the question of remedy that the club won. Since 1977 other cases, which have been settled out of court, recognise that in some circumstances a court will consider an injunction an appropriate remedy and that there is also a risk that a cricket ball could inflict an injury or damage which would result in considerably higher damages being awarded than the £400 which Lintz Cricket Club had to pay. Although, as the cases in this chapter show, sometimes it is the clubs who win and sometimes the recipients of unwanted cricket balls, the clubs have won the two 'Tests' played so far, although only by having the 'umpire's' decision reversed by a higher authority.

XIX

TWO DIVORCES

The marriages of cricketers, due to the nature of their occupation, are subjected to more strains than those of most men and this, added to all the usual reasons which lead to divorce, has resulted in many cricketers being divorced, some on two or more occasions. However, as mentioned in the Preface, matrimonial cases are outside the scope of this book, but I propose to make two exceptions. The first, which happened nearly a hundred years ago, because the divorce case in which he was involved constitutes a Test player's main claim to fame and the second because, although not concerning the first-class game, cricket was apparently the sole reason for a divorce being obtained.

Did they or didn't they?

The Test cricketer was Arthur Coningham, who played for his country in one Test only. This was the second Test in the 1894–5 series when Coningham took the wicket of A. C. MacLaren with his first ball in Test cricket, which was also the first ball of the match. On a difficult wicket England were dismissed for 75 and Australia did not fare much better, scoring only 123. In their second innings England scored 475, thanks mainly to Andrew Stoddart's 173, and went on to win by 94 runs. Coningham's contributions were two wickets for 76 runs and scores of 10 and 3.

Coningham was born in Melbourne in 1863 and later moved to Brisbane and played cricket for Queensland and on one occasion in a minor match scored 26, which was his side's total score. In 1892–3 he played for New South Wales and this seems to have been instrumental in his being chosen for the 1893 tour of England. In his book *With Bat and Ball*, George Giffen, another member of the side, writes:

The public did not improve the Eleven by its interference. We had our team picked, and the Cricket Council of Australasia, under whose auspices we travelled, had signified its approval, when Coningham, the ex-Queenslander, bowled pretty well for New South Wales against Victoria, and at once a cry was raised for his inclusion. The members of the Cricket Council took the matter up, with the result that it was practically put to us that we must take Coningham, and we did so against our own judgment. He was not a success in England, and the conclusion has since been arrived at by our leading critics, that, though brilliant at times, he is too erratic to be included in representative elevens.

It might have been fairer to say that Coningham was not given a chance to be a success in England as he was only selected for four of the twelve first-class matches and he performed reasonably well in these. However Coningham did achieve one distinction during the tour, he was awarded a medal for jumping into the Thames and saving a boy from drowning. As well as being a good all-round cricketer and a strong swimmer, Coningham was an excellent runner, a good shot, billiards player, oarsman and rugby footballer. He was also a chemist by trade, was known as a bit of a prankster and, perhaps surprisingly, was a teetotaller.

Coningham married Alice Dowling, who had been born and educated in England, at Bondi Church on the morning of 11 March 1893, the day on which the Australian team sailed for England and although they were married at a Protestant church, Coningham agreed that his wife could remain a Roman Catholic. One of the people whom Mrs Coningham came across in the Roman Catholic community was the administrator of St Mary's Cathedral in Sydney, the Reverend Doctor Denis Francis O'Haran and in 1900 Coningham sought a divorce on the grounds of his wife's adultery with O'Haran. Coningham claimed £5,000 damages (currently almost £200,000) and the custody of his two older children, but not of the youngest child, who had been born in November 1899 and of which Mrs Coningham said O'Haran was the father.

The case[1] opened in December 1900 before Mr Justice Simpson and a jury of twelve, all of whom were Protestants. Coningham, who was represented by Hyman Moss, told the court how, following the birth of his wife's third child, he had become suspicious of her and searched her boxes. Among other things he had found a signed photograph of O'Haran and on this slender evidence Coningham had confronted his wife and accused her of misconduct with the priest. Moss went on to relate how Mrs Coningham had confessed to adultery and said that if her husband would forgive her she would make a full written confession, which she did. In it Mrs Coningham said that O'Haran was the father of her youngest child, Vincent Francis, who had been named after him and that she and O'Haran, 'both know how deeply we have wronged you, but I have always been afraid you would kill him'.

After Moss had outlined the facts he examined Coningham who was then cross-examined by counsel for O'Haran. During his cross-examination Coningham admitted that after the start of the divorce proceedings he had continued to share a bedroom with his wife and this admission precipitated Moss's sudden departure from the court, thus leaving Coningham to conduct his own case. This was strange as the issue of condonation had not been raised and Moss was criticised by the judge for abandoning Coningham. The petitioner himself, however, seemed unperturbed and, as Pearl puts it:

> His ignorance of the ritual and refinements of the law was compensated by an extraordinary self-confidence and at times by an alertness in cross-examination worthy of a skilled and experienced counsel. But his greatest ally was his wife, who showed an unflagging enthusiasm and an uninhibited candour in cataloguing and cross-indexing her confessions of adultery.

In answer to questions from her husband, Mrs Coningham told the court how after a St Patrick's day concert in March 1897 she had gone with O'Haran to his office where he had

[1] The details of the Coningham case were obtained from *Wild Men of Sydney* by Cyril Pearl, which contains a full account of the case and of other cases in Sydney at the same period.

turned down the gas, kissed her and made improper gestures, only agreeing to turn the gas up again when she promised to meet him on the following Sunday. On the Sunday Mrs Coningham refused to go to O'Haran's office but he led her out of the cathedral, up a lane and down some steps into a dark room. Here, she said, O'Haran spread his coat on the floor and they committed adultery, according to Mrs Coningham 'forcibly, all through the night'. She then went on to relate how when she next saw O'Haran he had said to her: 'Now you are here we may as well indulge.' According to Mrs Coningham she did not take up his suggestion on that occasion, but when they next met O'Haran gave her a signed photograph and the pair then 'indulged'. They subsequently repeated the performance virtually every week, usually on a Friday – not one might have thought from an ecumenical point of view the most appropriate day, but apparently chosen because O'Haran went to confession on Saturdays.

After his wife's evidence had finished Coningham called a number of witnesses, including various people from the cathedral, but their evidence did not seem to advance his case, although a Doctor Frederick Marshall did testify that Coningham was unlikely to be Vincent Francis's father on account of an injury he had sustained from a cricket ball in January 1899, ten months before the boy was born. When O'Haran went into the box he denied all the allegations of adultery and other misbehaviour with Mrs Coningham and gave details of what he was doing on some of the occasions when adultery was said to have taken place. O'Haran also maintained that he had been chaste all his life, but Coningham did score a hit when he asked O'Haran if a couch had been removed from his office because it would not hold two people. 'It would hold two,' O'Haran replied: 'How did you know that?' Coningham asked. The priest did not reply.

In his final address on behalf of O'Haran, Jack Want, QC said that the whole case was a 'plant' and that Mrs Coningham had branded herself as being worse than a prostitute and was willing to throw her son to the wolves in an attempt to win £5,000 damages. In his turn Coningham told the jury that alibis of the likes of O'Haran, which were 'as cheap as bananas, fourteen in a box for sixpence', could not be believed when absolution was so readily available for sins that had been committed. Coningham denied charges of blackmail and said that he would leave it to the judge to apportion between his wife and children any damages which were awarded against O'Haran. 'I want none of his pelf,' he added. Mr Justice Simpson then summed up and the jury retired to consider their verdict. Almost twelve hours later they returned and the foreman announced that there was no hope of them reaching a unanimous verdict. Rumour later had it that the split had been eight to four in O'Haran's favour, but as the issue was not resolved he was neither exonerated nor condemned and the case had to be heard again. As the *Argus* said: 'Doctor O'Haran is a martyr indeed or else the cassock robes the rake.' During the three months between the two cases both sides were busy doing their best to ensure that their man would win the second hearing. Doctor Dill-Macky, a staunch anti-Roman Catholic who was head of the Presbyterian Church, organised a fighting fund for Coningham which, in addition to money, provided him with a revolver and ammunition. Coningham also received a series of anonymous letters from someone who apparently hated O'Haran, but only signed himself 'Zero'. Coningham replied to these letters, the contents of which were not of much use to him, by writing to 'Delta' care of the local post office.

By bribing one of the Coningham camp, O'Haran's supporters got to hear of this correspondence and one of them, Daniel Green, watched at the post office and saw someone collect one of the letters from Coningham. This person turned out to be a Roman Catholic priest who had a grudge against O'Haran, but with his unmasking the correspondence abruptly ended or would have done had not Green decided to take the priest's place and continue the correspondence himself. This enabled Green to feed Coningham with false information, including in particular the dates of two afternoons when Zero said he knew that O'Haran was alone in his office and could therefore have been with Mrs Coningham. Although initially reluctant, the Coninghams eventually agreed that Mrs Coningham would go into the witness-box and swear that she had 'indulged' with O'Haran in his office on these afternoons. Needless to relate, the afternoons in question, 1 and 30 April, were ones for which O'Haran had a cast-iron alibi. In addition, Green arranged for

Mrs Coningham's letters to be stolen from her lodgings and, so that nothing was left to chance, with the assistance of W. P. Crick the crooked Postmaster General of New South Wales, also arranged for letters and telegrams passing between the Coninghams to be diverted to Green for copying before they were delivered.

The second hearing began in March 1901 and Jack Want – now KC following Queen Victoria's death – again led for O'Haran, while Coningham again conducted his own case but without the loaded revolver which had been taken from him in court. The judge this time was Mr Justice Owen and much of the case followed the same course as the first hearing but, with the evidence of collusion between Mr and Mrs Coningham available to O'Haran's advisors, the cards were stacked against the Coninghams. Mrs Coningham duly 'admitted' that she had committed adultery with O'Haran on the afternoons of 1 and 30 April and, when confronted with the compromising letters, the Coninghams unwisely maintained that they were forged. Apart from the handwriting, the contents clearly showed that they were genuine.

Mr Justice Owen gave a short and clear summing up which, in view of the course the case had taken, inevitably favoured O'Haran. After an absence of two hours the jury returned with a unanimous verdict for O'Haran, although they also found that there was not enough evidence to establish conspiracy by the Coninghams. O'Haran had to meet his own costs and expenses, which in total amounted to over £3,000 (currently well over £100,000), but most of this sum was raised by his supporters.

On the evidence of the second hearing and in the light of the Coninghams' contention that there was no conspiracy between them, the jury were clearly right to find in favour of O'Haran. However, as the judge intimated in his summing up and as Pearl points out, the actions of the Coninghams were also quite consistent with O'Haran being an adulterer on the basis that, following the experience of the first trial, the Coninghams were determined that O'Haran should not get away with it again. But, perhaps unfortunately for them, this was not the way they decided to play it. As *The Australasian* commented after the case, 'we must take the jury's verdict or wait till the Day of Judgment.'

After the case the Coninghams emigrated to New Zealand, but their days in the divorce court were not over. In 1912 Mrs Coningham divorced her husband for committing adultery in a beach hut. As Pearl fittingly concludes his account of the case, Coningham had found the law of divorce was too much for him. 'In Sydney,' he told a reporter, 'my wife said she did and a jury said she didn't. In Wellington, I said I didn't and a jury said I did.'

Cricket co-respondent
The facts of the second case are less sensational, but more unusual. In 1981 Michael Rowley, who was 46 years old, worked for a steel company in Smethwick and lived in Wolverhampton. He had also been official scorer of the Stourbridge Cricket Club since 1960 and in twenty-one years had missed only one match – when he was at Headingley watching a Test against Australia. In 1964 he married his wife, Mildred, and she sometimes went to watch the club's matches. Gradually, however, Rowley's obsession with the game got the better of his wife, who said that her husband could remember scores and weather conditions from years ago but could not remember her birthday. Eventually, Mrs Rowley decided that 'cricket for breakfast, dinner and tea' was too much and she sought a divorce on the grounds of her husband's unreasonable behaviour. Meanwhile, in the summer of 1981, Rowley had moved out of the family home and pitched his sleeping bag in the club's pavilion. The case came up at Wolverhampton Divorce Court on 25 August 1981 and Mrs Rowley was granted a decree nisi.

Rowley was not, however, in court when the case was heard: he was at Torquay on a cricket tour with his club, playing under its touring name of the Worcestershire Marauders. Asked to comment on his divorce, Rowley admitted that his cricket club was the main reason for the break-up of his marriage and that he put his cricket before his family but, he added, 'I can't stop – we've got to get on with the game.'

XX

A FEW SUNDRIES

Lights out in Oxford

No really great cricketer has been endowed with a wider range of talents than Charles Burgess Fry and he certainly made wide use of his natural gifts. He left Repton for Oxford in 1891 with the top classical scholarship to Wadham College, beating, among others, F. E. Smith who was to enjoy a brilliant legal and parliamentary career and, as Lord Birkenhead, was Lord Chancellor from 1919 to 1922. Fry was up at Oxford for four years and in each of them won blues for cricket, athletics and association football. As an athlete he was a good sprinter and for a time held the world record for the long jump and as a footballer he won a Cup Final medal with Southampton, but it is as a cricketer that he is best remembered. His achievements are too many and too well known to need relating here but during an interrupted first-class career of thirty years he captained both Sussex and England and scored over 30,000 runs at an average of over 50, including 94 centuries of which 6 were scored in consecutive innings. Apart from his cricketing exploits, Fry was, among other things, a schoolmaster, author, journalist, League of Nations delegate and parliamentary candidate, but what he called his life's work was running the training ship *Mercury* on the Hamble river in Hampshire. However, except in relation to cricket, he never attained the fame which might have been expected but, as Fry says in his autobiography *Life Worth Living*, the fact that he did not attain the eminence in politics and the law of some of his Oxford contemporaries did not mean that he had done nothing with his life. Fry continues:

> Once, standing in the Mercury rose gardens at Hamble, Lord Birkenhead said to me, 'This is a lovely place and a fine show, C.B. But for you it has been a backwater.' 'The question remains,' I replied, 'whether it is better to be successful or . . . happy.'

The case in which Fry was involved took place in 1895, his last year at Oxford when he was at the height of his fame and three months before he, most unexpectedly and disappointingly, gained only a fourth-class degree. He was senior scholar at his college, had taken a first class in Classical Moderations and had captained the university at both cricket and football and had also been president of the University Athletics Club.

In his autobiography, Fry tells how F. E. Smith suggested to him that he 'could not jump and catch hold of the bracket arm of the first lamp-post in High Street, haul myself up, turn out the gas, and then light it again with a match from a box in my right waistcoat pocket'. Fry recounts that he 'immediately essayed the not difficult feat' and that just as he was relighting the gas-burner and looking down in triumph he found that his friends had disappeared and that he was being observed by a policeman. The consequence was that on Tuesday 19 March Fry appeared in the Oxford City Police Court charged with extinguishing five street lamps in the High Street on the previous Friday night. Police Constable Higgins said in evidence that he had seen Fry climb two lamp-posts and extinguish the lights and that there were three other lamps out further up the street. This differs slightly from Fry's own account of the case in that he says that he was apprehended when tackling the first lamp-post but the nature and location of the offence are not in dispute. At the Police Court hearing a Mr Marshall appeared on behalf of the University and applied for the case to be remitted to the Chancellor's Court on the ground that Fry was a member of the university. Marshall produced the charter under which the application was made and the bench, consisting of the deputy mayor and three justices, granted the application.

Apart from the identity of the defendant, the remission of the case to the Chancellor's Court is the main point of interest in this rather trivial affair. Under a charter of Edward III, which was granted in 1331, and another of Henry VIII, granted in 1522, the Chancellor of the University can claim exclusive jurisdiction over members of the university in certain categories of cases, including minor criminal offences. The second charter was confirmed by the Oxford and Cambridge Act of 1571 and it has been held that the privilege of the charter extends to a case where the plaintiff is resident outside Oxford but where the defendant is a resident undergraduate. The Court is, in fact, the Vice Chancellor's Court, the Chancellor not being a resident official of the University, and the rules under which it operates are largely those laid down in 1892 and are, therefore, still the same as those applicable in Fry's case. Although the court still exists and retains its jurisdiction, it seldom sits and I believe that the last time it sat was in 1968 to consider a case involving a dispute between an undergraduate and the landlord of his lodgings.

To revert to 1895, Fry relates that he had to stay up after the end of term as the Vice Chancellor's Court did not sit for about two weeks. When it did sit Fry's was the only case before the court and PC Higgins again gave his evidence and the Vice Chancellor said that he was very sorry to see a young man of Fry's ability and promise charged with these 'school-boyish tricks'.

To Fry's surprise and dismay, instead of being fined a nominal 1s. 6d. the Vice Chancellor fined him £2 plus 7s. 6d. costs with the alternative of fourteen days' imprisonment. Fry writes that he was 'severely tempted to subject the Vice Chancellor's Court to the absurdity of the second alternative', but a friend dissuaded him 'in an emphatic whisper' and also provided enough money to pay the fine. Perhaps Fry should have restricted his jumping to the long jump.

A wage reduction

The Amalgamated Society of Cricket Ball Makers was formed in 1897 as the trade union of people involved in that occupation. It was based in Tonbridge and, as might be expected, was a small union, usually having between 150 and 250 members. The years before 1914 also saw the formation of an employers' organisation, the Cricket Ball Manufacturers' Association, but the outbreak of the Great War sharply reduced the demand for cricket balls and many of the men making them joined the forces or went into other jobs connected with the war effort.

During the war the value of money more than halved and by 1919 the wage rates of cricket ball makers, most of whom were pieceworkers, had more than doubled to reflect this. The post-war demand for balls, however, and the fact that all, or virtually all, the ball makers were members of their trade union enabled the Society to negotiate further increases in the piece rates. In February 1920 the rates went up by 25 per cent and in October 1920 by a further 12½ per cent. These increases were not attributable to inflation, as the decline in the value of money was halted in 1918 and overall during the 1920s its value rose.

However, in 1921 competition from Australia and India forced English manufacturers to reduce the prices of their cricket balls and the employers sought to cancel the increases granted two years earlier, but this was opposed by the Society. On behalf of the employers, the Association applied to the Industrial Court, which had been set up under the Industrial Courts Act of 1919 to help settle disputes between employers and workmen. The Association applied for a reduction of 22½ per cent from 4 June 1921 and a further 15 per cent from 3 September, which would have had the effect of returning to the rates ruling in April 1919.

Representatives of the Association and of the Society appeared before the Industrial Court on 27 June 1921, which on the following day announced its decision in a nine-paragraph statement, which is reproduced in Hugh Barty-King's excellent history of cricket bat and ball manufacture.[1] Reference was made in the court's statement to competition from Australia and India and to the 'fall in the cost of living, as shown by the official index number' and also to the fact that under the terms of the 1919 agreement seven months' notice had to be given of a change in wage rates and that this had not been given. However, the court found that the provision regarding notice had not been strictly adhered to in the past either and, 'having carefully considered the evidence submitted and the contentions of the parties', reduced the increase of 37½ per cent to one of 22½ per cent with immediate effect and to one of 12½ per cent with effect from 3 September 1921. The employers thus achieved two-thirds of the reduction which they had sought.

It may seem strange in an age when, with one or two

[1] *Quilt Winders and Pod Shavers* by Hugh Barty-King, Macdonald & Janes, 1979.

exceptions, the value of money has fallen steadily year by year
over the past fifty years that a reduction in wage rates could even
be contemplated. This, however, was not uncommon between
the wars when the value of money rose in more years than it
fell, although these reductions often precipitated disputes with
those whose wages were affected. It seems that, perhaps, in
the cricket ball case there may have been a reluctance on the
part of some of the workers involved to accept the 'umpire's'
decision, as on 18 July 1921 *The Times* reported: 'The strike
in the cricket ball factory of Messrs Wisden and Co. has been
settled by arbitration before the Board of Trade.' On the other
hand the strike, which is not mentioned in *A Wisden Centenary,
1850–1950*, may have arisen over a completely different issue.

A cigarette at the Adelphi

English cricket in the late nineteenth century was notable
for several well-known brotherhoods associated with particular
public schools and among the best known are the Lytteltons
and Studds of Eton, the Fosters of Malvern and the Fords of
Repton. Five brothers who are less well known are the
Champains, all of whom were in the Cheltenham XI during
the last twenty years of Queen Victoria's reign and four of
whom subsequently played cricket for Gloucestershire.

The sons of Sir John and Lady Bateman Champain, one
of whom became bishop of Knaresborough and another a
brigadier, played in a total of only 149 first-class matches
of which one son, Frank, played in 114. Frank Champain
was an attractive attacking batsman and a superb fielder and
he was in the Cheltenham side for five seasons and on going
up to Oxford won a cricket blue for four years, being captain
in 1899 when he scored 120 against the Australians. He
played intermittently for Gloucestershire between 1895 and
1914, mainly under the captaincy of Gilbert Jessop, who had
been his rival captain in the 1899 University match. In his
autobiography, *A Cricketer's Log*, Jessop writes: 'I would as
soon watch Frank Champain score a hundred as I would
any other English batsman save Ranji. There was nothing
dilatory about his tactics, for he believed in putting the bat
hard against the ball and his late cutting was as crisp as that
of the Old Man's [W. G. Grace] himself.' Champain also twice

represented the Gentlemen against the Players at the Oval and, in addition, he was a fine rugger player, winning three blues for that game.

After he came down from Oxford, Champain became a schoolmaster, first at Wellington and then at Cheltenham, which he left in 1911 to take up fruit farming in British Columbia. He returned to England in 1913 and joined the staff at Sedbergh, but on the outbreak of the Great War he joined the army and was commissioned in the Rifle Brigade. On leaving the army in 1919 he went back to Sedbergh for a time before joining the staff at Bromsgrove, where he became a housemaster. However, less than three months after his fiftieth birthday, Champain's reputation and career prospects suffered a seemingly fatal blow when, on 23 August 1927, he was convicted at Bow Street Police Court of importuning and sentenced to three months' imprisonment.

According to the prosecution, on the night of Tuesday 9 August at the Adelphi Arches, which are near the Strand, Detective Handford, a plain clothes policeman, had kept observation on Champain and, at about quarter to midnight, Champain had offered Handford a cigarette and made certain suggestions to him. Champain denied having spoken the words attributed to him and evidence was given as to his character by Robert Routh, the headmaster of Bromsgrove, and by other witnesses, one of whom said that Champain was incapable of an unclean thought. The magistrate, Sir Chartres Biron, however, said that the facts left no doubt in his mind and he convicted Champain of being 'a rogue and vagabond' and of importuning. Champain was sentenced to three months' imprisonment, but he gave notice of appeal and did not, therefore, have to start his prison sentence immediately.

The appeal was heard by a bench of magistrates at the London Sessions on 21 September 1927, when G. D. ('Khaki') Roberts appeared for the Crown and the formidable team of Sir Henry Curtis-Bennett KC, J. D. Cassels KC[2] and Eustace Fulton represented Champain. Curtis-Bennett subjected Handford to a searching cross-examination during which he admitted that his evidence was uncorroborated, that Champain was sober –

2 Later Sir James Cassels.

contrary to suggestions made at the Police Court – and that he was the only person who had been importuned by Champain. Most damaging to the Crown's case, however, was that Curtis-Bennett showed Handford to be in a muddle over the time of the alleged incident and that his evidence about when it was supposed to have happened was inconsistent.

Curtis-Bennett then addressed the bench on the subject of Champain's character and reputation, outlining his sporting achievements and teaching career and mentioning that he had played for the Gentlemen, 'the second highest honour in the cricket world'. Various witnesses were called to testify as to Champain's high character, including Pelham Warner who said that Champain had always borne the reputation of being 'a thoroughly decent man', and Miss Lilian Faithful, a former principal of Cheltenham Ladies' College.

The bench retired for only ten minutes and returned to say that, having heard the cross-examination of one of the witnesses for the prosecution, they were unanimously of the opinion that it would be unsafe to convict Champain but thought it wiser that he should have been given the opportunity of giving evidence and calling his witnesses. Having heard his evidence and that of his witnesses, they also considered that he had proved his innocence and vindicated his character. Champain's appeal was allowed, his conviction and sentence quashed and, as the court considered it an exceptional case, he was also allowed his costs.

Champain, therefore, went back to Bromsgrove School for the autumn term with his reputation untarnished, although the case doubtless attracted a certain amount of comment from both pupils and staff. After leaving Bromsgrove, he became a master at Blundell's, which is at Tiverton, where he died on 29 December 1942 following a heart attack a week or so earlier. In his book *Gloucestershire Road*, Grahame Parker relates that when the white-coated ambulancemen arrived to take Champain to hospital he remarked, 'Ah, I see the umpires are going out.' Not quite his last words, but Francis Henry Bateman Champain seems to have died, as he lived, in the tradition of his generation – that of the well-bred and gifted public school amateur.

A reluctant replay
In 1988 Blackpool Cricket Club celebrated its centenary, which

was marked by a commemorative brochure and a special article in *Cricket World*. The club has been among the most successful in Lancashire league cricket and one of its first professionals was the eccentric Lancashire and England bowler Cecil Parkin. Other Test players who appeared for Blackpool include Harold Larwood, Ted McDonald, Jim Parks senior and Hanif Mohammad and in the last thirty years the club has won the Northern League championship several times, in addition to the Slater Cup and various other trophies.

On Sunday 10 July 1988 Blackpool played Barnsley in the sixth round of the Cockspur Cup National Club Championship at Barnsley. The match was affected by rain and at about ten minutes to ten the game had to end on account of the deteriorating light, although Blackpool had not bowled their full 45 overs. Nevertheless, it was thought that Blackpool had won the match on the faster scoring rate, as they had scored 93 all out in 35 overs, whereas Barnsley were 66 for eight after 38 overs when the game was abandoned.

However, the umpires reported Blackpool to the National Cricket Association for their slow over rate and the Association ordered the game to be replayed. Blackpool objected and decided to test the validity of the Association's decision in the courts and accordingly on 21 July the parties appeared in a three-hour hearing before Mr Justice Brown at Manchester. Sir Simon Brown decided that, in its capacity as the governing body, the Association had the right to order a replay and refused to set its decision aside. After the court's ruling the Blackpool Committee met and agreed to accept that the match should be replayed, as indeed they had to do if Blackpool were to remain in the competition.

The replay took place on Sunday 24 July at Barnsley and started at a quarter past ten in the morning so that the winner could play South Northumberland in the seventh round in the afternoon. According to the *Daily Mail*: 'The conflict had aroused such passion in Yorkshire that 37 people, a doberman and a red setter were there at Barnsley to see the start of a Blackpool innings which produced 121.' Barnsley were 115 for seven when the last ball of the match came to be bowled and a six would have given them victory on account of having lost fewer wickets, but no run was scored and so Blackpool won by six runs. In the afternoon they beat South Northumberland by nine wickets and so reached the semi-final of the Cockspur Cup. Thus was Blackpool Cricket Club's centenary year marked by an appearance in court and by winning two games of cricket on the same day, but not by winning the Cockspur Cup, as in the semi-final they lost to Wolverhampton by 23 runs.

The last word

On 20 August 1931 *The Times* reported that two boys, who had been summonsed at Old Street Police Court for playing cricket in the street, pleaded not guilty, saying that they had no bat and used only their hands. The magistrate read out the definition of 'cricket' from a dictionary as: 'A game much played in England and sometimes in America with a ball, bat and wicket.' 'That settles it,' he said, 'the boys are discharged.'

SOURCES AND BIBLIOGRAPHY

Apart from letters written to the author, the following is a virtually complete list of the books and other sources consulted:

Newspapers

The Argus. The Australasian. Birmingham Evening Mail (and Despatch). Birmingham Post. Bolton Journal and Guardian. Bury and Norwich Post. Chelmsford Weekly News. The Cheltenham Examiner. The Cheltenham Mercury. Church Times. Daily Express. The Daily Gleaner. Daily Mail. Daily Mirror (Australian). Daily Sketch. The Daily Telegraph. Doncaster and Thorne Advertiser. The Doncaster Gazette. Drewry's Derby Mercury. East Grinstead Courier. Essex Chronicle. Essex Union. Evening Argus. Evening News. The (Evening) Standard. Hants and Berks Gazette. Huddersfield Daily Examiner. The Ilkeston Pioneer. The Independent. The Leeds Mercury. The Mail on Sunday. Manchester Evening News. The (Manchester) Guardian. Melbourne Age. The Morning Post. News of the World. Northampton Chronicle and Echo. Northampton Mercury and Herald. Nottingham Guardian Journal. Observer. Oxford Chronicle and Berks & Bucks Gazette. Romford Times. Somerset County Gazette. The Southend Standard. South London Press. Staines and Egham News. The Sun. The Sunday Express. The Sunday Telegraph. The Sunday Times. Sun Herald. Sussex Daily News. The Sydney Morning Herald. The Times. Uxbridge Gazette. The Weekly Dispatch. The Weekly Journal or Saturday Post. The Whitehall Evening-Post. Worcester Evening News. Worthing Gazette. Yorkshire Post.

Journals and periodicals

Archaeologica Cantiana. Cricket. The Cricketer (International). The Cricket Quarterly. The Cricket Statistician. Cricket World. The Journal of the Cricket Society. Journal of the Demijohns C.C. The Law Guardian. The Law Society's Gazette. Playfair Cricket Monthly. The Solicitors' Journal. The Sporting Magazine. Sussex Archaeological Collection. Sussex Notes and Queries. Sussex Record Society.

Reference books

The Army List.
The Book of Sports, printed by Robert Barker, 1633.
The Concise Dictionary of National Biography, Oxford University Press, 1948.

The Dictionary of National Biography 1971–1980, Oxford University Press, 1986.

Halsbury's Laws of England, third and fourth editions, Butterworth & Co.

Hansard.

The Law Lists, Stevens & Sons.

Sport and the Law, Edward Grayson, Butterworth & Co., 1988.

Whitaker's Almanacks, J. Whitaker and Sons.

Who's Who, A & C Black.

Who Was Who, A & C Black.

A Bibliography of Cricket, compiler: E. W. Padwick, The Library Association, 1984.

Barclays World of Cricket, general editor: E W Swanton, Willow Books, 1986.

The Complete Who's Who of Test Cricketers, by Christopher Martin-Jenkins, Queen Anne Press, 1987.

Cricketers and the Law, J W. Goldman, Hodgson & Son, 1958.

Cricket Scores and Biographies, Longmans.

Curiosities of Cricket by An Old Cricketer (A. L. Ford), D. B. Friend & Co. 1897 (republished by J. W. McKenzie, 1978).

England v Australia, Ralph Barker and Ivring Rosenwater, B. T. Batsford, 1969.

The Kent C.C.C. Blue Book.

Sussex C.C.C. Official Hand-book and Guide.

Who's Who of Cricketers, Philip Bailey, Philip Thorn and Peter Wynne-Thomas, Newnes Books, 1984.

Wisden Book of County Cricket, Christopher Martin-Jenkins, Queen Anne Press, 1981.

The Wisden Book of Cricket Records, compiler: Bill Frindall, Queen Anne Press, 1986.

Wisden's Cricketers' Almanack, 1864 to 1988, John Wisden & Co. and others.

The World of Cricket, general editor: E. W. Swanton, Michael Joseph, 1966.

Other books

Allen, D. R. (ed.), *Arlott on Cricket*, Collins, 1984.

Altham, H. S., and Swanton, E. W., *A History of Cricket*, George Allen & Unwin, 1947.

Ashley-Cooper, F. S., *Cricket Highways and Byways*, Allen & Unwin, 1927.

Barnes, Sidney, *It isn't Cricket*, William Kimber & Co., 1953.

Barty-King, Hugh, *Quilt Winders and Pod Shavers*, Macdonald & Janes, 1979.

Beecher, Eric, *The Cricket Revolution*, Newspress, 1978.

Birkenhead, The Earl of, *Walter Monckton: The Life of Viscount Monckton of Brenchley*, Weidenfeld and Nicolson, 1969.

Blofeld, Henry, *The Packer Affair*, Collins, 1978.

Bolton, Geoffrey, *History of the O.U.C.C.*, Oxford, 1962.

Botham, Kathy, *Living with a Legend*, Grafton Books, 1987.

Bowen, Rowland, *Cricket, A History*, Eyre & Spottiswoode, 1970.

Box, Charles, *The English Game of Cricket*, The Field Office, 1877.

Boycott, Geoffrey, *Boycott, The Autobiography*, Macmillan, 1987.

Brearley, Mike, *Phoenix from the Ashes*, Hodder & Stoughton, 1982.

Brodribb, Gerald, *Hit For Six*, Heinemann, 1960.

Brooke, Robert, *John Edward Shilton's Book*, The Association of Cricket Statisticians, 1984.

Buckley, G. B. (Compiler), *Fresh Light on Pre-Victorian Cricket*, Cotterell, 1937.

Callaghan, John, *Boycott: A Cricketing Legend*, Pelham Books, 1983.

Cardus, Neville, *Autobiography*, Collins, 1947.

Coldham, James D., *Lord Harris*, George Allen & Unwin, 1983.

Cozier, Tony, *The West Indies: Fifty Years of Test Cricket*, Angus & Robertson, 1978.

Down, Michael, *Is It Cricket?* Queen Anne Press, 1985.

Ellis, Clive, *C.B.*, J. M. Dent & Sons, 1984.

Frith, David, *A Pageant of Cricket*, Macmillan, 1987.

Frith, David, *My Dear Victorious Stod*, David Frith, 1970.

Frith, David, *Thommo*, Angus & Robertson, 1980.

Fry, C. B., *Life Worth Living*, Eyre & Spottiswoode, 1939.

Gibson, Alan, *The Cricket Captains of England*, Cassell, 1979.

Giffen, George, *With Bat and Ball*, Ward, Lock, 1898.

Gilchrist, Roy, *Hit Me For Six*, Stanley Paul, 1963.

Gooch, Graham, *Out of the Wilderness*, Grafton Books, 1986.

Hadfield, John, *A Wisden Century*, Sporting Handbooks Limited, 1950.

Heyhoe, Rachael, and Rheinberg, Netta, *Fair Play*, Angus & Robertson, 1976.

Hills, Wallace H., *The History of East Grinstead*, Farncombe & Co., 1906.

Howat, Gerald, *Learie Constantine*, George Allen & Unwin, 1975.

Humphry, Derek, *The Cricket Conspiracy*, National Council for Civil Liberties, 1975.

Hyde, H. Montgomery, *Norman Birkett*, Hamish Hamilton, 1964.

Jessop, Gilbert, *A Cricketer's Log*, Hodder & Stoughton, 1922.

Lewis, Tony, *A Summer of Cricket*, Pelham Books, 1976.

Lewis, Tony, *Double Century*, Hodder & Stoughton, 1987.

McDonald, Trevor, *Clive Lloyd*, Granada Publishing, 1985.

Mahony, Peter, *Sundry Extras*, The Hambledon Press, 1984.

Mailey, Arthur, *10 for 66 and All That*, Phoenix Sports Books, 1958.

Manley, Michael, *A History of West Indies Cricket*, Andre Deutsch, 1988.

Marjoribanks, Edward, *The Life of Sir Edward Marshall Hall K.C.*, Victor Gollancz, 1929.

Marshall, John, *Sussex Cricket*, Heinemann, 1959.

Morrah, Patrick, *Alfred Mynn and the Cricketers of his Time*, Eyre & Spottiswoode, 1963.

Mosey, Don, *Botham*, Methuen, 1986.

Mosey, Don, *Boycott*, Methuen, 1985.

Moyes, A. G. *Australian Cricket, a History*, Angus & Robertson, 1959.

Odendaal, André (ed.), *Cricket in Isolation*, André Odendaal, 1977.

Parker, Eric, *The History of Cricket*, Seeley, Service, 1950.

Parker, Grahame, *Gloucestershire Road*, Pelham Books, 1983.

Patterson, M. W., *A History of the Church of England*, Longmans, Green, 1909.

Pearl, Cyril, *Wild Men of Sydney*, W. H. Allen, 1958.

Pollard, Jack, *The Formative Years of Australian Cricket*, Angus & Robertson, 1987.

Pollard, Jack, *The Turbulent Years of Australian Cricket*, Angus & Robertson, 1987.

Pullin, A. W. ('Old Ebor'), *Alfred Shaw, Cricketer*, Cassell, 1902.

Robertson-Glasgow, R. C., *More Cricket Prints*, T. Werner Laurie, 1948.

Robinson, Ray, *From the Boundary*, Collins, 1951.

Robinson, Ray, *The Wildest Tests*, Pelham Books, 1972.

Ross, Gordon, *A History of West Indies Cricket*, Arthur Barker, 1976.

Shawcroft, John, *Derbyshire Bowlers*, J. H. Hall, 1986.

Sobers, Gary, *Cricket Crusader*, Pelham Books, 1966.

Steel, A. G., and Lyttelton, R. H., *Cricket*, Badminton Library, Longman, 1888.

Stollmeyer, Jeff, *Everything Under the Sun*, Stanley Paul, 1983.

Swanton, E. W., *Gubby Allen, Man of Cricket*, Hutchinson, Stanley Paul, 1985.

Swinnock, George, *The Life and Death of Mr Tho. Wilson, Minister of Maidstone*, 1672.

Thomson, A. A., *The Great Cricketer*, Robert Hale, 1957.

The Times (contributors), *M.C.C. 1787–1937, The Times*, 1937.

Turner, E. S., *May It Please Your Lordship*, Michael Joseph, 1971.

Whitington, R. S., *An Illustrated History of Australian Cricket*, Pelham Books, 1974.

Williams, Marcus (ed.), *Double Century*, Collins Willow, 1985.

Williams, Marcus (ed.), *The Way to Lord's*, Willow Books, 1983.

Wynne-Thomas, Peter, and Arnold, Peter, *Cricket in Conflict*, Newnes Books, 1984.

Law reports

The reports consulted in connection with cases contained in the law reports are shown in the 'Reported Cases' section below.

Miscellaneous

The Index of Retail Prices. Certificates obtained from the General Register Office. Assizes' Records held at the Public Record Office. Kent Assizes Indictments. South Eastern Circuit Assizes Indictments. Surrey Quarter Sessions Roll. West Sussex Quarter Sessions Roll. Wanborough Manor Court Roll. Muster Rolls and Pay Lists of 11th Foot. The Hornsby Professional Cricketers Fund Scheme. *Historical Gleanings*, G. B. Buckley (compiler). Lexis Service. Butterworths Telepublishing. East London News Agency report. Papers relating to the case of *Railton and another* v. *Pehrsson*. Papers relating to the case of *Simmonds and Simmonds* v. *Uxbridge C.C. Conny*, David Lemmon, Cornhill 1988 Lord's Test Souvenir Programme. Diaries of the Reverend Vernon Royle. Letters written by F. R. Foster.

Reported cases

Those cases contained in the Law Reports are shown below with the references of the reports used and the chapter of this book in which the case in question appears.

Case	Reference	Chapter
Attorney-General v. *News Group Newspapers Limited*	[1987] Q.B. 1	XIV
Bolton and others v. Stone	[1949] 1 A.E.R. 237, [1950] 1 K.B.201 and [1951] A.C. 850	XVIII
Club Cricket Conference v. *The Commissioners of Customs and Excise*	[1973] V.A.T. Tax Reports 53	IV
Constantine v. *Imperial Hotels Limited*	[1944] 1 K.B. 693	VII
Fitch v. *Rawling, Fitch and Chatteris*	[1795] 2 Henry Blackstone's Common Pleas Reports 393 and [1775-1802] A.E.R. 571	X
Giles v. *London County Council*	[1904] 2 Knight's Local Government Reports 326	XVII
Goddard (Inspector of Taxes) v. *Ducat*	[1927] 6 Annotated Tax Cases 720	IV

Abbreviations

A.C.	–	Appeal Cases
A.E.R.	–	All England Law Reports
Ch	–	Chancery
K.B.	–	King's Bench Division
Q.B.	–	Queen's Bench Division
R.R.C.	–	Reports of Rating Cases
W.L.R.	–	Weekly Law Reports